CDMA

THE CANADIAN DIRECT MARKETING HANDBOOK II

Building

customer

relationships

BY MARILYN STEWART

Canadian Cataloguing in Publication Data

Stewart, Marilyn
    The Canadian direct marketing handbook II: building
    customer relationships

ISBN 1-895812-10-0

1. Direct marketing – Canada. I. Canadian Direct
Marketing Association. II. Title.

HF5415.126.S74 1998   658.8'4   C98-900401-5

This publication is designed to provide accurate and authoritative information on the subject matter covered. It is sold with the understanding that neither the author nor the publisher is engaged in rendering legal, accounting, or other professional advice.

Designed and edited by
Creative Publishing Solutions Inc.

Photography by
Thomas L. Sandler

Printed and bound in Canada by
The Delta Group

THE CANADIAN DIRECT MARKETING HANDBOOK II

Building customer relationships

CONTENTS

ACKNOWLEDGMENTS

A special thank you to the following chapter editors for their input and review.

Chapter	Editor
The Nature of Direct Marketing, Opportunity Evaluation, and The Marketing Plan	Anthony (Tony) Keenan, Chairman, Advisory Board, St. Joseph Printing Limited, Doug McCormick, Partner, iCom Inc.
The Role of the Agency	Trish Wheaton, Executive Vice-President, Director of Client Services, Wunderman Cato Johnson (Toronto)
The Role of Research	Ken Solmon, Vice-President, Director of Strategic Planning and Consumer Insight, Wunderman Cato Johnson (Toronto)
Lists	Ossie Hinds, Founder and President, Cornerstone, Linda Trauzzi, President, Watts List Brokerage Ltd.
Creative	Fransi Weinstein, Senior Vice-President, Creative Director, BBDO Response
Direct Mail	Mona Goldstein, President, Wunderman Cato Johnson, Toronto, Yvonne Nunnaro, Production Manager, OgilvyOne Worldwide
Telemarketing	Dorothy Millman, President, Phonettix Intelecom Ltd.
Direct Marketing Suppliers	Rich Bassett, President and CEO, Bassett Direct, Hugh Hilliard, Vice-President, Sales, Watts Direct Marketing Services Ltd.
Careers	Marnie Keith-Murray CMC, President, The Keith-Murray Partnership
Case Studies	Canada Post Corporation

INTRODUCTION

In the 1990s, the consumer has far more products to choose from and many more ways to shop for those products — giant malls, specialty stores, mail order catalogues, home shopping networks, and virtual stores on the Internet. Consumers are bombarded with messages through a growing number of channels — television, radio, direct mail, on-line computer networks, Internet, phone, fax, billboards, transit advertising, specialty magazines, and daily and weekly newspapers. Today's consumer can bank by phone or computer, from the home or office, from the car or from an airplane, at an automated banking machine, and occasionally at a branch.

There's little doubt that our customer is inundated with messages. And some of those messages are of no interest or relevancy to the customer, thereby creating consumer dissatisfaction.

Do you know how to break through the clutter and dissatisfaction and give your customers what they want, when they want, and how they want it? And once your customer has your product or service, do you know how to build an ongoing relationship and remain an important part of your customer's future purchase decision?

To develop any relationship, there must be two-way access and conversation. Does your customer have access to your company? If so, in how many ways? Do your best customers have easy access? How many customer calls do you take a week? A month? A year? Or are they deployed to someone else in the company?

The combination of less time, more ways to shop, and friendly technology gives today's customer more choices and today's marketers more challenges. But these challenges are filled with opportunity. Are you attacking these challenges with the best possible solution? Are you using all the resources available to you? Are database driven communications part of your media mix?

Are you still considering your customer as your target, rather than your partner? What can you do better to build important customer relationships with the right customers?

We have structured this book to give you some practical answers, ideas, and case studies. Not only do we examine the opportunities that exist in building better customer relationships, but we help you identify and market to your most profitable customers and retain and build customer loyalty through the relationship-building techniques of direct marketing.

According to the latest industry statistics contained in the 1997/98 Canadian Direct Marketing Association *Annual Fact Book*, 1996 was another double-digit growth year with 10 percent representing $11.2 billion worth of goods and services. The book states that 1997 is expected to reflect yet another double-digit growth year of 12.4 percent.

Interactive/on-line

The growth of Web sites in 1997 has transformed the Internet from a passive search for information, to an active participation in such successful sites as Columbia House, IBM, and Chrysler Canada. The Web is not yet a marketer's dream — but a big opportunity. We are not yet able to gather enough test information and case studies to dedicate a chapter to this exciting area of marketing. In the meantime, investigate your options carefully. Developing the right strategy and methodology will be the key to your success in this area. Your primary goal to ensure consistent Web-site success should be to develop a Web control package with a combination of the right creative and the right offer for the right audience.

I-mail, developed by Terry Shane, president of Westminster International, is a product that is being tested to support direct mail. Briefly, this is how I-mail works: a direct mail package is sent to households or businesses containing a unique Internet access address. Once a potential customer accesses the site, a completely personalised Web page appears in seconds. Shane says that by adding I-mail to your marketing mix you can add incremental response rates from five to 15 percent.

In the following chapters, you will discover basic techniques and tips that focus on opening the lines of communication between you and your customer: analysing customer behaviour, acquiring the right customers, rewarding loyal customers, and acknowledging customers' past behaviour patterns with targeted offerings based on customer insight, relevancy, and need.

The Canadian Direct Marketing Handbook II is all about putting the customer first. And in many of today's organisations, this is a bigger challenge than words can express. I hope this book helps make your decisions a little easier and your challenges a little less daunting. In the end, the customer is always right.

This book would not have been possible without the support and contribution of the Canadian Direct Marketing Association and its member companies. In particular, the individuals who stuck with the vision and the detail into the wee hours of the morning. Thanks to my niece Tracey Taylor, Sylvia Halligan, CDMA, and Marianne C. Kearney, Creative Publishing Solutions Inc., for unselfishly contributing their expertise. And my family, friends, and clients who supported me in this effort.

"All sectors of direct marketing are experiencing healthy growth rates.... On average, Canadians spend $389 per capita annually on goods and services marketed through direct marketing channels." John Gustavson, president and CEO of the Canadian Direct Marketing Association.

THE NATURE OF DIRECT MARKETING

2

THE NATURE
OF DIRECT
MARKETING

Once you have
seen the light, you
can't go back into
the darkness.

In Canadian boardrooms where the focus is on the customer, customer profitability, customer relationships, and customer loyalty, history shows that direct marketing is a misunderstood and undervalued part of the marketing mix. Today, its acceptance is based on being customer focused, its analytics and its return on investment (ROI) appeal in a marketing environment anxious to allocate budgets to better understand the true value of customers. The very nature of marketing measurability in all media brings direct marketing to the forefront. Before we begin to explore the exciting world of direct marketing, we should first examine what *marketing* is, then how *direct marketing* meets the objectives stated in the definition of marketing.

▶ The marketing concept

The marketing concept is one of the more popular ideas in business today. In fact, the marketing concept seems to be one of the most consistently repeated phrases around. But the more one hears it, the more one wonders how many people really understand what marketing is, how it works, and how one goes about it.

A great many people have a thorough understanding of marketing. But I suspect that among marketing professionals, there are those who do not. I continue to hear comments such as: "let's get a nifty logo" or "let's get a department store tie-in." Marketing, however, cannot be reduced to concrete activities; rather it is an all-consuming process.

The marketing concept involves the entire business process. It is, in essence, determining what the consumer wants, then providing it. In the late 1880s merchant Marshall Field said: "The customer is always right" and "Give the lady what she wants." Old Marshall Field was very much a modern marketer.

Marketing goes far beyond distribution, far beyond selling. Selling focuses on the needs of the seller. It is basically preoccupied with the seller's need to convert product into cash. Marketing, on the other hand, is based on the idea of satisfying the needs of the buyer.

Peter Drucker, the well-known professor, consultant, and writer on modern management, says that despite all the current talk about the marketing approach, marketing is still more rhetoric than reality to many businesses. Consumerism, he says, proves this. What consumerism demands is that business actually market — that it start out with the needs, the desires, and the values of the consumer. It demands that business define its goal as *the satisfaction of customer needs.*

Consumerism therefore doesn't ask: what do we want to sell? It says: these are the satisfactions the customer is looking for. And it says that the aim of marketing is to know and understand the customer so well that the product or service fits him or her perfectly, and practically sells itself — again, "Give the lady what she wants." And that is a long, long way from just a nifty logo or department store tie-in, and much closer to what direct marketing can accomplish.

▶ The direct marketing concept

The definitions of *direct marketing* that have been printed in various publications have, for the most part, sounded intricate and scientific and have never stressed the key ideas that make direct marketing unique and popular today. Bob Stone, chairman of Stone & Adler and author of *Successful Direct Marketing Methods*, and Pete Hoke, publisher of *Direct Marketing* magazine define direct marketing as:

> *An interactive system of marketing which uses one or more advertising media to effect a measurable response and/or transaction at any location.*

On the basis of this definition, a lot of time is spent conveying the idea that direct marketing is *interactive* and *measurable*. However, the key word in this definition is *marketing*.

Direct marketing meets the broader objectives of marketing, and is intimately focused on the fundamental goal of marketing: understanding and satisfying customer needs. Direct marketing assumes that customers have uniquely different needs and seeks to understand those differences as a means to customise products, offers, and messages to better satisfy customers. One truth direct marketing demonstrates over and over again, is that not all customers are created equal.

So, in this regard, I am closer to the definition David Shepard Associates coined in *The New Direct Marketing*, 2ⁿᵈ edition.

> *The new direct marketing is an information-driven marketing process, managed by database technology, that enables marketers to develop, test, implement, measure, and appropriately modify customised marketing programs and strategies.*

To implement the new direct marketing you need to know how to:

· Identify and gather relevant data about customers and prospects.

· Use database technology to transform raw data into powerful and accessible marketing information.

· Apply statistical techniques to customer and prospect databases to analyse behaviour, isolate relatively homogeneous market segments, and score and rank individuals in terms of their probability of behaving in a

Direct marketing meets the broader objectives of marketing, and is intimately focused on the fundamental goal of marketing: understanding and satisfying customer needs.

variety of predictable ways (responding, buying, returning, paying, staying or leaving, and so on).

- Evaluate the economics of gathering, manipulating, and analysing data and capitalise on the economics of developing and implementing data-driven marketing programs.

- Act creatively on the marketing opportunities that emerge from these processes to develop individual customer relationships and to build business.

This definition captures the essence of direct marketing based on *pertinent customer data and using database technology to transform raw data into powerful and accessible marketing information.* It is a way of thinking about your customers and their relationship with your product — a special area concerned with offering the customer a relevant product or service with the intent of building a long-term, two-way relationship with the *right customers.* And the acknowledgment of the importance of the relationship and the tools available to develop that relationship with the customer has certainly evolved over time. This was the very reason I got into, and have stayed in, direct marketing all these years. The challenge has always been to understand the customer's wants, needs, and values, coupled with the value of the customer, and how the product fits that customer through various life stages. As the customer has evolved, so too has direct marketing.

▶ The direct marketing evolution

There have been various terms used for direct marketing over the years. The one constant has always been the determination to better understand the needs of the customer — to move from a product focus, to a customer focus. This was seen as early as the 1700s when a Pennsylvania bookseller sent out a catalogue, listing 600 titles, so that people who lived too far away to travel to his shop, could buy his books by mail.

The bookseller's name was Benjamin Franklin, and his catalogue is the first recorded use of direct marketing. His modest catalogue was the catalyst for the development of mail order, direct mail, and direct marketing as we know it today.

Since that time, the definition of direct marketing techniques have exploded. They've gone from direct mail to telemarketing to direct response television (DRTV), and now the new medium, the Internet. Direct marketing became a serious marketing discipline at the turn of the century when companies, such as Sears and Eaton's sent out mail order catalogues to rural communities. The industry has been expanding ever since. But it was not until the late 1970s and into the 1980s that direct marketing really exploded in Canada. And from then until now, the definition of direct marketing has evolved, and at times, gets rather complex.

In the 1960s and 1970s, the popular terms were direct mail, direct mail marketing, direct response, then direct marketing. In the 1980s, thanks to publications such as the *Harvard Business Review*, the industry took on a whole new set of new terms: database marketing, relationship marketing, and loyalty marketing. In the 1990s, one-to-one marketing was the hot topic in Canadian boardrooms and among authors, such as Don Peppers. And customer relationships and customer bonding became the new buzz words.

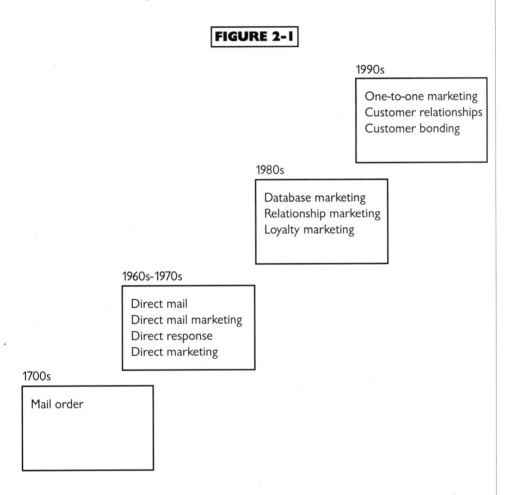

FIGURE 2-1

1990s
One-to-one marketing
Customer relationships
Customer bonding

1980s
Database marketing
Relationship marketing
Loyalty marketing

1960s-1970s
Direct mail
Direct mail marketing
Direct response
Direct marketing

1700s
Mail order

▶ Junk

This term has also been around since the 1700s. It is a term that was once considered a joke. I have never considered it a joke. Junk communications of all sorts should be the nemesis of your existence. It is not that mail, or print, or television spots, or junk e-mail (spam), or junk faxes, or junk automated phone calls, don't look or sound good, it is that they are unasked and unwanted communications that are not relevant. It is not the method of communication that makes it junk, it is that the communication piece itself is *not relevant to the customer.*

And not relevant does not describe colour, shape, size, or personalisation. It can be the best looking communication piece, but if it is not relevant to your customer's needs, it is considered junk.

Junk communications is the result of a bad strategy — a result of a sloppy marketing plan, without support of specific customer information, data, or behaviour. It is the result of the drive to sell products, as opposed to a drive to meet customer needs. What is junk for me, may not be junk to someone else. The junk judgment is based solely on need and relevancy. Junk will disappear when direct marketing is embraced as a strategy, and not executed as the work of a tactician.

In direct marketing, each communication contains an *offer* and a *response mechanism* that allows, not only the measurement of the effectiveness of advertising, but also demands that we become both a good listener to the customer's needs and knowledgeable about customer individuality. This forces the focus to customer *behaviour*, not just customer *attitude*.

▶ Direct marketing vs general advertising

Direct marketers are most often asked about the difference between direct marketing and *general* or *awareness advertising*. Figure 2-2 illustrates the key differences.

The late Andrew Kershaw, managing director of Ogilvy, Benson & Mather (Canada), summed it up nicely in 1965 when he addressed the Advertising and Sales Club of Toronto on the subject of direct mail:

> *The power of direct mail is unique in selecting respondents in clearly defined categories of consumers — and to yield immediate, concrete measurements of effectiveness. Above all, it is capable of meticulous testing with much less likelihood of muddied results than we are used to in advertising research. The enormous future growth of direct mail will rest on these foundations.*

What Mr. Kershaw could not have known is this growth has become even more necessary, given the reality of our ever-changing, knowledgeable, and demanding consumer. Today's consumers demand more value. Their definition of quality is evolving, personal convenience is no longer a luxury, and customer service is a must. Customer service is big business today. Direct marketing methods deliver that convenience coupled with value, quality, and customer service guarantees, while still building and focusing on the long-term customer relationship.

FIGURE 2-2

DIRECT MARKETING	GENERAL ADVERTISING
1. The primary objective is response	1. The primary objective is to build product and brand awareness
2. Asks for an immediate response or acknowledgment	2. Builds awareness over time
3. Sells to individuals	3. Sells to the masses
4. Offers are targeted to individuals	4. One offer for everyone
5. Captures customer information and behaviour on a database	5. Customer remains a stranger
6. Builds long-term relationships	6. Constantly reselling
7. Gives opportunity for two-way communications	7. One-way communications
8. Provides mechanisms for immediate response	8. No response mechanism
9. Immediate evaluation	9. Longer-term evaluation

Direct marketing and advertising should also be assigned different and defined roles (Figure 2-3) in your communications mix. As you examine the roles and how they affect overall consumer behaviour, you can then appreciate the impact and power of these different approaches to communication when they are used in concert with each other to complement or support your strategy.

FIGURE 2-3

DEFINING THE ROLES

DIRECT MARKETING	ADVERTISING
Acquire potentially profitable customers	Build awareness of brand and image
Turn non-profitable customers into profitable customers	Establish image and corporate values
Acknowledge, retain, and reward profitable customers	Attract new customers and make existing customers feel good about their choice

▶ The 3 key drivers of direct marketing are:

1. The ability to isolate customers and put them on a database

Direct marketing gives you the opportunity to capture the initial customer information and ongoing changing behaviour, and create a two-way dialogue.

2. Build customer relationships

Based on database analytics, you are able to choose the individual customers with whom you want to build an ongoing relationship, by listening to what they say either in words or behaviour. Customer relationships are not built on one-time communications, but rather on ongoing, relevant communications. No relationship happens overnight. You must continually work at it.

3. Build profitable customer relationships

By developing an ongoing, open relationship with your customer, you are able to determine profitability or potential profit based on customer value to your company. The combination of recency of purchase (R), frequency of purchase (F), and the monetary value (M) gives you the initial view of customer profitability. The combination of customer profitability and product/service relevancy, gives you the potential for moving your customer relationship up the ladder to customer loyalty.

▶ Calculating the lifetime value of a customer

By David Beaton, Blitz Data Customers By Choice

An introduction

This section looks at the profits, costs, and revenues of a business in a context that may be unfamiliar to you. Developed by direct marketers over a number of products and industries, lifetime value is a means of calculating the economics of a given business based on the relationship the business has with its customers — the fundamental difference in direct marketing.

Direct marketing can be thought of as the art and science of building relationships with customers. Direct marketers see a "single sale" as part of an ongoing process of serving a customer need. Today's sale leads to others in the future, channelled through the product delivery and communication program the direct marketer creates to facilitate the process. Further, measuring success only in terms of sales is insufficient for most purposes. It is critical to measure the impact on profit based upon the actions of marketers and their customers over time.

Direct marketers have found that traditional tools that account for profit and loss do not reflect, or are insensitive to, this multi-year, multi-sale, bottom-line approach. In its place, various means of calculating the sum of the costs and benefits of the relationship a business has with its customers emerges over time. Most use similar methods and concepts. The following summarises the key features the analyst should be aware of when calculating the lifetime value (LTV) of a customer.

1. Applications

Before defining how to calculate LTV, let's spend a minute discussing how the analysis is applied. Examples of the uses to which such calculations are put are:

- Setting new accounts acquisition allowances that reflect the contribution to profit of new customers over appropriate planning horizons

- Calculating the anticipated impact of changes in pricing, costs, or credit policies on unit and total business profit

- Setting selection criteria for targeted marketing efforts

- Calculating the acceptance criteria for granting credit to new customers or increasing credit limits on existing customers

- Identifying profitable opportunities to convince lapsed customers to begin buying again

- Assigning an asset value to your existing customer base

2. The elements of LTV

2.1 Expected lifetime

The one approach that most distinguishes this type of profitability calculation from more traditional approaches is the concept of the *expected lifetime of the customer relationship.*

Every customer with which your business has a relationship represents an opportunity to make new sales in the future. The customer value is not merely the sum of what customers have purchased in the past. The LTV approach allows the analyst to estimate what future sales could be and to add that value in weighing the worth of the customer.

The first step, then, is to estimate how long the average relationship with your customers will be. This period is referred to as the *expected lifetime.*

To reach this number, it is necessary to determine what percentage of customers from a base of new accounts maintain and sever this relationship with you each year, either voluntarily, through their own actions (e.g., writing to the customer service department to notify it that they no longer wish to purchase from your company) or involuntarily, through the actions of your firm (e.g., a cut off of their credit privileges by the accounting department).

Let's assume you publish a magazine. Several years ago, a group of 100 customers subscribed to your magazine.

· All were for a period of one year

· In the first year after their initial enrolment, several cancelled their subscription

· Several more never paid for their initial order and consequently your company cancelled their subscription

· At the end of the first year, 90 subscribers renewed for the second year

· In the second year, 10 more subscribers cancel for a variety of reasons

· Let's assume 10 cancel for each year of the next five years

If we were to chart this progression, it would look something like this:

A hypothetical attrition curve

Starting group	100 customers
After first renewal	90
After second renewal	80
After third renewal	70
After fourth renewal	60
After fifth renewal	50
After sixth renewal	40
After seventh renewal	30

As the hypothetical attrition curve chart illustrates, only 30 percent of our original group of 100 is still subscribing after eight years. If, at this time, we wanted to calculate the average time this group of customers had been subscribers, we would sum up the number of customers each year and divide by 100.

If we assume all newly enrolled customer groups behave in the same way, the average expected lifetime, in this case, would be 5.2 years.

If we assume the group will not age another year, we could use the value 5.2 as the expected lifetime of this group. However, we may know this is not the case. The remaining 30 subscribers may continue to age, adding to the existing average lifetime of the group. To calculate expected lifetime in this case, we need to estimate how long this process might continue.

To do this, consider several factors. The first is whether there is some finite limit to the relationship beyond which it is unlikely to continue. For example, our group of 100 may have an average age of 35 years. We may know from research that it is extremely unlikely that a subscription will continue after the reader reaches the age of 65. Our upper limit to ageing, in this case, will be 30 years.

Second, consider your organisation's planning horizons. It may be extremely impractical to consider profits from a relationship 30 years from now when the model is being used to calculate acquisition margins for the coming fiscal year. To some extent, discount rates in the model take this time effect into account (as we will see later), but the analyst may want to impose a more restrictive condition, for the sake of erring on the conservative side. For this reason, a maximum horizon should be agreed on with management, reflecting the degree to which management wants to recognise events far in the future when considering actions on today's business.

The representative attrition curve

Our aim in calculating an attrition curve for this model is to arrive at numbers representative of the customer relationship across the full range of operation of the business, and in consideration of the most recent customer behaviour. To do so, several dimensions of behaviour will need to be investigated and a blend of learning from this exercise brought to bear to arrive at a representative curve.

Factors that have been known to affect the shape of attrition curves are market conditions, the economy, enrolment methods, market penetration, and policy changes that govern the ongoing relationship. It is advisable to calculate a number of attrition curves across dimensions that the analyst believes to be important, given firsthand knowledge of the business. Once this is done, the resulting curves should be compared and distilled into one, or a small group of curves for the next step.

To create one curve that represents many will require judgment as to what most represents the state of the business at this time. For example, if it is found that attrition curves from enrolment several years ago imply a much shorter lifetime than more recent curves, and if this trend can be explained in terms of shifts in marketing and credit practices or market factors that are sustainable, then the analyst is justified in calling for a longer expected lifetime for the *representative* customer.

The calculation of expected lifetime is a critical one for the purposes of assessing profitability. It may often be the case that the finances of the relationship promoted by many direct marketers show losses in the first year, or the first few purchases, followed by increasing unit profits. This is especially true of many continuity sales, such as books or records, and of many financial sales relationships, such as credit cards. It may take several years to break even, and several more to become profitable. The longer the expected lifetime after break even, the more profitable the present value of it is. With this in mind, you should select time horizons and attrition curves with care.

2.2 Customer behaviour

Once we know how long we can expect to maintain a relationship with our customers, we need to know what we expect will happen over the course of that relationship.

- What actions will the customer take that will, in turn, generate revenues for our business?

- How many actions can we expect the customer to make?

- What actions can your customers take that will generate costs, without associated revenues for the firm?

- How many such actions will take place over the customer's lifetime?

It is the sum of these actions that will determine the costs and revenues our firm will realise over the course of doing business with our customers. This sum is referred to as *customer behaviour*.

After identifying these actions, we must assess how frequently they occur relative to our *average* customer. That is, not all customers will behave in exactly the same way. Some will purchase regularly, pay their bills on time, rarely return merchandise or complain to customer service. Others will generate credit problems, be infrequent or low-value purchasers, and regularly return merchandise. It is the average of this behaviour that allows us to construct a picture of a representative relationship. This representation takes into account the relative probabilities of most, if not all, significant customer behaviour.

To illustrate how to incorporate behaviour into our model, we return to our hypothetical group of 100 subscribers. Let's assume, for the sake of simplicity, that there are only three actions subscribers can take, and they take these actions only on the date their subscription comes up for renewal.

The actions taken are:

1. Pay for another year of the magazine, by cheque, in advance

2. Cancel their subscription

3. Write to customer service with an inquiry about their account. Following an explanatory letter, they pay their subscription for the next year, by cheque. Now we need to know how often this behaviour occurs relative to a group average. Of the 100 subscribers that come up for first year renewal:

- 80 pay to renew
- 10 pay after correspondence
- 10 cancel
- Similar observations are made for each year of renewal
- The numbers are converted to a percentage of the year's starting group

Now we have some information to add to our attrition curve.

TABLE 2-1

ATTRITION CURVE WITH BEHAVIOUR ADDED

Year I	Renew %	Cancel %	Renew with correspondence %
100	80	10.0	10.0
90	80	11.0	9.0
80	80	12.5	7.5
70	80	14.3	5.7
60	80	16.7	3.3
50	80	20.0	0.0
40	75	25.0	0.0
30	75	25.0	0.0

Now that we understand how many years subscribers have been with us, and how they have behaved over this period, we are ready for the next step in the calculation.

2.3 Allocating revenues and costs to behaviour

The LTV approach conforms with traditional financial analysis when it comes to assessing the costs and revenues of the operation. However, instead of performing this compilation over the traditional one-year period or in relation to each of the business cost centres, we assess costs in relation to the customer behaviour that generated them in the first place. The time frame that is relevant is the *expected lifetime* as calculated in the first step. The behaviours to which costs will be assessed are outlined in 2.1.

Revenues are allocated to the model at the time they occur. In our example, we assume our only revenues come from the payment of the $50 subscription at the time of renewal.

There are three costs that must be allocated to the LTV model: *variable, fixed,* and *semi-variable*. For the purposes of the LTV analysis, *variable costs* are defined as those that change in direct proportion to customer behaviour. The costs of processing subscription renewals would be treated as a variable cost.

Fixed costs are those that remain unchanged over a wide range of customer behaviour. To decide whether costs should be treated as fixed for a LTV calculation, you must first decide for what purpose and over what time period the calculation applies. In the long run, all costs can be treated as variable, even those that appear to be fixed over the short-term. For example, the costs of the building in which we house our magazine operation may appear, on first glance, to be a fixed cost. Heat, light, and mortgage costs are incurred whether the business grows rapidly or shrinks at the same pace, especially over the next few years of operation. However, over the course of many years, we can see that "housing" can be treated as a variable cost — that is, we could move the operation to larger or smaller quarters as business growth dictates. So, you must review each cost carefully to decide whether to treat it as fixed or variable in the context of the LTV calculation being performed.

If a cost is to be fixed for the calculation, a means must be found to either allocate it to the business or treat it as a cost beyond the scope of the calculation itself. Allocation methods vary in complexity and are beyond the scope of this discussion. In general, though, the analyst must decide which treatment would result in a fair portrayal of costs, again in the context of the calculation being performed.

We may decide the fixed cost should be beyond the scope of the calculation. In this case, the outcome of the calculation is a statement of profit that does not take into account all of the costs of doing business. We call the LTV number a contribution to profit and overhead because of this effect.

Semi-variable costs are costs that change in some proportion to changes in customer behaviour, but which have a significant fixed-cost component.

An example may be the customer service department we referred to earlier. Over most levels of customer activity, the staffing costs of the department will be fixed. Beyond this range, we could add staff in proportion to the level of correspondence coming in. This portion is a variable cost. The sum of these two is, of course, a semi-variable expense. Allocation methods for the fixed portion of this cost are treated as the fixed costs already outlined. The variable portion is used to define cost changes outside of the range covered by the fixed cost staffing.

In most cases, allocate all of the variable and semi-variable costs of the operation to the LTV calculation. This way, all of the costs normally associated with a traditional profit and loss statement are included in the LTV approach. As we have seen, however, the means of allocating and summing these costs may vary significantly from traditional profit and loss approaches.

▶ Timing

The LTV model is time-sensitive — that is, behaviour and the costs associated with it are projected over the expected lifetime of the customer. For some businesses, this means projecting many years into the future. For every year after the current one, costs and benefits are discounted to arrive at their equivalent present value. The rate used for discounting varies; many companies use their capital costs.

▶ Putting it all together — a sample LTV calculation

After determining our customer's expected lifetime and assessing behaviour over this period, and allocating the costs of doing business to this behaviour over the relevant time periods, we are ready to calculate a hypothetical LTV. For the sake of illustration, let us return to our magazine subscription example. Remember. The behaviour and costs associated with it are greatly simplified. Table 2-2 on the following page calculates the lifetime value on the basis of behaviour, revenues, and costs used in this case.

TABLE 2-2

AN EXAMPLE OF THE LIFETIME VALUE OF A MAGAZINE SUBSCRIBER

YEAR:	1	2	3	4	5	6	7	8
Revenues:								
Percentage of starter group paying	100	90	80	70	60	50	40	30
Renewal fee	$50	$50	$50	$50	$50	$50	$50	$50
TOTAL REVENUES:	$50	$45	$40	$35	$30	$25	$20	$15
Costs								
1. Acquisition costs	$30							
2. Product costs, annual	$30	$30	$30	$30	$30	$30	$30	$30
3. Cancellations								
Percentage cancelling	10	11	12.5	14.3	16.7	20	25	25
Cost per cancellation	$10	$10	$10	$10	$10	$10	$10	$10
TOTAL CANCELLATION COSTS	$1	$1.10	$1.25	$1.43	$1.67	$2	$2.50	$2.50
4. Renewals								
Percentage renewing with correspondence	10	9	7.5	5.7	3.3	0	0	0
Percentage renewing without correspondence	80	79	77.5	75.7	73.3	70	65	65
Cost per renewal without correspondence	$2.00	$2.00	$2.00	$2.00	$2.00	$2.00	$2.00	$2.00
TOTAL RENEWAL COSTS	$2.60	$2.48	$2.30	$2.08	$1.80	$1.40	$1.30	$1.30
TOTAL COSTS PER YEAR	$63.60	$33.58	$33.55	$33.51	$33.47	$33.40	$33.80	$33.80
Revenue per starter group	$50.00	$45.00	$40.00	$35.00	$30.00	$25.00	$20.00	$15.00
Costs per starter group	63.6	30.222	26.84	23.4598	20.0796	16.7	13.52	10.14
Gains (losses) per year	($13.60)	$14.78	$13.16	$11.54	$9.92	$8.30	$6.48	$4.86
Discount factor	0.86956	0.75614	0.65751	0.57175	0.49717	0.43232	0.37593	0.32690
Net present value per annum	($11.83)	$11.17	$8.65	$6.60	$4.93	$3.59	$2.44	$1.59
Net present value	$27.14							

As you can see, the LTV of a representative subscriber is $27.14

▶ The direct marketing success formula

Direct marketing plays an ever-increasing and important role in today's marketing mix. However, there is little documented reason for its success. Why is direct marketing so successful? Many experts will tell you there is a formula for success, and the formula includes the constant refinement of all marketing variables: product, service, offer, price, and media to better satisfy customer needs. It is how you apply the formula that will make you successful in direct marketing. The success formula is centred around offering the *right* product or service, to the *right* audience, with the *right* creative, via the *right* media, with the *right* proposition or offer, in the *right* format, with the *right* level of campaign integration, which has the *right* tests built in for growth, being managed by the *right* systems, and resulting in the *right* analysis.

10 Rs for success

1. The *right* audience

Direct marketing allows you to offer special products to specific segments or target groups. Use this advantage. Design programs that appeal to a target defined more specifically than "male/female, 18-54 years of age, and still breathing." Does your product have a different benefit for seniors than it does for young professionals? Your ability to select your audience and truly target it with relevancy, is the key advantage of direct marketing.

2. The *right* product or service

One reason for direct marketing's success is that it delivers *quality* merchandise to the consumer, at home, or in the office, based on good value. You may want to add the word *unique*. "Me-too" products with no unique selling proposition (USP) are not successfully marketed directly to the consumer. *Direct marketing is not the vehicle to dispose of products that have been unsuccessful elsewhere. Nor is it the place to get rid of damaged goods.*

3. The *right* media

Your product, audience, budget, and expected response rates will play a major role in the selection of your media. Remember. You have direct mail, telemarketing, print advertising, preprinted inserts, broadcast, and the Internet from which to choose. Some products that cannot achieve a reasonable cost per order in print may be suitable for television. Allow your up-front analysis (that is, analysis done before the campaign) determine which direct marketing vehicle allows you to reach your target efficiently and effectively based on your stated objectives in your marketing plan.

4. The *right* proposition or offer

You may have chosen the right audience and media, and have done all your up-front analysis, but without an effective, unique offer, you will not convert your prospect. Many years ago, "free" was touted as one of the best offers available. That is not the case today. Today's consumers believe in price and value. Review your product attributes, do your research, and determine what the best offer is for your product — then test.

5. The *right* creative

Your creative product, regardless of the format you choose, should reflect your corporate image and demonstrate your consumer promise. The *right* creative is more centred around creative that is relevant to your target audience, respects your brand position, and differentiates you from competitors. It treats the consumer with respect, is easily understood, incorporates the principles of direct marketing, and asks for the order over and over again.

6. The *right* format

The available formats are varied in direct mail, print advertising, and broadcast. Should your direct mail package be delivered in a 6 x 9, 9 x 12, or a No.10 envelope? Does your product or service need a four-colour brochure, a two-colour insert, or just a letter and response form? Should your print advertising be carried on-page or should it be an insert? Should your television spot be 60 seconds, 90 seconds, or 120 seconds in length? Or perhaps a 30-minute infomercial is best suited to your objectives. Of course, costs, strategic testing, and expected response rates will have a dramatic influence on these decisions.

7. The *right* campaign integration

If direct marketing is but one discipline in your marketing mix, be sure that your brand message is consistent, your timing is complementary, and your analysis is set up to track each component separately. Advertising and direct marketing are strong companions. In the case of testing a multi-media direct marketing campaign, be sure your analysis reflects and supports your testing objectives.

8. The *right* tests

The number of tests you can conduct are endless. Be sure your tests are designed for easy reading of results. More important, be sure you *test for the big things, for big success*. Execute tests that will make a difference to your future marketing plans. Some big tests could include, customer segments, price testing, offer testing, media/list testing, and benefit statement (creative) testing.

9. The *right* systems

Before you offer your product via direct marketing, be sure you have the right systems to cope with and track response as well as offer superior customer service. Not the least of these is the input and control of a customer database.

10. The *right* analysis

When we talk about analysis, we speak of *up-front* (before your campaign) and *back-end* analysis (after your campaign). Direct marketing lives and dies by the numbers, but the proper interpretation of the numbers is not always obvious. Whether your analysis defines the behaviour difference between buyers and trials, or the cost difference between lead-generation and a closed sale for your sales force, the need for analysis applies. Be sure to include in your analysis the lifetime value of your customer. And while skill in numerical analysis is a necessity, it will not be sufficient unless the analysis is directed and supported by a deep understanding and commitment to the customer's needs and behaviour.

Figure 2-4 on the following page serves as a guideline for you to focus on this process and evaluate your expected results.

FIGURE 2-4
THE DIRECT MARKETING ACTIVITY CHART

Up-front planning

1. **The right product**
   - what product/service
2. **The right audience**
   - potential (universe) market
   - target customer, new and/or existing
3. **The right media**
   - past results
   - required frequency
   - cost per order (CPO) expectations
4. **The right offer or proposition**
   - what must be tested: price, offer, media
   - when, where, and how to test
5. **The right creative**
   - past results
   - target (segment) attitude
   - primary benefit
6. **The right format**
   - past test results
   - budget
   - expected cost per order (CPO)
7. **The right integration**
   - is this a multi-media campaign
   - is other advertising running at the same time
8. **The right tests**
   - what will be tested: price, media, offer, format, audience
   - when and how to test
9. **The right systems**
   - who will track response and how
   - who will update the database and when
   - who will produce reports and when
   - if using telemarketing, who will train and write the script and supply answers for consumers
10. **The right analysis**
    - what has to be done
    - who will do it
    - what is the expected ROI
    - expected change in customer behaviour
    - projected overhead

Organising

1. Selecting the *right product/service*:
   - price
   - quality
   - unique selling benefits
   - quantity needed
   - delivery method
   - payment terms
   - storage arrangements
2. Selecting the *right audience*:
   - existing customers, what segments
   - lapsed customers, what segments
   - new customers, rented from whom, what definitions
3. Selecting the *right media*:
   - personalised direct mail
   - print advertising
   - free falls (FFIs, FSIs)
   - coupons, merchandise stuffers
   - householder mail
   - catalogue
   - television
   - radio
   - phone
   - Internet
4. The *right media* Buying:
   - where
   - when
   - for what length of time (frequency)
   - from whom
5. The *right creative and offers*:
   - what is the market strategy
   - offer definition
   - price parameters
   - available terms of payment
   - what is the idea
   - who will write it and when
   - who will design it and when

Systems: Implementing

1. Processing orders/leads
2. Database update and reports
3. Arranging fulfillment, packaging, addressing, shipping
4. Handling of cash and credit cards, banking arrangements
5. Accounts receivable:
   - invoicing
   - use of credit cards
   - use of payment plans
   - collection policies
   - dunning
6. Customer service:
   - inquiries
   - quality problems
   - back-up service, internal or external

Back-end analysis-evaluating

All aspects:
- audience
- product
- media
- offer and timing
- creative
- format
- integration
- tests
- systems
- analysis

Planning the next campaign

OPPORTUNITY EVALUATION

3

Corporate and product or service opportunities in direct marketing are bountiful. Each and every company must examine these opportunities for itself.

The success of new entrants relies on embracing direct marketing as a strategy based on the proper analysis and the strength of implementation. Opportunity evaluation therefore occurs on the *corporate level* and must fulfill the overall corporate objectives, rather than your individual business unit goals on a one-off project basis.

This chapter deals with how to evaluate the potential of direct marketing for your company. Whether this is a first-time project for your company or an introduction of a new product or service idea, the analysis should be done with the same completeness.

My personal guidelines are:

Mine the power of profitable passions;
build on strength, not structure; and
cultivate people — delegate process.

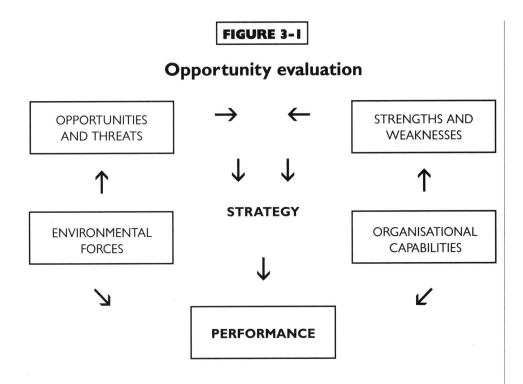

FIGURE 3-1

Opportunity evaluation

OPPORTUNITIES AND THREATS	→ ←	STRENGTHS AND WEAKNESSES
↑	↓ ↓	↑
ENVIRONMENTAL FORCES	**STRATEGY**	ORGANISATIONAL CAPABILITIES
↘	↓	↙
	PERFORMANCE	

▶ Environmental forces

This is your opportunity to examine what you can quantify about the structure and dynamic of the direct marketing opportunity under consideration.

Your first examination should be an overall analysis and understanding of the current state of the industry and the macroenvironment in which your firm does, or will, operate.

The direct marketing environment

· What business category does your product or service fit into?
· What are the primary drivers of the category?
· Is the category customer driven or knowledge driven?
· Who are the competitors (define the barrier to entry and the barrier to exit)?
· Define and research consumer attitudes — positive and negative
· Define geographic impact: local, regional, national, international
· Determine allocation of resources
· What are the profit differences from your existing business?

Before you can make direct marketing a part of your company strategy, you must take a critical look at your business in order to determine whether direct marketing can indeed work for your company needs as well as your individual products or services categories. Direct marketing must fit into your company philosophy. This commitment must be made in the boardroom and acknowledged and embraced as an important component of your company strategy. It must become a way of doing business that is seamless.

▶ Your company

After examining the direct marketing environment, you should then proceed to a careful and complete analysis of your own company's operations, and the environment in which it functions. This will allow you to determine whether direct marketing can be a profitable component of your overall marketing strategy.

When analysing your company's situation, look at past trends as well as present performance: examine and compare past and present sales and profits, media mixes, and methods of distribution. This should give you a good indication of where your company is going and what kind of investment you can afford to make in the future. Also remember that an important part of the company definition involves an equally careful examination of the marketplace and the environment in which your company presently operates.

First examine your overall corporate objectives, which are part and parcel of your company philosophy:

- **Short-term:** up to one year

- **Mid-term**: two to three years

- **Long-term:** up to five years

- **Quantitative:** total sales, gross margin, net profit, and return on investment

- **Qualitative:** defined as a new market entrant, protecting an existing market, expanding your existing market, or extending your current product or service line

▶ Strengths and weaknesses, opportunities, and threats (SWOT)

The SWOT analysis plays an important role in ascertaining the answers to some very specific questions. It is a process that is helpful at all stages of corporate growth and expansion. It is imperative to your success that the corporation understand and acknowledge what it is good at and what it needs to improve.

The next step asks more specific questions about all the components of your present company situation:

Industry sales and size

What is the size of the present market for this type of product or service?

You may wish to consult sources, such as Statistics Canada, trade associations, market research, and your own company files. Your answer should be a combination of gathered intelligence.

Competition

Is there really an opportunity for another entry into the marketplace? Are there already too many competitors, each of whom may have a very small share? Have you ranked your competition fairly and honestly? Can you employ an effective strategy or address a market niche not currently filled?

Market composition

Who buys this type of product? Why do they buy it? Where do they buy it? Do customers presently respond to direct marketing campaigns for this product/service? Is there a seasonal factor to consider?

Uniqueness

Can you offer something unique, or are you duplicating someone else's offer? What is your unique selling proposition (USP)? Do you plan to dominate the market? If so, how? What role will innovation play in your market position? How will you outperform the competition?

Comparative value

Can you offer greater value than your competition? What is your point of difference, and can it be clearly communicated as a customer benefit? Will your prospects perceive your product as a better value?

Customer service

Are systems in place to deliver products or services to customers, and handle fulfillment of orders quickly and efficiently? Can you efficiently handle customer correspondence, phone inquiries, and picking, packaging, and delivery of the product? Are you equipped to build an ongoing relationship with the customer? (That is, do you maintain a suitable database?) Are you equipped to win over customers from the competition, if necessary? Should you seek outside help? If so, from whom, and how much will it cost?

Repeat orders

Will your first sale lead to repeat sales? Is it a single-product offering, or is there an opportunity for sales continuity programs? Can you organise and operate an efficient follow-up system and offer ongoing offers to your customer base? Do you have, or will you develop, other product lines that can be cross-promoted to a customer base?

Technology

Do you have the technology, or the skills to develop the needed technology to compete? What are the hardware, software, and competency criteria and how do you stack up?

Profit margin

What is the potential profit? Is your margin large enough to make your total investment worthwhile? Does it reflect industry standards for the category? How much money must you invest up-front to realise your profit objectives? How long will it take? Can you afford to wait for your return on investment? Can your projected profit meet your corporate guidelines for success? Do the associated costs cancel out the anticipated benefits?

▶ **Organisational capabilities**

A direct marketing strategy must reflect a logical search for a match between external opportunities and internal capabilities. When one of these opportunities change, the company must be flexible enough to adapt.

Business unit strategy

A business unit should be developed around your new direct marketing mandate, objectives, and expected return on investment.

Core competencies

An assessment of existing skills within the unit must be examined, and if necessary, a commitment to training existing staff members and/or a search for additional staff must be undertaken to complete the required skills of the business unit. People create strategy so, it's people that will make the difference in how the task is accomplished.

Assign a champion

Every strategy needs its champion. Selection of this individual should be centred around great communication skills, leadership skills, and a passion for direct marketing success.

When this phase of your opportunity evaluation is complete, analysis of these quantitative and qualitative factors will allow you to clearly define your company — its image, its strengths and weaknesses, the opportunities and threats, and its organisational capabilities. It will also allow you to differentiate yourself from your competitors and carve out a niche in the direct marketing universe. It should clearly define and evaluate your future market opportunities.

If this process leads you to decide that direct marketing is a feasible strategy for your company, you must determine how you will enter the marketplace. You may already have existing products or services through which you can accomplish your stated objectives, or you may be embarking on a new product launch. No matter what the case, the process of evaluation should be the same.

Product or service selection can be accomplished in either two ways:

1. Select your product or service to market, then target your campaign to the appropriate audience.

2. However, in today's customer-driven environment, delineation of a target market opportunity, then identifying an appropriate product or service niche, gives any company a position of strength from which to operate.

1. Your product or service line

The recent and rapid extension of direct marketing has introduced an enormous variety of products and services into the marketplace, *servicing both the business and consumer marketplace.*

The likes of IBM, Bell Canada, Royal Bank, General Motors, and Honda, have all proudly joined the ranks of corporations successfully incorporating direct marketing into their marketing plans. They have realised that their products have a target audience, and they are committed to building a long-term relationship with their customers.

The adoption of direct marketing techniques does not guarantee success. Only analysis of your product or service will lead you in the right direction. What direct marketing does offer is the opportunity to *selectively* reach those segments of the total population that are most likely to buy and to build a relationship with your valuable customer segments.

Here are some guidelines to consider when evaluating the potential of products and services to be sold by direct marketing:

Value

You must offer a distinct price, and/or great value, as a major selling feature. Your price, though it need not be a bargain, must nevertheless be perceived as offering "value." The effect of pricing and price packaging should be considered carefully. In the idea of value, there are other ingredients than mere price. Often, convenience, service, and your corporate guarantee will be significant add-ons with respect to perceived value. Product/service uniqueness and desirability can also increase value to customers.

Retail failures

Some failed retail or branch service/products may be ideal for direct marketing remedies. One should first determine, through research, why the public shunned the product in the first place. Depending on the case — e.g. untrained retail or branch staff who are unable to properly assist the consumer or retail counter staff take too long to produce required information or consumers preferring to have their partner present when the buying decision is made — identifying such obstacles is crucial to product understanding and product complexities. Direct marketing may help, but it will never make a bad product good.

Exclusive product or service

Certainly a product or service that can be sold exclusively via direct marketing will have more appeal than one widely available. If it is not possible to avoid a price comparison, the direct marketer can put together a special package offered exclusively to the target audience. A successful offering can be for example, a quarter-point savings on your RSP or an added bonus, often related in some way to the product and relevant to the audience.

Speciality items

A product or service that appeals to a special segment of the market, such as seniors or professional women, is often an ideal candidate for direct marketing.

2. Your target market

Before you embark on your direct marketing campaign, you must create in black and white a clear definition of the type of people who are most likely to be your customers. Are your best prospects seniors, professionals, such as doctors and lawyers, or DINKS (double income, no kids)?

Clear delineation of your audience will help you target your campaign directly to your best prospects and fully support the direct marketing advantage of selecting and testing your audience. Pinpoint your offer to those consumers who are most likely to respond and plan to constantly refine your target definition based on market experience, customer feedback, research, and testing.

Effective targeting of your high potential customer base is the most important step in a successful direct marketing campaign. You can begin by establishing a list of the primary characteristics of your customer or prospect. Develop this list by:

- Analysing your own company records

- Conducting market research

- Analysing your past experience (if any) on the basis of the similarities and differences between the type of people who have received your offer in the past and have responded, and those who received your offer and did not respond

Company or organisation sales records will reveal significant details about your present customers. Well-conducted market tests will further show the characteristics of buyers versus non-buyers.

You should be able to classify your prospects in the following ways:

Present customers

Your best prospect will be your past satisfied customer. The more recently and frequently that customer purchased from you, the better the prospect.

Direct marketing buyers

Generally speaking, anyone who has made a purchase by means of any direct response vehicle is more likely to respond to another offer via the same vehicle. Remember. Direct response buyers have made a commitment to do business through the mail, phone, or Internet and therefore tend to respond more readily than someone who has never done business that way before.

Friends and neighbours of buyers

If you can reach the friends and neighbours of your present customers, or have them reach for you, chances are they will want to buy your product or service, too. Imagine the power of a friend's endorsement. As you examine the opportunity of the power of referrals, remember it also works in the reverse: if customers are dissatisfied with you, they can probably take a number of customers with them if they defect.

Demographically delineated audiences

Attempt to define, by experience, testing, or research, whether the people most likely to buy your product or service can also be described in terms of the following types of factors:

1. Geographic: region; province; city, suburb; urban, rural; house, apartment

2. Socioeconomic: sex; marital status; age; income; occupation; education

3. Psychographics: lifestyle; interests; attitudes

If once you've defined your company, selected a product or service, and decided on its appropriate target market, you conclude that direct marketing offers your company valuable potential, then the next step is to *decide how to market your product or service* — that is, develop a marketing plan.

▶ Summary

Before you embark on your marketing plan, let's quickly review some of the steps we have covered so far:

- You have completed an opportunity evaluation that involves an assessment of your company's position in the marketplace, its objectives, its product or service line, and its target market.

- You have analysed and taken into account your past and present corporate positioning and performance, and your plans and objectives for the future.

- You have made a corporate commitment to direct marketing.

- You have identified your champion.

- You have set your corporate objectives and have defined the role of direct marketing in meeting these objectives.

- You're ready to do your first marketing plan.

THE MARKETING PLAN

4

YOUR MARKETING PLAN

I n progressing from opportunity evaluation to your *marketing plan*, you now turn from overall corporate definition to a specific marketing campaign.

This chapter deals with how to plan and prepare for a profitable campaign when significant potential exists. It is designed to help you define a marketing plan and determine what preliminary actions (tests) and decisions are necessary before you invest significantly in direct marketing. At the end of this chapter, you will find a sample marketing plan (Figure 4-3). Although every marketing plan will not look like the one shown, this one illustrates the information you need.

A good plan can mean a successful direct marketing campaign — successful in its accomplishments, in its lessons and test results. Ill-conceived or improper planning and poor control implementation are frequently the principle reasons for failure. Therefore, one must take the time to plan carefully. Remember. Planning is the least hard cost in your campaign — it takes place before you commit to large expenditures.

▶ What is a marketing plan?

A marketing plan should be a concise working document that is designed to be used as a constant reference. It is a detailed document, but not a cumbersome document. A marketing plan should define:

- The type of business you are in (products, competition, market, environment)
- Your specific campaign objectives (what you want to accomplish)
- The major problems and opportunities you face
- Your strategy (how you will accomplish your campaign objectives, capitalise on your opportunities, eliminate the problems, and minimise the risks)
- When and where your strategy will be executed (your tactics)
- Who is responsible for carrying it out
- Measurement criteria (financial, non-financial, quantitative, qualitative)

Your specific campaign should be a direct evolution from the corporate objectives assessed in the *opportunity evaluation*. The two should be consistent and complementary in objectives, target audience, and success measurement.

In the case of a company that has many campaigns in preparation simultaneously — American Express Personal Card, Gold Card, Platinum Card, Optima Card, No Fee Card, Corporate Card, and American Express Air Miles Card — each plan should be an integral part of an overall marketing plan. Overall objectives are defined at the higher corporate level, then broken down for each business unit. At each product level, a strategy and action plan are developed and passed back up through the organisation for approval of budgets, resource commitment, consistency, and impact analysis within the broader corporate objectives.

▶ Contents of your marketing plan

Although there are different possible ways to put your marketing plan together, it should be organised more or less as follows:

1. A summary of current market position
2. Problems and opportunities
3. Marketing objectives
4. Marketing strategy
5. Marketing tactics (plan and budgets)

1. Summary of current market position

Your definition of the company's image and performance should be based on the following considerations:

- Definition of your market and key competitors
- Definition of your recent performance versus that of your key competitors
- Performance of specific programs over the past year
- Overall market performance (growth, profitability)
- Results of any tests
- Your recommendations

2. Problems and opportunities

It is important to list major problems and key opportunities that your business currently faces and their impact as they apply to your category. Define only the opportunities that are unique to your company, product, or service. These should include:

- Sales trends
- Competitor's activities
- Legislation and mandatories (legal requirements)
- Consumer attitudes

3. Marketing objectives

After analysing the current market situation and defining problems and opportunities, assess the key *objectives* for the short-term, mid-term, and long-term. Your objectives should be stated in specific, *measurable* terms, and should be stated both for your *test* and for your *roll-out* campaign (a subsequent, higher volume campaign, based on what you learned from your previous test).

Figure 4-1 presents some sample objectives. You will notice that the purpose of your test is merely to "test the waters," and that your roll-out objective is stated in clearly defined terms since it must be based on results from your test. Do not attempt to have a roll-out objective in a test situation. Remember. Direct marketing success is based on the ability to track and interpret test results.

You may wish to test other factors, such as price or response rates from different media, but these additional tasks, though spelled out in your list of objectives, should be given secondary importance. Achieve your major objectives first, then fit in your other tests as your plan and budget allows. Your campaign objectives should be simply stated. Nothing flowery — just the facts.

FIGURE 4-1

EXAMPLES OF MARKETING OBJECTIVES

SELLING A PRODUCT

Test objective
To find out if you can profitably sell a pocket calculator to your present customers

Roll-out objective
To sell 2,000 model WP1 calculators at $65 for a contribution to profit of $20,000

GENERATING LEADS FOR YOUR SALES FORCE

Test objective
To find out if you can generate qualified leads for your sales force at a lower cost per qualified lead (or resulting sale) than present lead-generating methods

Roll-out objective
To generate 40 qualified leads per week, for eight members of your sales force in the central Ontario division, for the periods January through June, and September through November

FUNDRAISING

Test objective
To assess the results of mailings to rented outside lists, such as doctors, lawyers, and accountants

Roll-out objective
To raise $50,000 in the fall of 1998 via direct mail by mailing to successful rented outside professional lists, such as doctors, etc.

4. Marketing Strategy

Once you have defined your objectives, you must determine how you can accomplish them. The marketing strategy development process should provide you with an outline of how to address your objective(s). It states that you are going to accomplish something by doing something. The strategies developed must not only accomplish the objectives set, but also do so as efficiently and cost-effectively as possible. Only your best strategies should be selected.

They should identify:

What to sell (product or service):

· Name of your product or service

· Description of your product or service

- Price, incentives, and other details of your offer

To whom to sell (target audience):

- The primary users of this product or service

- Those most likely to purchase

- Geographic, demographic, and psychographic characteristics of high-potential buyers and past purchase behaviour

Where to sell (medium):

- The medium or combination of mediums to be used

- The methods to track and measure effectiveness

When to sell (seasonality):

- The best season, month, or week in which to sell

- How much control can you have over the timing of each medium? (If you use more than one medium, can you integrate the campaign?)

How to sell:

- What is your offer?

- Is it competitive?

- Is there a point of difference, and can you capitalise on that difference?

- What is your creative approach: does your "creative" sell? Does it have the selling components needed to get a "yes" response? Is the customer's commitment clearly stated on the response form? Is the response mechanism clear and easy to understand? Is your guarantee an important part of the offer?

By defining your marketing strategy, you create the framework for the execution of your campaign. The next step, your detailed tactical plan, should be developed by the individuals responsible for the production of your campaign.

5. Marketing tactics

Plans and budgets

Now that you have identified your best strategies, you must break down each strategy into a detailed, tactical plan. Each individual plan will have its own objectives, budget, timetable, and measurement criteria. The process, therefore, is to:

1. Define the individual campaign

2. Specify the potentially profitable tests

3. Identify separate campaigns or identifiable parts of campaigns, such as lists, print ads, or telemarketing, in order to facilitate future analysis

4. Develop execution schedules for each campaign

5. Set the criteria for the follow-up campaigns

6. Specify how your campaign will deliver on the budget objectives (determine offer, price, and fixed and variable costs)

7. State how you propose to track and measure the results of your campaign (inquiries, orders, costs per order, sales units, net revenue, gross profit, net profit) and ask again whether these are consistent with your corporate objectives

This type of financial planning must be done for both your test and subsequent roll-out, to assess not only current, but future potential profit also.

▶ Format of your marketing plan

Your marketing plan should always be in written form. The advantage of having a formal, written plan is considerable.

· It provides a precise understanding of, and promotes agreement on, the objectives, the background facts, and assumptions upon which they are based, and the decisions made to achieve your targets.

· It provides a written outline of your action plan for each campaign, including budgets and forecasts — things that should be reviewed and critiqued on an ongoing basis.

· It is a valuable reference document, and a protection against loss of experience and valuable information, and against the loss of the agreed-upon, long-range plans.

· It provides a guideline system for planning and executing campaigns, for measuring results so that you can learn from your mistakes and build on your successes, and for taking corrective action.

· It is a living, active, document.

In short, an agreed upon plan is a *commitment to do something, to measure the results and to document lessons learned from your efforts.*

▶ The marketing planning cycle

The written format ensures that actual results can be compared against projections. As such, it provides an excellent guideline for future planning. The marketing plan for any current year will comprise the results of past campaigns and tests, and information about changing market conditions and competitive activities. Similarly, the results of this year's marketing activities will make up the data for decisions pertaining to next year's plans. Thus, the planning of your campaign is a continuous job. It consists of a cycle of activities into which new information, data, and insights are continuously assimilated.

FIGURE 4-2

THE MARKETING PLANNING CYCLE

9. **Evaluate results** in light of current market environment	→ 1. **Analyse** the total market
↑	↓
8. **Collect** data (internal and external)	2. **Evaluate** results
↑	↓
7. **Service responses** and **follow up**	3. Reach **conclusions**
↑	↓
6. Conduct **campaigns**	4. Set **new** objectives
↖ 5. **Plan and budget** ↙	
←	

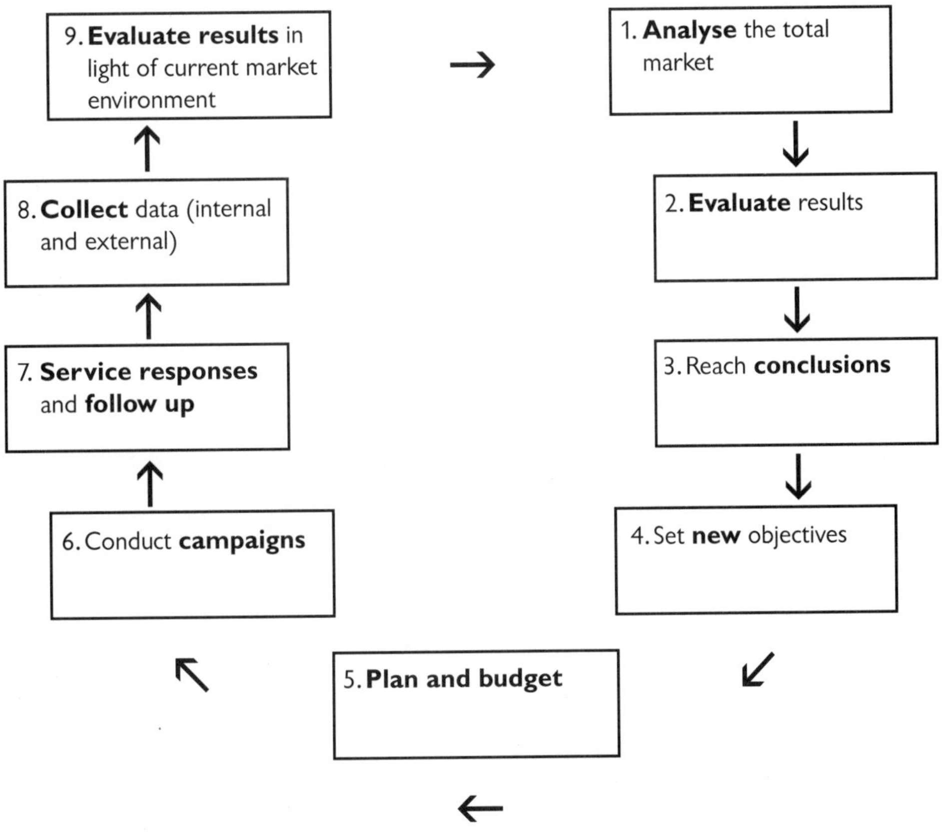

▶ Summary

Whereas *opportunity evaluation* considers overall corporate operations and objectives, a *marketing plan* deals with a specific marketing campaign within your corporate context.

A marketing plan is a concise working outline that:

- Defines the company's position

- States specific campaign objectives

- Identifies problems and opportunities

- Outlines a strategy for accomplishing the campaign objectives

- Designates areas of responsibility

- Defines measurement of success criteria

The advantages of a formal written plan are:

- It defines specific objectives and ties them to approved budgets

- It charts your course to meet specific project aims and schedules

- It helps you manage your program in an orderly, professional way

- It saves you time during implementation: a full year's activity is spelled out in advance — as opposed to hectic, last minute, one-shot programs

- It saves you money by pre-planning and co-ordinating your purchase power

- It assures the best possible creative output: writers, art directors, and production managers will have enough time to think ahead and perfect their contribution

- It serves as an ongoing catalyst for growth

- It establishes, at the outset, the integrated role direct marketing plays in your company's overall marketing and media planning

- It gives you a year-by-year comparison of results for future planning, budgeting, and ongoing analysis

SAMPLE MARKETING PLAN

Company/division:	The ABC Company — Special Projects
Campaign plan No.:	SP — 135
Issue date:	March 15, 1999

Distribution list: P. Adams, Marketing; T. Brown, Customer Service; F. Cooper, Database Manager; T. Drake, Fulfillment Operations; J. Edwards, Director of Finance.

1. Title: "The 2000 Executive Diary"

2. Background:

In the past five years we have had virtually no competition in the marketplace and still we struggled to meet our sales volume. This year, with the influx of two strong competitors, our challenges will be even greater. Our two formidable competitors are offering their diaries to their existing customers (strong crossover with ours) for $16.99 and $18.99 respectively. We cannot compete with these prices, so our strength must come from our quality of product, customer service, and the unique additions we have made to this year's diary series. In order to combat the competition, we will also mail earlier this year, in the hope that our past customers will remain loyal to our product and its features that serve them in their daily business life. We will also test some outside lists that will allow us to extend our reach. Due to product price increases, we will also test a price increase in a strongly competitive market.

3. Objectives

Annual plan: to sell 200,000 copies of The 2000 Executive Diary at $29.95 each (price includes $2.50 postage and handling (P & H) costs).

This plan:

(a) To sell 100,000 copies of The 2000 Executive Diary at $29.95 each (includes $2.50 P & H) and generate a gross margin of $1,198,000 (40 percent) and a contribution to net profit of $300,000 (10 percent).

(b) To test selling to prospects via rented mailing lists and print advertising.

(c) To test The Executive Diary in an IBM compatible software application priced at $29.95 each (including P & H of $2.50).

(d) To test the effect of offering an extra item free as an added incentive to the printed diary version only.

(e) To test the effect of increasing the price on the printed format to $34.95 plus P & H costs of $2.50.

(f) To design and test access to The Executive Diary offer on our home Web page.

4. Mail date

August 10, 1999. Print advertising will be on the newsstand in August issues. Our Web page will be available on August 10, 1999.

5. Offer and target segments

- We will test the profitability of offering an IBM compatible format of The Executive Diary in appropriate business publications at the price of $29.95 (including P & H).

- To our existing customer segments who have purchased from us over the past five years, we will offer The 2000 Executive Diary with the purchaser's initials gold-stamped for $29.95 (including $2.50 P & H). This offer will be made to 460,000 past customers and represents Cell 1 of the mailing.

- We will test the profitability of a free, added gift of a pocket notepad (cost $1 each), in direct mail to 20,000 past customers (Cell 2) and to 20,000 test cells randomly selected from outside lists (Cell 3).

- We will test a higher price of $34.95 + $2.50 P & H to 20,000 past customers (Cell 4) and to 20,000 names from outside lists (Cell 5).

- We will select a total of 480 names from outside lists that match the profile of previous buyers (Cell 6 through 10).

- We will mention our Web site in each of our efforts and track the number of hits. Although we will not incorporate a response mechanism into the Web site, we will allow for a surprise gift (cost $1) in each of our offer if customers indicate they have seen our site in the special box provided on all order forms.

6. Format

(a) Direct Mail

Based on our past tests of creative and format, the control mailing package will consist of:

- Outer mailing envelope with teaser copy
- Two-page letter

- Two-colour brochure
- Order form
- Business reply envelope (BRE)

Note: See Schedule 1, "Test Cell Formats"

(b) Advertisement

We will run two 7 x 10 black-and-white advertisements in two business publications with the standard offer, and a full-page advertisement in the *Financial Post* for our software application option. All advertisements will include a coded order coupon, a special box if they've visited our Web site, our Web site address and, a toll-free, 1-888, direct order number.

Recommended publications are based on readership profiles, response estimates based on discussions with our direct marketing agency, and maximum cost per order (CPO) estimates. Planned ads are:

Publication	Cost	Circ.	Est. Response		Coupon Code	Est. CPO
Canadian Business	$ 3,000	64,000	0.8%	512	OF11	$ 5.86
Executive	$ 3,000	40,000	1.4%	560	OF12	$ 5.36
Financial Post	$ 9,200	280,000	0.5%	1,400	OF13	$ 6.57
	$15,200	384,000		2,472		

(Note: the cost of publications and their associated circulation are used as examples only and are not meant to reflect any pricing or circulation for this, or any year.)

7. Forecast response

(a) Direct Mail
(b) Rationale for Estimated Response

Projected Response

Cell			Response	Orders
Cell 1:	460,000	existing customers	12.0%	55,200
Cell 2:	20,000	past customers with premium	14.0%	2,800
Cell 3:	20,000	outside lists with premium	10.0%	2,000
Cell 4:	20,000	past customers price test	10.0%	2,000
Cell 5:	20,000	outside lists price test	7.0%	1,400
Cell 6:	20,000	outside list test	8.5%	1,700
Cell 7:	20,000	outside list test	8.0%	1,600
Cell 8:	20,000	outside list	7.5%	1,500
Cell 9:	20,000	outside list	8.0%	1,600
Cell 10:	380,000	outside lists	7.9%	30,200
Total				**100,000**

1. Response from actives is based on our average response for similar creative and an identical offer made for the 1999 The Executive Diary.

2. Cell 2 is based on our previous response, adjusted upward conservatively because of the premium.

3. Cell 3 is based on Cell 2 response, adjusted downward because an outside list was used.

4. Cells 4 and 5 are based on the response rate, conservatively adjusted downward to take into account the price increase.

5. Cells 6 through 10 inclusive have been selected because of their profiles and that of our target market appear to match reasonably closely, and because the potential for future volume campaigns is quite large. Although no specific information is available to us, we feel, on the basis of discussions with the list broker and of previous list experience, that the response rate should be achievable.

8. Order processing and reporting

(a) Order handling plans

Based on past experience, we expect 60 percent of the orders to come in via our toll-free, 1-888 number and 40 percent via return mail.

We will use our internal telemarketing group for the initial response and have back up in place with our approved external call centre. Customer screens have been created, a script has been prepared along with a list of questions and answers (Q & As). Training will begin the last week of July. Both telemarketing groups share the on-line credit card approval responsibilities and database updating responsibilities.

Orders received by the processing department each day will be sorted according to direct mail order form, print ad coupon, or customer inquiry mail (white mail), and batched according to source code. The department should ensure that the customer's name and address are complete for those orders accompanied by full payment by cheque or money order. Make any necessary corrections by comparing the order, payment, and mailing envelope. At this stage the database will be updated. These payments are to be separated from the orders and transmitted to finance. The actual order must be marked "Paid" at the time it is separated from the payment. All credit card orders will be processed through one telemarketing station and source codes assigned.

All mail orders received with partial payment or without any payment are to be forwarded to the customer service department for follow-up, together with the mailing envelope. All requests for further information are to be forwarded on a daily basis to customer service.

Any customers who indicate they have seen our Web site will be tallied and a surprise gift will be shipped with the order. These stats should be recorded separately and indicated on the appropriate customer file in the database.

(b) Statistical reporting

The processing department should record each source code order according to order form, coupon, or white mail. The number of orders received for each code should be counted and the totals recorded on the media analysis sheet. The total number of orders for each code should be extended and total value of the orders recorded on the media analysis sheet, a copy of which is transmitted to finance for reconciliation with the daily deposit. These data screens have already been designed and are in place for training purposes.

(c) Fulfillment reporting

Completed orders should be transmitted to the shipping department for the preparation of shipping labels on a daily basis, and must be in the hands of shipping no later than 2 p.m. on the day of receipt. Our goal is to ensure a one-day turnaround wherever possible to support our goal of excellent customer service.

(d) Customer service

All mail forwarded to customer service is to be sorted into the following categories:

1. Incomplete orders: these are to be dealt with by contacting the customer directly to complete the order. This initial response should be completed by phone during business hours.

2. Requests for information: these are to be dealt with immediately by phone.

3. Customer letters requiring payment information: these are to be processed by the department after obtaining the necessary information from finance.

4. Customer letters requiring shipping information: these are to be processed by the department after obtaining the necessary information from the shipping department.

5. Returned merchandise: this should be listed on a "Returns Screen Report," which should be transmitted to the department daily. The returned merchandise should be forwarded to receiving for inventory update.

(e) Bill me later

Not accepted. If orders are received requesting this option, customer service is to advise the customer that this option is not available and offer other methods of payment. This initial contact should be made by phone if the number is available or as a fall back by mail.

CAMPAIGN SP-135
PROJECTED SALES
TEST CAMPAIGN

Direct mail	Units	Selling price	Sales
Cell 1	55,200	$ 29.95	$ 1,653,240
Cell 2	2,800	29.95	83,860
Cell 3	2,000	29.95	59,900
Cell 4	2,000	34.95	69,900
Cell 5	1,400	34.95	48,930
Cell 6	1,700	29.95	50,915
Cell 7	1,600	29.95	47,920
Cell 8	1,500	29.95	44,925
Cell 9	1,600	29.95	47,920
Cell 10	30,200	29.95	904,490
	100,000		**$3,012,000**
Print media	2,472	29.95	74,036
TOTAL SALES	**102,472**		**$3,086,036**
Less: returns, cancellations, and bad debts			369,606
NET SALES			**$2,716,430**

Cost of sales

102,472 units @ $13.88 each	$1,422,311
4,800 premiums (Cells 2 and 3) @ $1 each	4,800
5,000 surprise gifts (.05 of 100,000 @ $1 each	5,000
TOTAL COST OF SALES	**($1,432,111)**
GROSS MARGIN	**$1,284,319**

Less: promotion costs
Direct mail:

1,000,000 pieces @ $450/M	$450,000
Media costs	15,200
Creative and production costs	12,000
TOTAL PROMOTION COSTS	**$477,200**
Less: Fulfillment costs @ $5/unit	500,000
TOTAL COSTS	**($977,200)**
NET PROFIT CONTRIBUTION:	**$307,119**

Note: Projected returns, cancellations, and bad debt estimated at 8 percent based on last year's performance. Revenue of $2.50 for P & H ($8,500) of cells 4 and 5 are not reflected in these figures. If the higher price of $34.95 proves successful, revenue will be included for the roll-out campaign. Roll-out projections should be done based on the annual goal of 200,000 diaries sold. Both test and roll-out costs are prepared at this initial stage of planning.

SCHEDULE 1
CAMPAIGN PLAN NO. SP-135
TEST CELL FORMATS
DIRECT MAIL

Cell Description	Size	Source	Outer envelope	Letter	Brochure	Order form	BRE
1. Control	460M	House list	OE-1	L-1	B-1	OF-1/1	BRE-1
2. Premium test -1	20M	House list	OE-2	L-2	B-2	OF-2/2	BRE-1
3. Premium test -2	20M	Outside list (nth select)	OE-2	L-3	B-2	OF-2/3	BRE-1
4. Price test 1	20M	House list	OE-1	L-4	B-2	OF-3/4	BRE-1
5. Price test 2	20M	Outside list (nth select)	OE-1	L-5	B-2	OF-3/5	BRE-1
6. List test 1	20M	Outside list 1 (nth select)	OE-1	L-6	B-2	OF-1/6	BRE-1
7. List test 2	20M	Outside list 2 (nth select)	OE-1	L-6	B-2	OE-1/7	BRE-1
8. List test 3	20M	Outside list 3 (nth select)	OE-1	L-6	B-2	OF-1/8	BRE-1
9. List test 4	20M	Outside list 4 (nth select)	OE-1	L-6	B-2	OF-1/9	BRE-1
10. Balance of outside lists	380M	Outside lists	OE-1	L-6	B-2	OF-1/10	BRE-1

Total quantity   1,000M

Note: We have allowed for two versions of the outer envelope (OE) to capitalise on the premium (cells 2 and 3) opportunity. The letter will be used to reflect customer, non-customer, price testing, and premium testing. There will only be two versions of the brochure: one with gold initials and one without to capitalise on efficiencies. All order forms will be laser personalised. This personalisation will include list and offer coding. Materials are being coded to facilitate insertion at the lettershop stage.

THE ROLE OF THE AGENCY

5

THE ROLE OF THE AGENCY
Consultants and freelancers

As in marriage, you have to work hard to find the right partner, then work harder to keep the relationship together.

In the early 1970s, who would have believed the Canadian direct marketing agency would play such an important role in the missionary work so crucial to the rapid growth of our business and so critical to recruiting, training, introducing new clients to the discipline, and developing a unique Canadian creative product.

In 1972 Lester Wunderman opened the first direct marketing agency in Canada. It was headquartered in Montreal, and even then, the agency knew it was bound for a very exciting future. That core group, which included me, is still very active in the industry today. By 1977, I unabashedly ventured out with two other partners, to open Canada's third direct marketing agency.

That's right, in 1977 there were still only three direct marketing agencies in Canada, no advertised Canadian consultants, and no acknowledged Canadian freelancers. But today, when you select an agency, consultant, or freelancer, you have a much broader field to study and broader expertise to absorb and examine. As with all relationships, you must first examine what your needs are, quantify them, then venture out to meet or exceed your expectations.

In this chapter, we will address some key areas related to successfully choosing and working with an agency, consultant, or freelancer. We will explore:

- Your options
- Your needs
- Guidelines on how to choose a partner
- How to brief your chosen partner
- Compensation arrangements
- Keeping the partnership together

Selecting a partner should be as important to you as relocating your office, buying a new home, selecting a school for your child's education, or planning for your retirement — all very important decisions in your life that can lead to pleasant memories, personal growth, riches, or sheer disaster. The quality of your agency selection often dictates the quality of your subsequent business life, the impact of your brand, and your own professional growth. Take time and get all the facts before you start out.

First, do you really need an agency (or a new agency), or should you develop your own in-house resources? Is there a role for a consultant? Should you include a role for freelancers? Or is there a unique combination that's right for you?

▶ Considering your options

If you already have an agency, be sure that it is a change you want. The time you have invested in your present agency relationship and the agency's learning curve are only two of the considerations before deciding to move on. Before dissolving the relationship, you should sit down with your existing agency partners and have a frank discussion about your expectations and their strengths and weaknesses. Perhaps they can make some changes that better suit your future needs. If you are satisfied that they are not able or willing to make the needed changes, advise them you are going to embark on an agency search. This should be done before you go into the marketplace to conduct an active agency search. Give them permission to participate in the new agency search, or terminate their contract (90 days notice is acceptable) if they do not have a chance to win. There are some real fundamentals to explore before settling in with a new partner.

For certain products or corporate situations, the bulk of the direct marketing work is best done in-house, with one's own, trained resources. This is not to say that going to an outside agency once or twice a year for an idea-driven campaign is not a good concept. But it is meant to point out that in some fields, such as publishing, there is so much product knowledge to absorb and so little time for an outside agency to absorb it. This, coupled with the need for instant feedback on results and the necessity for frequent communication with customers, may mean that an agency is not willing to keep up with the fast-paced needs of such a company unless a dedicated team and an appropriate budget is assigned.

In these circumstances, the best contribution an outside agency can make is to give you those one or two big campaign ideas a year that make the difference, not only in increasing your response rates, but also in positioning your product. The agency involvement can be very valuable in setting the stage for your next breakthrough, be that in the creative approach, in positioning your product, or in your expressed offer and audience opportunity.

Martin Smee, former direct mail manager, circulation, at Maclean Hunter Limited, explains:

> "Some 40 years ago, we decided at Maclean Hunter to go the route of an in-house direct marketing department, but we also made use of the strengths of an ongoing relationship with a consultant, freelance writers, and designers, as well as direct marketing agencies.

> "The sheer volume of business alone forced us to develop our own staff. A typical magazine group, with new incentive programs and rate changes to cope with every year, has to write, design, and alter some 40 programs annually, involving up to 120 component parts. Imagine what it was like with six magazines.

> "In addition to sheer volume, in-house has a much better grasp of Audit Bureau of Circulation regulations, Department of Consumer and Corporate Affairs guidelines, the legalities of sweepstakes and contest promotions, sources of imported premiums,

Your consultant, in addition to your agency, should provide you with a pipeline of information about your competition and the industry in general.

coupled with an intimate knowledge of the strategies behind renewal series, gift campaigns, pricing policy, and price comparisons. They are also far better informed of a magazine's editorial policy and market niche.

"The one person you should always have to help you is a consultant. He or she is your conscience, your employee who is beholden only to you when it comes to assessing the true value of a program and the value of work, from copywriting and design right up to lettershop. Your consultant, in addition to your agency, should provide you with a pipeline of information about your competition and the industry in general. There are a number of very good consultants to choose from.

"For a small operation, a quarterly visit from a consultant would suffice; where a large number of programs are going on all the time, a regular, monthly visit might be called for. But, in any event, in helping you to plan your overall marketing strategies, an experienced consultant is worth his or her weight in gold.

"With a multiplicity of clients, a good direct marketing agency has a breadth of experience with all media and different creative approaches that the average direct marketing manager cannot hope to equal, plus a knowledge of specialised markets, such as that in French-speaking Quebec.

"Developing in-house staff is a long-term project. Consultants, freelancers, and the agency may be the best training tools you can hire. For any direct marketing operation that starts off relatively small and grows, my recommendation would be to begin with a consultant (who could be a person or an agency) and a freelance writer/designer. From there, the development of in-house staff can be more beneficial. The expanded use of an outside direct marketing agency would be the next step. A judicious mix of in-house, consultant, freelance, and agency talents will use the strengths of all sources and would undoubtedly lead to a more successful and profitable direct marketing operation.

"I would never keep a direct marketing operation exclusively in-house, regardless of its size or expertise."

Another business category that may fall into the same logic is the catalogue business. It is dependent on fast turnaround times and instant decisions based on results. In most cases, catalogues are written, designed, photographed, illustrated, typeset, colour-separated, printed, and ready for delivery to the customer within 13 weeks.

But here too, the outside agency can be invaluable for that big strategy idea, the creative breakthrough, the use of new media, or new benefit testing. In these cases, it is not whether you should use an agency, it is defining how best to use an agency and its core talent.

▶ Small budgets, big needs

Your second consideration must be the size and allocation of your budget. There is really no budget too small for an agency, it really comes down to the amount of work required for that budget. Many marketers ask what too small a budget means. There is no fixed answer. Too small can be too small a budget for simply too much sporadic activity over a 12-month period — thereby not allowing an agency to properly staff for your projected needs nor to maintain an acceptable profit margin on your business.

If you have a small budget and big needs, consider including consultants and freelancers in your partner search. As is the case with any partner selection, invite only trusted consultants and freelancers with good reputations, the relevant credentials for the job, and whose references can be verified.

Remember. It is as important to check the references of a consultant or freelancer as it is to do your homework before the selection of an agency partner. Don't be embarrassed to call the clients with whom your prospective consultant or freelancer has worked. Ask about personality traits. Was he or she easy to work with? Did he or she get along with others involved in the job? Did he or she meet deadlines? Was he or she interested in response rates after the program was completed? Would the client use him or her again?

By highlighting these two examples, I in no way imply that agencies cannot turn on a dime, deliver miracles, or contribute to either publishing, catalogues, or small budgets in a very, very big way. It is merely an illustration of ensuring you select a partner that meets your needs, while still developing the skill set of your internal team.

Assuming, however, that you are going to use an outside agency, the next section is mandatory reading before selecting your new partners.

▶ Guidelines to choosing an agency

Most clients and agencies agree, there are at least three levels to every agency selection, whether originally designed that way or not: capabilities, strategic insights, and the creative product.

Preparation

First, it's important to create an internal agency search team (AST). An AST is responsible for the search, partner evaluation, selection, and eventually input into the agency's annual performance evaluation.

Most clients and agencies agree, there are at least three levels to every agency selection: capabilities, strategic insights, and the creative product.

Include all key personnel who are responsible for, or will interface with, the customer through marketing, finance, customer service, research and product development, and any other related activities particular to your company.

- Assign a team leader
- Assign responsibilities
- Assign critical dates

Remember. This team should stay in place until well after the agency selection has been made. Each member should make at least a one-year commitment, and responsibilities should include input into the first agency performance evaluation or review. Then with your corporate objectives and communication plan in hand, determine which services your company requires, and prioritise them.

Needs analysis

The AST may decide to complete one integrated needs analysis or have each member independently complete the requirements as it understands the needs of both the company and its customers. Either way, make this a totally consultative process, taking advantage of each contributing area of expertise. Consolidate the input.

FIGURE 5-1

NEEDS ANALYSIS

1. Assignment:
☐ Corporate   ☐ Single product/service   ☐ Multi-products/services

2. Does your company already have an agency relationship?
☐ Yes   ☐ No
If yes, does it have a reputable direct marketing affiliate?
☐ Yes   ☐ No

3. Do your needs and culture require a:
☐ Small agency   ☐ Medium agency   ☐ Large agency

4. Specific product/service experience:
☐ Important   ☐ Not important

5. Corporate culture:
☐ Important   ☐ Not important

6. International network of services:
☐ Important   ☐ Not important

7. What strengths do you have internally?
☐ Marketing strategy   ☐ Customer service   ☐ Customer database
☐ Sales support   ☐ Telemarketing   ☐ Shipping
☐ Other:_____

8. What services are required from the agency?
☐ Direct marketing   ☐ Advertising   ☐ Public relations
☐ Sales promotion   ☐ Database management   ☐ Research

9. Do you need internal help to implement a direct marketing strategy?
☐ No   ☐ Yes
If yes,   ☐ Direct marketing staff training   ☐ Internal systems

10. The chosen partner must be knowledgeable brokers in:
☐ Setting the strategy   ☐ Creative development   ☐ Account management
☐ Production services   ☐ Database   ☐ Print media
☐ Broadcast   ☐ New media — Internet   ☐ Systems and procedures
☐ Product development

▶ To do list

The next task on your list should be your phone to do list.

☎ One of the first calls to make is to the Canadian Direct Marketing Association (CDMA). On the basis of its database of direct marketing agencies matched to your needs, it will supply you with a list of member agency names, phone numbers, and recommended contacts. Although most agencies are CDMA members, you may want to expand your search.

☎ Call the president, vice-president, or director of marketing of a company whose advertising you respect and ask that person for the name of his or her agency.

☎ Consult trade publications such as *Canadian Direct Marketing News (CDMN), Strategy Direct Response, Marketing Magazine,* and *Marketing Direct* (a *Marketing Magazine* supplement).

After you've compiled a list of names from these phone calls, you should have a list of agencies that adhere to direct marketing ethics and principles and are able to give you sound, strategic business advice. If the AST members have a short list of their own, add the recommended agencies to your list. Care must be taken to ensure that your preliminary list of agencies meets your total needs.

☎ If you can screen calls well, and have completed your needs analysis, you may want to add one more phone call to your list; call the trade publications or put out a press release, stating your needs and your decision to do an agency search. Once published, the phone calls should come pouring in. You may be overwhelmed by the response, but it will give you an opportunity to review the completeness of your list.

☎ Next, place a phone call to the suggested contact at each agency and arrange for a credentials presentation. Indicate exactly what you are looking for: agency credentials, experience in your product/service category, case studies of existing business that may relate to your product or service, and possibly, their preferred method of compensation. This presentation will be compiled based on the information you give about your needs: what your product/service is, your key marketing challenges, what needs you have as a company, whether your company has worked with an agency before and if so, which one. Also share who will be attending the initial meeting and the selection criteria for the successful agency.

Although this initial contact can be done by phone, you should send a written confirmation and include a business overview of your company and products. Schedule a convenient date for your agency visit, allowing the agency at least two weeks to prepare. (This is necessary because the agency is staffed to service its existing client roster, and existing clients must come before potentially new clients. When you are an existing client, you will expect and demand this same courtesy.)

Round one

When it's time for your agency visit, you should know exactly what credentials you are looking for. The agency credentials should demonstrate all three important ingredients: capabilities, strategic insight, and associated creative. Most of this will be demonstrated through the use of relevant client case studies.

Prior to looking at your agency evaluation checklist (to be presented shortly), there are two very important questions to consider.

1. Do you like these people? You will have a successful partnership only if you are partners with people you like. Be people-selective and people-sensitive.

2. Who will be your senior contact person? Is he or she in the room? Can you relate well to this person? Will you be able to pick up the phone as quickly in times of distress as you will in times of triumph? This aspect of the relationship is of prime importance in your selection.

Only after you are comfortable with the people should you focus on the checklist for evaluating the agency, its resources and appropriateness for your business objectives. Build your agency evaluation around your needs analysis.

FIGURE 5-2

AGENCY EVALUATION

Agency name: **Date:**
Contact name:
Phone number: **Fax number:**

1. Is the agency staffed with direct marketing professionals?

2. Does the agency have experience and expertise in developing strategic direct marketing plans?

3. Does the agency have a track record for producing programs or campaigns that sell?

4. Does the agency use testing to find the approach that ensures not only immediate success, but long-term profitability? What other research methods does it employ?

5. Has the agency recently been awarded new business from its existing clients?

6. Does the agency understand all direct response media as needed by your business — not just direct mail, but also television, magazine, newspaper, alternative media, telemarketing, take-ones, statement stuffers, and catalogues? Is it creative in its media buying? Is it up-to-date with new technology and how it can be applied to your business?

7. Does the agency have experience in the development and utilisation of a database as a marketing tool for building relationships with key customer segments? Has it specifically addressed its database capabilities?

8. Does the agency give you a good balance of marketing versus creative expertise?

9. Does the agency have a point of view on your competitors? Was that point of view well researched?

10. Can the agency give you the added benefit of related resources if you need them — including image advertising, sales promotions, public relations, and market research?

After you have evaluated each agency's credentials, ask for client references — and be sure to check them. If you are seriously considering having one of them as your business partner, it's better to know what kind of partner the agency has been to other companies before you add it to your agency short list.

Round two

Your short list should now be just that — short (maybe three or four agencies). Within this short list you should have all the resources you need for a successful partnership. But you are only going to choose one, so what's next?

1. Ask each agency for an organisation chart. This should identify the key contacts for account, creative, production, media, and financial services.

2. Determine the primary responsibilities of the people in these groups.

3. Ask for a flow chart of how a job goes through the system, and note any quality control check points.

4. Find out what reports you can expect from the agency, and how often.

5. Ask for a walk-through of the agency — its hallways, boardrooms, and offices. Ask to be introduced specifically to the team that will work on your business and get a better understanding of what other accounts they work on. (You can tell a lot about an agency by the mood of the people and their degree of enthusiasm.)

When all is said and done, you should still have the same agencies on your shortlist — now you just know them a lot better. You could make your final decision at this point. But if you don't feel you have enough information, then you may choose to move to the next step.

The next step could be to brief all remaining agencies on your product and assign a problem for each of them to solve. The same problem should be given to all agencies, in exactly the same manner, with exactly the same information. Do not show any favouritism. If you show favouritism, your product will suffer.

The document describing your product and the test problem is called the agency brief.

The agency brief

Although there are many variations on an agency brief, there are clearly some items of information that must be included. The quality, clarity, and value of this information will be reflected in the final product.

Be very specific. This is not the time to ask for creative ideas. Your purpose in this brief should be to judge the quality of each agency's strategic thinking and problem-solving capabilities. Strategy should always be approved first. In fact, I personally would "penalise" the agency that did speculative creative prior to an approved strategy — that is, I would tend to move it down the list. As a good partner, you should not expect creative before strategic thinking is approved.

Now that all agencies have been briefed, allow them at least three weeks for presentation. Meanwhile, expect phone calls and enquiries from the agencies. Only one (senior) person from the AST should be assigned to answer all the questions. If various people are assigned, the answers may vary and be unintentionally misleading; one person will deliver consistency and ensure fairness.

This job of dealing with questions from the agencies requires absolute confidentiality, and the AST member responsible must show no favouritism. It is always best to have the person who prepared the agency brief be responsible for answering the questions. This is the ideal situation.

Round three

During your selection process, the AST may feel there is (or almost is) a tie between at least two (and maybe three) of the agencies when evaluating which one will be the best partner for the company, and which one will produce the most relevant (best) work. If the team cannot decide, it's time to ask for execution of the marketing strategy. In a brief discussion with each agency contact, you should inform them of the tie and ask whether they would be willing to put creative ideas behind the strategy that they presented. You should be prepared, at this point, to offer a flat fee for a creative execution; this demonstrates your respect for the amount of work involved in the process. The fee need not be high, but make it fair.

Final selection

You've now tentatively chosen your agency on the basis of your needs, people/interpersonal skills, professional skills, quality of thinking, and possibly creative execution. However, there is still more work to do. One of your first discussions should centre around compensation.

Compensation

There are as many possible compensation arrangements as there are agency and client relationships. Your preference may not be mentioned here. You may choose to present a new formula to your agency. Discussed here are three formulas that do work — that is, they can be expected to align with both your objectives and those of the agency: successful relationships and corporate profitability.

1. Agency Fees

The agency presents a fixed, averaged hourly rate based on an agreed to project list. This hourly rate may be calculated as one fixed hourly rate for all agency personnel or separate rates for each contributing department. I like the arrangement for one fixed averaged hourly rate. This calculation ensures you are getting senior management involvement on your account, on an ongoing, consistent basis. After all, on the fixed averaged hourly rate, you can get a senior person for the same rate as a junior. Both these calculations allow the agency to project your staffing requirements for the upcoming years and ensure you get consistent, well-trained people on your account, which will make your life much easier.

2. Fees and commission

This combination, in some situations, makes sense. The agency proposes to work for hourly rates for specific parts of your program, such as planning, account management, creative concepts, and creative development. In addition, it receives a commission to support media buying, production estimating, and buying of other outside services. These outside services can include, but are not limited to, personalisation, film, printing, all media buying, list rental, and lettershop services.

The difficulty in making this arrangement work fairly is that the print quantities involved are sometimes small. Targeted mailings of 20,000 pieces do not yield much commission. The investment of time, both yours and that of the agency, is the largest in the test phase of any program. The long hours involved in the important, up-front strategic work will be realised in your successful roll-out plans. You may want to consider paying fees on the initial test and a commission rate on the roll-out portion.

Your circumstances, and that of your chosen agency, may be such that you both feel this is a viable arrangement. Agree on what is best for both of you, but with this combination, allow for some flexibility.

3. Monthly retainer

This is a fixed amount paid to the agency on a monthly basis, calculated over a 12-month period, based on an agreed-to scope of work. Within this arrangement, you should still reconcile the amount paid monthly to the hours spent on the account. Although some months may vary in the amount of activity over a six-month period, it should average out over the 12-month period. Ask your agency, up-front, which hourly rate will be used for its reconciliation and how often the reconciliation will occur.

4. Performance bonus

An incentive bonus, based on performance, can accompany any of these compensation arrangements. Predetermine measurement criteria, benchmarks, and value must be agreed in advance.

Along with covering compensation, you should also request information on its financial systems. This should include, but not be limited to, how you are billed and when you are billed. At this time you should introduce the agency's financial person to the contact in your finance department. These two individuals should be responsible for working out a financial system that best suits both your needs.

Another important element in your success is the quality of the people you assign to interface with the agency. Appoint an agency liaison, a senior level person, who is the keeper of the relationship. Juniors just will not do! They cannot possibly have the training, and experience necessary to approve strategies, creative and expenditures.

Also, make the approval processes as simple as possible. Ensure there is a senior person on your team responsible for approval and attending all agency briefings. This will save you, and the agency, time and money.

Nurturing the relationship

Now that you have chosen your partner and the systems are in place, you are now ready to start work. In all your dealings with the agency, remember that you took a long time to choose this agency. Do your utmost to be a good client, and your agency should do its best to be a good agency.

The principles of open dialogue, honesty, and full disclosure will encourage hard work. There will be good times and bad times. The good news and the bad news should bring the same reaction from you and your agency — find a solution, do not place blame.

Periodic evaluations

You need to evaluate your agency at least once a year. In fact, in the beginning of the relationship, I suggest you evaluate it within the first six months. This evaluation should be in writing, and be honest and fair. Point out the good aspects of the relationship and indicate the areas in which you'd like to see some improvement. Give concrete examples for both. Be open as well to the agency's evaluation of your people, systems, and how they can better work in harmony. If you are forthright with your agency, you should expect the same in return.

With this foundation in place, you and your agency can look forward to a long and happy partnership.

THE ROLE
OF RESEARCH

6

Direct marketing is years ahead of traditional advertising in its analysis of response rates, cost per order, media effectiveness, and comparative offer testing. Direct marketers have, in the past, relied solely on in-market testing to prove the effectiveness of a campaign's target audience, benefits, price value, offer, and creative positioning. The area of market research is just beginning to find its rightful home in the direct marketer's arsenal.

The unique research applications can assist in answering some important questions. What does the customer look like for this product? What are the customer's hot buttons? How should the product be configured to best suit the customer's needs? Which media, or combination of media, is most relevant to effectively reach the potential customer and get a response?

If you could obtain answers to these questions directly from the consumer, you'd be hooked on market research. Many direct marketers have no retail channel or direct sales force from which to get personal customer feedback. Most have never seen their customers face-to-face. So a face-to-face encounter could become habit-forming, especially when the insights lead to significant improvements in a direct mail package, print campaign, or television script. Raising response rates by fractions will make a difference to your bottom line.

Ken Solmon, vice-president, director of strategic planning and consumer insights, Wunderman Cato Johnson, says:

> "We've not invented any startling new techniques, but we have, in part, through trial and error, come to understand that there is a wide range of direct marketing issues that can be successfully explored in qualitative and quantitative research."

Although they are not new techniques, it is the direct marketing application of the techniques, and the structure in which the techniques are developed, that interests me — and should interest you.

It's too expensive and risky to produce a slick, direct response television (DRTV) commercial and wait to see how it does. The same holds true for direct mail, where the issue may not only be production costs for several testing versions of a mailing, but the needed time to fully read back-end results and the value of the newly acquired customers.

As costs rise and time lines shrink, we need more efficiencies. And market research may be able to provide them. With more and more products vying for a customer's attention, direct marketers should look to some traditional research methods, applied in a unique way, to enhance their customer knowledge. Some of the research methods to consider are: focus group testing, concept testing, trade-off analysis, simulated test market modelling, and communication testing.

In addition, there's the issue of product pricing: how can I be sure I'm maximising my profit before I test. Testing response rates in the mail within two or three different pricing structures may not be acceptable to company's that are not willing to configure internal systems to accommodate various offer levels and various levels of offer profitability — these offers often staying on the database for a number of years. Specific market research techniques can also assist in directionally setting the best price and value package for the consumer.

Direct marketers who are too slow to take advantage of the tools and skills offered by the specialised market research community risk being left behind. Not all market research firms are created equal. To find the right partnership with the right skills and experience, you should conduct a search in the same way as you would to secure any partnership. The ideal selection criteria would be to include this expertise in your needs analysis within your agency search.

One of the direct marketing agencies implementing these unique research applications is Wunderman Cato Johnson (WCJ). WCJ is a sister company of Young & Rubicam Advertising and has an international commitment to direct marketing and to building brands. In 1994, Young & Rubicam Advertising successfully launched Brand Asset™ Valuator and began to investigate its unique applications for direct marketing.

Without giving away any trade secrets, the process of building brands, the Brand Asset™ Valuator, is reflected through a progression of four primary measures or pillars. These measures are used to evaluate current brand performance, identify core issues for the brand, and evaluate brand potential.

Brands can be elevated by these individual measures. But more important, the relationships between the pillars show the true picture of a brand's health, its intrinsic value, its muscular capacity to carry a premium price, and its ability to fend off competitors.

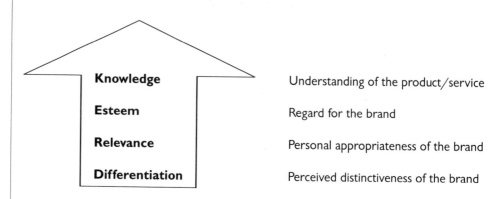

FOUR PRIMARY ASPECTS

Knowledge	Understanding of the product/service
Esteem	Regard for the brand
Relevance	Personal appropriateness of the brand
Differentiation	Perceived distinctiveness of the brand

The 4 primary aspects of building a brand based on the Brand Asset™ Valuator are:

1. Differentiation is first

The starting point for all brands is *differentiation*. It defines the brand and distinguishes it from all others. *Differentiation* is how brands are born.

As a brand matures, Brand Asset™ finds that *differentiation* often declines. It doesn't have to happen. Even after reaching maturity, with good management, a brand can perpetuate its *differentiation*. A low level of *differentiation* is a clear warning that a brand is fading.

2. Relevance comes next

Differentiation is only the first step in building a brand. The next step is *relevance*. If a brand isn't relevant or personally appropriate to consumers, it isn't going to attract and keep them — certainly not in any great numbers.

Brand Asset™ shows that there is a distinct correlation between *relevance* and market penetration. Relevance drives franchise size.

3. The basis of esteem

Brand Asset™'s third primary measure is *esteem* — how much consumers like a brand and hold it in high regard. In the progression of building a brand, it follows *differentiation* and *relevance*. It's the consumer's response to a marketer's brand-building activity.

Esteem itself is driven by two factors: perceptions of quality and perceptions of popularity. And the proportions of these factors differ by country and culture.

Brand Asset™ tracks the ways in which brands gain *esteem*, which helps us consider how to manage consumer perceptions. Through Brand Asset™, we can identify opportunities for leveraging a brand's *esteem*.

4. Knowledge is the successful outcome

If a brand has established its *relevant differentiation* and consumers come to hold it in high *esteem*, *brand knowledge* is the outcome and represents the successful culmination of building a brand. Knowledge means being aware of the brand and understanding what the brand or service stands for. Knowledge is not a consequence of media weight alone. Spending money on a weak idea will not buy *knowledge*. It has to be achieved.

A good example of qualitative research for direct marketing can be seen in the development of the DirectProtect campaign for The Co-operators Group. WCJ's efforts were proceeded by two series of focus groups. The first was exploratory in nature to determine how the consumer dealt with home and auto insurance. The second series was to explore alternative creative approaches.

The insights came when WCJ put this learning together with some earlier direct marketing qualitative work. The results of its efforts not only brought product success and consumer satisfaction, but an unqualified win of The Canadian Direct Marketing Association's 1996 Gold RSVP award in the financial service and insurance category. Plus it won the industry award for The Best of the Best category, which is given to one outstanding program for the year.

Through the co-operation of The Co-operators Group, WCJ, and Canada Post, we are able to share with you a case study on this unique and successful campaign.

Background

Canada's home and auto insurance industry was poised for the invasion of chartered banks into this competitive field. Based on the experience of the U.K. insurance industry — in which direct advertisers now account for up to 30 percent of auto insurance sold — Canadian banks had the potential to capture a significant share of the home and auto market at the expense of traditional agents and brokers. The Co-operators Group, Canada's third largest home and auto insurer, wanted to preserve its dominant position in the Canadian marketplace. Anticipating the use of direct marketing by the new entrants, The Co-operators Group implemented a strategy of distribution channel dominance. The company established a direct marketing operation to complement its existing agent, broker, and group-sales channels.

CO-OPERATORS GROUP CASE STUDY

Objectives

- Position The Co-operators as a leader in the insurance industry
- Create a direct distribution channel
- Establish DirectProtect, an insurance-by-phone service, as a leading insurance brand

Strategy

Consumer research guided the development of television and print creative.

- **Research showed:** Consumers were concerned that insurance-by-phone would lack the friendly, personalized service available from traditional insurance brokers.

  Creative response: A friendly, approachable "Tiny Man" who emerges from a telephone receiver to help the consumer decipher the insurance policy.

- **Research showed:** Consumers disliked the uncomfortable sense of obligation that often comes with dealing "face-to-face".

  Creative response: "Tiny Man" emphasized the ease of getting an expert quote from DirectProtect by phone in just a few minutes, with no obligation to buy.

Program in Action

The core offer consisted of a no-obligation home insurance quote by phone. Additional offers were tested, including an auto insurance quote offer and a smoke alarm premium with the home insurance quote.

High levels of reach and frequency were employed across all media to quickly establish the Direct Protect brand. The media plan was developed to sustain DirectProtect's profile throughout the campaign period.

Network and spot television (1,500 GRPs) was used to establish the brand and support the print advertising; highly rated, prime-time properties were bought. Print, including direct mail, was employed to generate response and to support the brand advertising. A total of 18 million inserts were distributed over the three-month launch period. Finally, a public relations initiative targeted all major media outlets in Ontario.

Results

During launch period

- Average calls from new prospects: 302 per day (50% over target)
- Resulting cost per order: 80% less than budget
- Increased traffic at offices was an additional, unexpected benefit of the campaign

Results of tracking research, after 3 months

- Awareness of DirectProtect: 25% (from a starting point of zero)
- Percentage of aware consumers who say they'll call for a quote: 23%

Trade/industry response

- Articles published about DirectProtect: 3 (approx. 1 million consumer/trade impressions)
- Winner of Canadian Direct Marketing Association 1996 RSVP Award, plus Best of The Best Award
- Industry observers heralded DirectProtect as the beginning of a revolution in the way insurance is marketed, and The Co-operators group as its leader

The Co-operators Group fortified its position in the Canadian insurance market by marrying the principles of direct marketing to those of brand building – firmly establishing a new channel to the consumer.

Keys to Success

Brand Advertising and Direct Response Advertising
Given the reluctance of consumers to switch insurers, a key aspect of the program strategy was to sell the ease and speed of getting a "no obligation" quote from DirectProtect, with the payoff being better coverage at lower cost. This message was communicated through a combination of brand advertising and direct response advertising.

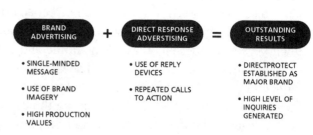

BRAND ADVERTISING	+	DIRECT RESPONSE ADVERTISING	=	OUTSTANDING RESULTS
• SINGLE-MINDED MESSAGE • USE OF BRAND IMAGERY • HIGH PRODUCTION VALUES		• USE OF REPLY DEVICES • REPEATED CALLS TO ACTION		• DIRECTPROTECT ESTABLISHED AS MAJOR BRAND • HIGH LEVEL OF INQUIRIES GENERATED

Please contact your Canada Post Corporation representative to receive copies of other case studies in this series.

LISTS

7

LISTS

Lists are one of the

most important

components to your

direct marketing

success.

Your marketing plan defines, not only *what* product you are going to market, but also *to whom* you are going to market. Your choice of lists is one of the most important elements of your campaign. Your efforts, no matter how gallant, will fail if you do not locate the best prospects.

Technology and its direct marketing application has dramatically enhanced list management, list selection, segmentation, profiling, and analysis. Based on the high cost of acquiring new customers, a better understanding of list data and list practices will allow for better marketing definition and decisions for both your company and your product.

A list is defined as a collection of customer data that has been gathered for a specific purpose. The benefit of the list to marketers is that it allows them to target their marketing efforts based on basic customer insights. How marketers apply that insight to their program is what makes their program unique.

We will review two types of lists: your house list or customer database (your internal list) and outside list rental.

▶ Your house list

Your house list may be compiled of customers, leads, and prospects. Customers are defined as individuals who have made a purchase from your company. A lead may be someone who has shown an interest in your product, but has not yet purchased. A prospect is an individual who has characteristics that match your best or loyal customer profile.

Before you start collecting names, you must decide what type of customer information you need (and will use) to support your marketing objectives both in the short- and long-term. Design your house file based on your projected needs, not your short-term needs. Many companies decide against capturing prospects based on the sheer volume of names and the cost and time involved in data capture. So, set your marketing objectives first and build a strong foundation from which to capture customer information.

An acquisition cost is your first expense in developing your house list. This expense represents your cost of acquiring customers' names, addresses, purchase habits, and any other relevant data as defined in your marketing objectives. Your second expense will be based on your decision as to whether you will build and maintain your house file (the basis for a customer database) in-house or use an outside supplier. Many companies make their decision to build their house file or database using an outside supplier based upon cost considerations, such as hardware, expertise, staff commitment, and staff training. This decision is also a result of recognising that their internal systems and expertise may be too heavily focused on finance, payroll, and inventory control.

As marketing needs lean more toward utilising database information, you must decide what your needs are: a house list of customers' names, addresses, and phone numbers, or a database in which you will also capture purchase behaviour, age, sex, birthday, occupation (the list can be endless according to your needs). And if you are a business-to-business marketer, you may want to add industry type, company size, number of employees, title, fax number, and direct dial phone number. By making decisions at the design stage, you will be able to collect as much customer information as possible early in the relationship.

The more you know about your target audience, the easier it will be for you to design campaigns that are specifically tailored to your customers' needs. Consequently, your campaigns will be more relevant to your customer, increasing your response rates and delivering a successful return on investment for your company. This target audience knowledge will also support your customer-service programs and allow you to be more specific in your offer and proactive with the right customer-service programs.

In addition to demographic and purchase behaviour, include:

- Source of customer name
- Date of entry into the file
- Date of each purchase, which will allow you to select your names by purchase, recency, and frequency
- Purchase price

There are several other ways for you to build your house file. I have often discovered customers' names and addresses on coupons under some unsuspecting person's desk gathering dust. No matter what form they come in, these are your customers' names and addresses. They have previously bought or tried your product, and they are of great value.

So, you should be looking around your premises for all respondents to all your marketing efforts, including advertising, sales promotion, public relations efforts, and don't forget about the sales force customers and leads. Even warranty cards and your finance department will yield a reliable list of customers.

Not only must you consider the content of your house file or database, but also the format of your information. Don't try to reinvent the wheel. Always use a fixed field format. That is, each item should appear in exactly the same field for each customer entry. This allows easy access to the proper data when preparing mailing or telemarketing file tapes for your campaigns. More important, this format also allows you easy access to data for segmenting, profiling, and modelling.

No customer record should go on file without a postal code. Not only does the postal code give you insight into the customer, but it also allows you to mail at the third class bulk postage rate, thus saving you money.

After your house list or database is in order, you should consider whether it will be an income generator for your company or not. For your house list to be an income generator, you must agree to rent it for use by other direct marketing firms. If you decide to put your house list on the rental market, you can employ an in-house list manager or decide to select one of the reputable list management firms to work on your behalf.

FIGURE 7-1

THE BENEFITS OF AN IN-HOUSE AND OUTSIDE LIST MANAGER/BROKER

	In-house	Outside
Profitability	No management or rental fee to outside list manager	A management and/or maintenance fee
	Increased overheads	No additional overheads: rental fee paid by list renter
Control	Under your internal control	May be replaced if performance is unsatisfactory
	You may need to invest in training and build internal controls and billing	Already trained. Needs only to be trained on your list and its unique characteristics
Revenue	Only handles one list: yours. Needs to develop outside contacts in order to drive sales, and develop advertising to promote the list	Have large, knowledgeable, and reputable sales force with a reputation for quality list rental — actively promote lists

▶ Renting out your house list

Ossie Hinds, founder and president of Cornerstone, which has a list management division in Toronto, says there are about 2,300 Canadian lists in rental circulation with about 40 percent coming under U.S. ownership. Each company must decide for itself if renting out its mailing list to other companies meets its overall business goals. If you decide to make your house list available to the market, be sure you have secured your customers' permission to pass along their names. Be sure to read the CDMA Code of Ethics and Standards of Practice located in the Appendix. It states the obligation you have for protection of personal privacy on behalf of your customer.

As the list owner, you hold the final approval of any product or service being offered, and the method by which your customers will be marketed. Your list may be used for a direct mail program, a telemarketing program, or a combination of both. It can also be used as a list source to enhance another company's database or for research purposes.

In additional to a new revenue stream, there are other benefits to renting your house list. By letting other marketers rent your list, you can help increase response rates because you'll have to keep your list active — updating and cleaning your list for address correction. Remember. You'll always have the choice to approve or reject the company that wants to rent your list. No one else gets to make that decision. So, you are still in control of your customers. Each company must decide for itself as to whether its list will be available to other marketers.

▶ The list broker

We have previously referred to list brokers in this chapter. List brokers are a valuable source of information and it is in your interest to make them your partner and your confidant.

A list broker:

- Acts as liaison and arranges all rental transactions between list owners/managers and list users

- Publishes lists, rate cards, and catalogues describing each list, its price, and other user data

- Can pass on recommendations for your specific needs, protect your product, and protect your usage date, ensuring your offer is exclusive to the target audience

- Tracks your list and selection usage in order to avoid duplication in the roll-out of a successful campaign

- Does follow-up work to ensure tapes arrive on time for your planned mail date

- Conducts analysis and makes recommendations for your next wave of usage

- Collects payment and remits to the list owner

By making the list broker your full partner, you shouldn't leave him or her in the dark about your objectives, mail date, expected response rates, and any past successes or failures. All this information is shared in confidence, just as you would share with any other member of your marketing team. For a list broker to be as effective as possible, there needs to be a working atmosphere of trust between the two of you — trust to share the needed information, such as response rates, ranking of lists, dollars per thousand generated for each list, and so on. This information is between you and the broker. This is trust. This trust must never be violated.

Since time is everyone's enemy, give your list broker enough time to do a good, professional job. Involve the broker at the beginning; from the development of a marketing plan through to the creation of the offer and the mailing package. When planning a campaign, brief your list broker immediately and have him or her prepare a complete list recommendation. This will ensure you have the latest costs and pricing for each of your selected lists. This involvement should evolve all the way through to results analysis and profitability. For the list broker to do his or her job and assist in delivering results, he or she needs the following basic information from you, and probably more.

1. What is the purpose of the rental — direct mail, telemarketing, data enhancement exercise or research?

2. What is the control offer?

3. What tests are being conducted?

4. What are the planned quantities?

5. Which format do you need the names in?

6. Which lists have been used in the past? How did they perform?

7. Do you want to do a merge-purge of all outside lists against each other?

8. Do you want each list coded separately for tracking and measurement?

9. What selections do you want within the lists?

10. What is your projected return on investment?

11. What is your budget?

12. What is your preferred delivery date?

List brokers offer updated data on the lists in the market by issuing list cards, and a list catalogue available either on a disc or in paper format. These are available to you at no charge. Be sure you are on all the list brokers' mailing lists and maintain this updated data in a numerical format in your office or on a diskette for easy reference.

All list brokers are not created equal. Check with your direct marketing associates and get referrals. Check for confidentiality, experience in your category, commitment to results, and reliability for recommendations and delivery.

▶ Types of outside lists available for rental

There are two types of lists you should consider for your marketing efforts:

1. Direct response lists
2. Compiled lists

1. **Direct response lists** are made up of individuals at home or business addresses that have previously responded to a direct marketing offer by mail, phone, space advertising, television, catalogue, or a co-op mailer. Any subscriber to newspapers, magazines, books, or record clubs, or anyone who purchases products or services that are fulfilled by using the mail or a sales call, will appear in this category. Also in this category will be large databases (primarily consumer), which are the culmination of questionnaires sent across the country.

   Such individuals may be present or past responding customers; the response may have generated an order or just an inquiry or a lead. In all cases, these individuals and companies are predisposed to doing business by the mail or phone.

   The respondents who have made a recent purchase, likely defined as the last six months, should be your first choice. These names are often called hotline names. Responders who have made a purchase within the last 12 months, should be your second choice. The selection criteria of six and 12 months is based on the recency theory that the more recently customers have made a purchase or commitment, the more likely they are to buy again, quickly.

   You will also come across a group of names that are identified as inactive. This term refers to the fact that the customers' last purchase was made longer than 12 months ago or has cancelled a recent subscription or purchase commitment.

   Responder lists are updated frequently. In the case of monthly publications, the lists are updated monthly or quarterly. Of course, list owners can only update their lists as their subscribers advise them of a change of address or when a new subscriber is added. These updates are made as quickly as possible since it is in the publication's best interest to mail only to updated lists each time the publication is printed.

   There are some types of products or services that do not require monthly updates in order for them to be considered current. Be sure to ask the question: when was the list last updated? Remember. Responder lists are preferred, and should produce better results than the compiled list category.

2. **Compiled lists** should therefore be your second choice. List compilers gather this information from almost every available public source: phone

directories, city directories, real estate directories, professional listings, business and industrial associations, to name a few. But the weakness with compiled lists is that they do not carry with them the qualifier of whether this person has done business by the mail. This is a critical distinction.

If you do choose compiled lists, select as much customer detail as possible in order to strengthen your target audience definition. Updates to compiled lists can only be made when the information is publicly available. This may only be every 18 months to two years. As an alternative, a professional list compiler may be able to do custom compiling for clients with special requirements. Ask your list broker for details.

FIGURE 7-2

RESPONSE LISTS VS COMPILED LISTS

Benefit	Response lists	Compiled lists
Responsiveness	Usually outpulls compiled lists	
Universe		Generally delivers more name volume
Selectivity	Good psychographic selections about individuals, their lifestyle and purchase pattern	Good demographic selections about individuals
Cost		Can be less expensive to rent
Unlimited use	Rented for a specific purpose	Negotiable
Volume discount	Negotiable	Negotiable

According to the 1996/97 List Usage Survey commissioned by CDMA, responding companies state that outside list rental makes up 53 percent of their marketing efforts. This indicates to me either an increase in a customer acquisition strategy or the need to rent outside names to enhance a company's existing database structure and content. In addition, 31 percent of respondents indicate an average increase in their use of outside rented lists over the previous year. The research goes on to state that an increase in mailing quantity/frequency, list segmentation, testing, and the need for business growth were the most popular reasons given for an increase in the use of outside lists. I would also add that this increase in usage fully supports the quality of outside lists and the response rates they deliver when used properly.

▶ List formats

There are three basic list formats available for rental:

- Labels
- Magnetic tape or cartridge
- PC computer disc

You must decide which format you need *before* you order the lists. Work closely with your printer and lettershop or call centre to determine which format is most suitable for their needs.

Labels

This is the standard hard copy format for most label-addressed mailings. This format is referred to as 4-up cheshire labels. These labels are on a continuous form with 44 addresses to a page (four across and 11 down). These labels are not perforated or glued and therefore can only be applied by machine. This immediately defines your use.

At a premium price, this same type of labels can be obtained on pressure-sensitive stock, which can then be affixed by hand.

Magnetic tape

This format is preferred for any list manipulation, such as merge-purge, and laser addressing for personalising components of a mailing package. If you are planning a telemarketing campaign, many call centres will also prefer this format because it gives them easy access to customer information and gives them the ability to develop the call screen programs quickly and efficiently. If you are using a computer service bureau, check the required specifications before you order your lists. Most computer service bureaus work with 9-track, 1600 BPI tape. However, 800 BPI and 6250 BPI, and IBM 3480 cartridges are also used. Many delivery dates have been missed by ordering the wrong format.

Personal computer disc

Lists are often available on disc. Ensure you are able to read or convert the supplied file. Remember. State your preferred format early on in the process.

▶ Selection and segmentation within the rented list

Many lists are enhanced with demographic or lifestyle information so you can select lists that match or closely match your preferred customer profile. If a list offers selections, it means that the list owner has divided his or her list into various categories.

List brokers' rate cards itemise the various selections. Some selections may be: city, province, postal code, phone number, active, expires, gender, sex, income, phone sold, direct mail sold, dollars spent, cash order, credit card order, business category, business size, number of employees, etc.

List owners charge an additional fee per thousand names for each of these selections — an expense well worth your consideration. The more targeted your campaign, the better chances of higher response rates. These rates for selections are clearly indicated on each rate card. Your partnership with the right list broker can have a major impact on understanding and applying the right segments from each available list for campaign success.

Linda Trauzzi, President of Watts List Brokerage Ltd., Toronto, says the demand for selects is driven more by brokers than mailers. It's the broker's job to know how to tailor particular lists or segments to suit a mailer's need. We've always chosen lists based on the availability of segments.

▶ How much do lists cost to rent?

On average, the basic list rental price ranges from $50 to $120 per thousand names for compiled lists and $80 to $250 per thousand names for responder lists.

The following selections will increase this basic list rental price:

- Special selections. They can cost $10 to $20 per thousand for each selection and there may be a maximum selection charge on some lists.

- Magnetic tape, cartridge or diskette. If you order these, you may pay a tape charge of $20 to $50 per reel.

- Shipping, courier, and customs brokerage charges.

- U.S. lists. Many lists are payable in U.S. funds. Be sure to check the currency payment carefully.

- Minimum requirements. Most, if not all list owners have minimum name rental requirements. If you rent less than the minimum, you must still pay the minimum stated amount.

You may also want to consider renting names on a net name basis. This simply means that you pay only for the unduplicated names you actually use. This arrangement is based on a merge-purge, and can be very attractive. Net names can be negotiated on an 85 percent net name arrangement.

Here's an example of how net name arrangements can work:

If you rent 100,000 names, and after the merge-purge with your house list, you can only mail 85,000 names (based on 15,000 name duplication), you pay only for 85,000 names, plus a running charge for the 15,000, which were identified as duplicates. If you mail less than the 85,000, due to an even higher duplication factor, you must still pay the rental based on your 85 percent agreement. But you have saved the cost of 15,000 names.

▶ Timing for receipt of list rental

Your critical path must include two to three weeks for delivery of your rented lists. This is one of the first factors in planning a direct marketing campaign. There are several reasons for this range of time:

- Local delivery of tapes can be completed in a short time frame. Lists from the U.S. or abroad will and do take longer.

- Your added selections within each list can add processing time and will add to your delivery time.

- Shipping and any customs clearance will also add to your delivery time.

- Most list orders are run and prepared on a predetermined schedule. Your list order may have missed a scheduled computer run and will need to wait for the next scheduled run.

- List owners will protect mailing dates to ensure the best possible results for the user

In CDMA's List Usage Survey, responding companies indicate the heaviest promotion months occurred in September, October, and November. September was the number one month for direct marketing programs. The second busiest phase was during the winter months of January, February, and March.

▶ List protection

As you can tell by now, lists are an extremely valuable commodity. A system of seeding is used to protect against unauthorised use, theft, or even the repeated use of a mailing list, which was only rented for one-time use.

Seeding is the planting of predetermined names on a mailing list to readily identify its user. The use of the rented list is tracked, and can be used as court-safe evidence of unauthorised use.

Do not allow your mailing list to go outside without incorporating even the simplest system of seeding. Seeding will ensure that you know every time the list is used, by whom, for what, and in particular, how often. You will also find seeding a helpful method of tracking post office delivery dates.

▶ Testing

1. Be sure the test lists are representative of the entire list (universe)

Regardless of your test quantities, spend time reviewing the list universe. Ascertain the entire quantity of names available to you for roll-out, based on your selections or segmentation, before you decide on the test list quantity.

2. Ensure your test selections are statistically significant in the roll-out phase

As previously mentioned in this chapter, selections or segmentation within a list allow you to better target your core audience. When making your test selections, ensure there are enough of the same type of names left over for your roll-out. If you do not ascertain this up-front, and your selection is successful, you will have no similar names left for your roll-out.

A simple example of this can be expressed as:

List A

Total universe of names	200,000
Selection: female, names only	90,000

List test should be taken based on 10 to 20 percent of the 90,000 female names available — not based on the universe of 200,000 names. Standard test size is 5,000 names. You can still accomplish your goals by step-testing.

If you take the same list selection and add a provincial overlay to your selection:

List A

Total list universe of names	200,000
Selections: female	90,000
Ontario only	54,000

By adding the incremental select (living in the province of Ontario) your total universe of names available for testing is reduced to 54,000 names. As a result, your test should be based on 10 to 20 percent of 54,000 names not 90,000.

3. Keep track of the portion of the list used for testing

If you wish to re-use names on a test list, have the list broker ask the list owner to keep a record of the portion of the list used for the test. Then the names can be eliminated from any subsequent tests or when using the entire list.

If you are ordering lists yourself, you must advise the list owner in advance.

4. Track overall campaign results. Track each list separately

Track the results of each list and any selections, separate from overall campaign results. Your overall campaign results may come in at five percent, but the important element in achieving that five percent was made up of a multitude of individual lists and list segmentation. Analyse which individual list worked best, which selections worked best, and eliminate the poor performers from the roll-out. By eliminating the poor performers, you increase your chances for predictable response rates in the roll-out.

▶ Reading test results

Success is not measured by up-front response rates alone. The combination of response rate and return on investment is the calculation that drives the decision for a roll-out — this is referred to as front-end and back-end results. Table 7-1 on the following page is based on a single test mailing and does not reflect or include the lifetime value of each customer acquired.

TABLE 7-1

FRONT-END RESPONSE VS BACK-END PERFORMANCE

Program detail	LIST A Response: 6% Cancels: 10% Bad debts: 5%	LIST B Response: 7% Cancels: 10% Bad debts: 5%	LIST C Response: 8% Cancels: 20% Bad debts: 10%
Front-end response			
1. Mail quantity	10,000	10,000	10,000
2. Gross orders	600	700	800
3. **Gross sales ($)**	**24,840**	**28,980**	**33,120**
4. Promotion cost/M	420	420	420
5. Promotion costs	4,200	4,200	4,200
6. **Cost per order (CPO)**	**7.00**	**6.00**	**5.25**
List "C" appears to be the winner			
Back-end performance			
7. Revenue per order	41.20	41.20	41.20
8. Cancels	60	70	160
9. Bad debt	30	35	80
Cost per sale			
10. Cost of goods	9.00	9.00	9.00
11. Promotion costs	7.78	6.67	6.56
12. Overhead @ 10 percent	4.12	4.12	4.12
13. Fulfillment, shipping, etc.	4.40	4.40	4.80
14. Bad debt	4.12	4.12	8.24
Total:	29.50	28.31	32.72
15. **Profit per sale**	**11.98**	**13.09**	**8.68**

Considering only front-end response rates, List C would be the clear winner. But when analysing the back-end performance of each list, customers acquired from List C carry the combination of higher cancellations and bad debt ratio. List B is the clear winner based on acceptable levels of cancellations and bad debt yielding a better profit per sale.

▶ Summary

Let us now review what we've learned about lists:

1. The heaviest promotion months are September, October, and November; with September being the number one month.

2. The second heaviest months for promotion are January, February, and March.

3. Your house file is your own list, which is comprised of existing customers, leads, and possibly prospects. Your house file should contain as much behavioural information as possible in order to facilitate the selection and testing of specific customer segments.

4. If you decide to put your house list on the market for rental be sure you have your customers' permission to pass along their name (check the privacy code) and that you seed your names for ease of tracking usage.

5. Lists are one of the most important elements in your direct marketing campaign.

6. Outside lists are rented, not bought.

7. There are two categories of mailing lists:

    - Direct response lists (responder lists), which are comprised of names of individuals who have previously done business via the mail, phone or both.

    - Compiled lists, which consist of names gathered from many different public sources, such as phone or trade directories.

8. In the testing stage, your first consideration should be given to a direct response list.

9. Merge-purge (duplication elimination) is a computer process, which prevents multiple mailings to an individual by eliminating duplicates, when more than one list is joined together to form one all-encompassing mailing list. Duplicates can be identified within each list as well as across all lists.

10. Selects within a rented list increase your targeting and can reduce waste, thereby giving you the best chance to increase response rates.

11. Net name arrangements based on 85 percent mailing quantities, can save you time and money. Be sure to ask your list broker about these arrangements prior to renting the lists. This cannot be negotiated after the list rental transaction is complete.

12. Analyse the universe of a mailing list, less your selections, before choosing your test configuration.

13. Analyse each list in your campaign separately.

A good list professional can be your staunchest ally in exploring the viability and direction of your direct marketing program.

14. Test results should be evaluated based on up-front response rate and back-end performance.

We should also review the role of the list broker in your business:

- If trusted list professionals are brought in at an early stage, they can often bring the project into much sharper focus, drawing on knowledge of similar efforts by other marketers.

- The list professional can reach out to his or her network of friends, associates and contacts within the business community to provide the marketer with a broad base of advice.

Direct marketing's phenomenal growth over the past few years has tempted thousands of companies to spread their wings in this complex and intriguing field. Established firms with excellent reputations in other areas, such as publishing or retail, are now trying to branch out. But it isn't easy to succeed in this increasingly competitive field. A good list professional can be your staunchest ally in exploring the viability and direction of your direct marketing program.

TESTING: THE BASIC PRINCIPLES

8

Testing is the backbone of direct marketing success. This chapter will introduce you to testing, and will specifically concentrate on direct mail testing in order to demonstrate some very important basics. These direct mail principles extend to lists, both rental and in-house, direct response television, print, and telemarketing. Each chapter on these topics contains a section on testing.

What makes direct marketing unique is not only the opportunity to test, but the commitment to testing. In this chapter you will gain an understanding of the purpose of testing, test planning techniques, planning imperatives as well as tips for increasing response rates.

It is within this chapter that you will discover the answer to the most asked question: what response rate do you think I'll get?

Testing for the direct marketer should be considered an addiction. As I look around the industry today, far too many companies are risking too many dollars on promotions that do not contain test cells. The need to understand the principles of testing must be made a priority.

You will be introduced to five basic principles for testing, including the theory of probability and the arithmetic of testing. Don't let the introduction of math scare you. Testing is the only way to look at your product and examine your audience. Testing reinforces that thinking, and proves it in the numbers. Imagine, never having to listen to someone say: "I don't like that approach." Testing results will humble even the most experienced marketer.

▶ What is testing?

Testing is the process by which you expose your material to a representative sample of your potential audience, in order to measure results prior to large expenditures and/or any specific program design commitments.

As a manager, you need to determine whether your company's budget is being wisely spent. How do you justify, for example, spending $400,000 on a mailing of 1,000,000 pieces based on an acquisition strategy? How do you know if you have reached your potential customers? The answer lies in testing.

In this case, you take the best representative cross-section or sample of the 1,000,000 names, deliver your mailing to that cross-section, and measure the results. If they are good, and the test has been properly planned and executed, you can proceed with your roll-out mailing with a strong degree of confidence that your $400,000 will be well spent. If the test results do not measure up to your success model, you have limited your exposure to a moderate test-size budget and should now look for other ways to spend the balance of your $400,000 profitably.

Testing can be broken into two categories:

- **Product (or viability) testing**, in which you measure the basic viability of the product

- **Comparative testing**, in which you isolate one component of your direct mail package, change it, and test the effect of that change

Product testing

Your first test may be a product test. Obviously, product testing and comparative testing are interrelated; the success of the viability test will be determined in part by your choice of premium, your mailing package design, and so on. You must therefore use your best ammunition in your first test. Select your strongest possible offer and mailing package at the most attractive price.

If you think that spending an extra $40 per thousand on your mailing package may make a significant improvement in your response, then spend it. If the test does not show promise, you can be certain that no reasonable amount of comparative testing will make the product profitable.

On the other hand, if the first test does work, you can then go to work using comparative testing to see whether you can save money by using a less-expensive mailing package.

Comparative testing

One of the unique advantages of direct mail is the ability to conduct comparative tests. Not only do you want to spend your $400,000 budget profitably, but you want to be sure that you have maximised your profit potential by using the best and most effective combination of price, offer, target audience, and mailing package. You should, therefore, conduct comparative tests that will measure the cost effectiveness of changing one element, while keeping all others constant.

For example, assume you are selling a $20 vinyl jacket via the mail. You plan to offer a booklet premium to your 1,000,000 potential customers. First, you must determine whether the increase in jackets sold will be sufficient to justify the incremental cost of the premium. You therefore undertake a comparative test. One half of your test group will receive the premium offer and the other half will not.

The results of this test might look something like this:

Assumptions

1. Your house list (or potential outside list rental) is 1,000,000 (universe)

> Direct mail provides us with the unique ability to test and measure results precisely.

2. Your product selling price is $20

3. You have selected 40,000 names that are representative of your 1,000,000 universe

4. Your mailing costs are $400/M

TABLE 8-1

COMPARATIVE TESTING — JACKET TEST MAILING

Description	Offer A No premium	Offer B Premium
Number of pieces mailed	20,000	20,000
Mailing costs @$400/M	$8,000	$8,000
Number of replies	600	800
Percent response	3	4
Average cost per response	$13.33	$10
Premium cost per response	N/A	$1
Total cost per response	$13.33	$11

If your advertising costs were increased to $1,000/M, this may be a very different outcome. Therefore, some principles of testing must also be applied to the selection of the right vehicle for the right product.

Results

If you assume the quality of response is equal, then you have two reasons for going with the premium offer for your roll-out mailing:

1. You will make an additional $2.33 profit for every jacket sold

2. You will increase jacket sales from 30,000 (three percent response) to 40,000 (four percent response) in your roll-out campaign; a 33 percent increase in sales

Because of uncertainties in the marketplace and a high risk of jumping from a 40,000 test to a major 1,000,000 mailing, roll-outs are often done in two, three, or four stages.

And if your direct costs of product and fulfillment are $10 per jacket, then your simplified profit and loss comparison, projected to your 1,000,000 mailing will look like Table 8-2 on the next page.

TABLE 8-2

JACKET MAILING
SIMPLIFIED PROJECTED PROFIT AND LOSS

Description	Offer A No premium	Offer B Premium
Revenue:		
30,000 jackets @ $20	$600,000	
40,000 jackets @ $20		$800,000
Cost:		
Direct costs @ $10	300,000	400,000
Promotion costs:		
@ $13.33 per jacket sold	399,900	
@ $11.00 per jacket sold		440,000
TOTAL COSTS	$699,900	$840,000
MARGIN	($99,900)	$ 40,000

This increased margin, or, contribution to overhead and profit, is dramatic. Comparative testing demonstrates the cost effectiveness of the premium offer.

Test for the big things

Far too much money has been wasted on tests that have no real chance of making a significant difference to results. Every test you do costs money. There are more important variables to test than a green reply envelope versus a pink reply envelope. Concentrate your efforts on getting the consumer to open your package before you worry about the colour of the reply envelope. Test only those things that will make a difference to your profit and loss statement. You will need to have a constant vigil on this point, not only within your organisation, but with your outside consultants.

Direct mail provides us with the unique ability to test and measure results precisely. Direct mail testing is a wonderful hunting ground as well as a wonderful crutch for any manager. Remember. Before you set up a test, or authorise a test, ensure the results will be meaningful and make a significant difference to your bottom line.

There are three good reasons for limiting your test to the big things:

- **Tests cost money**
  Every test requires about 200 replies to be statistically valid; at a two percent assumed response rate, this means you need to mail at least 10,000 pieces to get reliable results (see Probability Table). Every additional item tested, therefore adds 10,000 pieces to the size of your mailing, increasing your test costs.

It's important to note that your test should avoid all possible bias. Otherwise, you will be making roll-out decisions based on misleading information.

- **Too many tests muddy the waters**

  The more elements you test, the more complex your tests will get and the more management time you will require to control them properly and read the results correctly. It is unfortunate, but true, that tests are often conducted in such a way that you can't see the forest for the trees so, the tests results become redundant. You will have wasted time and money.

- **Complex testing makes mistakes likely**

  The more tests you have, the more error-prone the tests will become. Errors are likely to be made in execution. Incorrect test analysis can have disastrous results.

  So, to keep your tests simple and error-free: keep your test costs down and test for the big things — those that will make a difference to your bottom line.

▶ 5 planning techniques for lists

It's important to note that your test should avoid all possible bias. Otherwise, you will be making roll-out decisions based on misleading information. Your test sample must truly be a representative cross-section of your universe (roll-out) population. Your target audience plays an important role in your success — more than just the names you choose, but also how you choose the names.

1.   Make sure your tests avoid all possible bias

Your test sample must truly be a representative sample and cross-section of your universe.

2.   The number of test names you select in each segment must be in direct proportion to the number of names in your roll-out

Your list sample must be geographically representative between regions of the country and between rural and urban. Edmonton may not perform as well as Vancouver; Toronto may perform better than rural Ontario; rural Canada may perform better than urban Canada.

3.   Your list sample must be representative of your universe by tenure

New names may outperform old names; loyal customers may outperform everyone on the list and cloud the potential segments.

4.   Your list sample must be representative by source and product

Names that are generated from a number of sources, such as direct mail, phone, or TV may respond differently. Similarly, you may get very different results from names who have spent $200 and names who have spent $10.

5. Your list sample must be representative by category

If you are renting a magazine list, active names may respond differently than the inactive category of names; repeat subscribers differently than the new; free trial subscribers and fully paid subscribers.

Once you have ensured your list is representative, be sure to keep the following tips in mind when you are planning and executing your tests:

· **Your test components must be identical to those you plan in your roll-out**

Your mailing package, price and offer must not change in any significant manner from test to roll-out.

· **Comparative testing requires that every component, except the piece being tested, remain the same**

When you are comparative testing, test only one thing at a time. If you introduce two variables into your test, you will not know which one has made the difference.

· **Roll-out decisions must be based on test results adjusted for seasonality and timing**

There is only one component that cannot be kept constant — timing. A test mailing in February 1999, will only give you results that apply to February 1999. The results do not apply to any other month of the year, or, for that matter, any other year. Use your business judgment and examine the test results and project your roll-out. The 1997 CDMA List Usage Survey indicates the heaviest months for list usage are September, October and November. The second busiest period is January to March. This may help guide your seasonality decision.

If your test results are strong, you have a safety margin that will encourage you to proceed aggressively to the roll-out. If your test results are marginal, you will want to judge the market conditions under which the test was made.

Therefore, the economy and the psychology of the marketplace at the time of testing, and at the time of the projected roll-out, are therefore critical factors in your decision. And over and above these conditions, there is the influence of seasonality. Certain seasons will pull significantly better than others, depending on your product or service.

· **Your sample size must be sufficiently large enough to give you the degree of accuracy for which you are looking**

TESTING: THE BASIC PRINCIPLES

The larger the sample, the more accurate your results. Unfortunately, for your test budget, it takes a significant increase in the number of pieces mailed to achieve a modest improvement in accuracy of results. In deciding on the number of names to test, you will always have to balance the need for accurate results against the need to control costs.

▶ Probability theory: determining sample size

The size and accuracy of your test will be governed by the statistical theory of probability. Using the probability table (Table 8-3), you can determine the number of names you need to mail to give you the level of accuracy you require. In other words, the answer to: how big a test is big enough?

To answer that question, you must first ask yourself how accurate you need your test to be. Of course, we'd all like it to be 100 percent accurate, but short of mailing the entire list, that is impossible. So, you compromise and decide on two things: the confidence level and the level of variance that you are willing to accept.

Acceptable confidence level

Most direct marketers work with a confidence level of either 95 percent or 99 percent; which means you are prepared to accept the fact that your test results will fall within the probability table limits either 95 percent of the time, or 99 percent of the time.

At the 95 percent level, you accept the fact that there is always a five percent chance that your roll-out results will be better (or worse) than you have forecasted in testing. In the Canadian marketplace, the 95 percent confidence level is adequate for almost all purposes. The cost of getting the extra accuracy of 99 percent confidence level is really too high — you may have to mail approximately 75 percent more mailing packages to move from 95 percent to 99 percent confidence level.

Acceptable limits of error

A test's level of variance, or limits of error, is the range of its possible deviation from accuracy. If the limit of error on a projected 2.0 percent response is +/- 2 percent, then your actual test results may vary from a 1.8 percent to 2.2 percent (usually expressed as "2% +- 0.2").

Obviously, the lower the limit of error, the better. Unfortunately, the only way to reduce the limit of error is to increase the size of your test mailing. You must therefore decide what degree of accuracy you need and what limit of error you are prepared to accept.

How to use the probability tables

Although we do not use the 99 percent confidence level limit table as an example herein, it appears on page 103 for your reference.

Assume you have best-guessed a three percent response, and you accept the 95 percent confidence limit and a limit of error of +-.3 percent. Follow this procedure:

1. Go to the table with the 95 percent confidence level (Table 8-3) on page 101.

2. Select the three percent (3.0) response line from the "R" column on the left side of the table.

3. Move over to the .30 limits of error column. Here you will find your test quantity of 12,419 pieces, or to round up, 12,500 pieces are to be mailed.

If you do get three percent on your 12,500 test, then there is a 95 percent probability that a future volume mailing, under identical conditions will produce a response between 2.7 percent and 3.3 percent, give or take 0.3 percent.

What happens if you only get two percent results on your 12,500 test? In that case:

1. Go to the table with the 95 percent confidence level (Table 8-3).

2. Select the two percent response line from the left-hand column.

3. Follow the line until you reach the quantity closest to 12,500 pieces mailed.

Your mailing quantity falls roughly halfway between the .20 and .30 columns. Your variance is therefore approximately 0.25 and you are now able to say that your 12,500 test has produced a two percent response, with a 95 percent probability that future volume mailings will produce a response range between 1.75 percent and 2.25 percent (+-.25). With these results, you should re-do your product profit and loss statement to find out whether you have a viable product or not.

In similar fashion, the 95 percent tables show that a 30,000 (29,407 in the table) mailing, yielding a two percent response will be accurate between 1.84 and 2.16 percent, and one of 10,000 (9,997 in the table) mailing yielding 2.4 percent response will be accurate between 2.1 and 2.7 percent.

Note that the size of your test does not depend in any way upon the size of list you are testing. A test of 5,000 names gives the same level of accuracy for a 1,000,000 name list as it does for a 50,000 name list. But there is one important difference.

TABLE 8-3

95% PROBABILITY TABLE — SAMPLE SIZES FOR RESPONSES BETWEEN 0.1% AND 4.0%
(CONFIDENCE LEVEL 95%)

R (Response)	LIMITS OF ERROR (EXPRESSED AS PERCENTAGE POINTS)														
	.02	.04	.06	.08	.10	.12	.14	.16	.18	.20	.30	.40	.50	.60	.70
.1	95,929	23,982	10,659	5,995	3,837	2,665	1,957	1,499	1,184	959	426	240	153	106	78
.2	191,666	47,916	21,296	11,979	7,667	5,324	3,911	2,994	2,366	1,917	852	479	307	213	156
.3	287,211	71,803	31,912	17,951	11,488	7,978	5,861	4,487	3,546	2,872	1,276	718	459	319	234
.4	382,564	95,641	42,507	23,910	15,303	10,627	7,807	5,977	4,723	3,826	1,700	956	612	425	312
.5	477,724	119,431	53,080	29,858	19,109	13,270	9,749	7,464	5,987	4,777	2,123	1,194	764	530	390
.6	572,693	143,173	63,632	35,793	22,908	15,908	11,687	8,948	7,070	5,727	2,545	1,432	916	636	467
.7	667,470	166,867	74,163	41,717	26,699	18,541	13,622	10,429	8,240	6,675	2,966	1,669	1,068	741	545
.8	762,054	190,514	84,673	47,628	30,482	21,168	15,552	11,907	9,408	7,621	3,387	1,905	1,219	847	622
.9	856,447	214,112	95,160	53,528	34,258	23,790	17,478	13,382	10,573	8,564	3,806	2,141	1,370	951	699
1.0	950,648	237,662	105,628	59,415	38,026	26,407	19,401	14,854	11,736	9,506	4,225	2,376	1,521	1,056	776
1.1	1,044,656	261,164	116,072	65,291	41,786	29,018	21,319	16,322	12,897	10,446	4,643	2,611	1,671	1,160	853
1.2	1,138,472	284,618	126,496	71,155	45,539	31,624	23,234	17,788	14,055	11,385	5,060	2,846	1,821	1,265	929
1.3	1,232,097	308,024	136,899	77,006	49,284	34,225	25,145	19,251	15,211	12,321	5,476	3,080	1,971	1,369	1,006
1.4	1,325,529	331,382	147,280	82,845	53,021	36,820	27,051	20,711	16,364	13,255	5,891	3,314	2,121	1,473	1,082
1.5	1,418,769	354,692	157,640	88,673	56,751	39,410	28,954	22,168	17,515	14,188	6,305	3,547	2,270	1,576	1,158
1.6	1,511,818	377,954	167,980	94,489	60,473	41,995	30,853	23,622	18,664	15,118	6,719	3,780	2,419	1,680	1,234
1.7	1,604,674	401,168	178,297	100,292	64,187	44,574	32,748	25,073	19,811	16,047	7,132	4,012	2,567	1,783	1,310
1.8	1,697,338	424,334	188,592	106,083	67,894	47,148	34,639	26,521	20,955	16,973	7,543	4,243	2,716	1,886	1,385
1.9	1,789,810	447,452	198,868	111,863	71,592	49,717	36,526	27,966	22,096	17,898	7,955	4,474	2,863	1,988	1,461
2.0	1,882,090	470,523	209,121	117,631	75,284	52,280	38,410	29,407	23,235	18,821	8,365	4,705	3,011	2,091	1,536
2.1	1,974,178	493,544	219,352	123,386	78,967	54,838	40,289	30,846	24,372	19,742	8,774	4,935	3,158	2,193	1,611
2.2	2,066,074	516,518	229,564	129,129	82,643	57,391	42,165	32,282	25,507	20,661	9,182	5,165	3,306	2,295	1,686
2.3	2,157,778	539,444	239,753	134,861	86,311	59,938	44,036	33,715	26,638	21,578	9,590	5,394	3,452	2,397	1,761
2.4	2,249,290	562,322	249,920	140,581	89,972	62,480	45,903	35,145	27,769	22,493	9,997	5,623	3,599	2,499	1,836
2.5	2,340,609	585,152	260,068	146,288	93,624	65,017	47,767	36,572	28,896	23,406	10,403	5,851	3,745	2,600	1,911
2.6	2,431,737	607,934	270,192	151,983	97,269	67,547	49,627	37,996	30,021	24,317	10,807	6,079	3,891	2,702	1,985
2.7	2,522,673	630,668	280,296	157,667	100,907	70,074	51,483	39,416	31,144	25,227	11,211	6,307	4,036	2,803	2,059
2.8	2,613,416	653,354	290,380	163,339	104,537	72,595	53,335	40,834	32,264	26,134	11,615	6,534	4,181	2,904	2,133
2.9	2,703,968	675,992	300,440	168,998	108,159	75,110	55,183	42,249	33,382	27,039	12,017	6,760	4,326	3,004	2,207
3.0	2,794,328	698,582	310,480	174,645	111,773	77,620	57,026	43,661	34,497	27,943	12,419	6,986	4,471	3,105	2,281
3.1	2,884,495	721,124	320,499	180,281	115,380	80,125	58,867	45,070	35,611	28,845	12,820	7,211	4,615	3,205	2,355
3.2	2,974,470	743,618	330,496	185,904	118,979	82,623	60,702	46,476	36,721	29,745	13,220	7,436	4,759	3,305	2,428
3.3	3,064,254	766,063	340,471	191,516	122,570	85,118	62,535	47,878	37,830	30,642	13,619	7,660	4,903	3,404	2,501
3.4	3,153,845	788,461	350,427	197,115	126,154	87,607	64,364	49,278	38,936	31,538	14,017	7,884	5,046	3,504	2,574
3.5	3,243,244	810,811	360,360	202,703	129,730	90,089	66,188	50,675	40,040	32,432	14,414	8,108	5,189	3,603	2,647
3.6	3,332,452	833,113	370,271	208,278	133,298	92,568	68,009	52,069	41,141	33,325	14,811	8,331	5,332	3,702	2,720
3.7	3,421,467	855,367	380,163	213,842	136,859	95,041	69,825	53,460	42,240	34,214	15,207	8,554	5,474	3,801	2,793
3.8	3,510,290	877,572	390,031	219,393	140,412	97,507	71,638	54,848	43,336	35,103	15,601	8,776	5,616	3,900	2,865
3.9	3,598,921	899,730	399,878	224,932	143,957	99,969	73,446	56,233	44,430	35,989	15,995	8,997	5,758	3,998	2,938
4.0	3,687,360	921,840	409,706	230,460	147,494	102,426	75,252	57,615	45,522	36,874	16,388	9,218	5,900	4,097	3,010

TABLE 8-4

99% PROBABILITY TABLE — SAMPLE SIZES FOR RESPONSES BETWEEN 0.1% AND 4.0% (CONFIDENCE LEVEL 99%)

R (Response)	LIMITS OF ERROR (EXPRESSED AS PERCENTAGE POINTS)														
	.02	.04	.06	.08	.10	.12	.14	.16	.18	.20	.30	.40	.50	.60	.70
.1	165,709	41,427	18,412	10,357	6,628	4,603	3,381	2,589	2,046	1,657	736	414	265	184	135
.2	331,087	82,772	36,787	20,693	13,243	9,197	6,756	5,173	4,087	3,311	1,471	827	529	368	270
.3	496,132	124,033	55,126	31,008	19,845	13,781	10,125	7,752	6,125	4,961	2,205	1,240	794	551	405
.4	660,846	165,212	73,427	41,303	26,434	18,356	13,486	10,325	8,158	6,608	2,937	1,652	1,057	734	539
.5	825,228	206,307	91,692	51,577	33,009	22,923	16,841	12,894	10,187	8,252	3,667	2,063	1,320	916	673
.6	989,279	247,320	109,919	61,830	39,571	27,480	20,189	15,457	12,213	9,893	4,396	2,473	1,582	1,099	807
.7	1,152,997	288,249	128,111	72,062	46,120	32,027	23,530	18,015	14,234	11,530	5,124	2,883	1,845	1,281	941
.8	1,316,384	329,096	146,265	82,274	52,655	36,565	26,864	20,569	16,251	13,164	5,850	3,291	2,106	1,462	1,074
.9	1,479,439	369,859	164,381	92,465	59,178	41,095	30,192	23,116	18,264	14,794	6,575	3,698	2,367	1,643	1,208
1.0	1,642,163	410,541	182,463	102,635	65,687	45,616	33,513	25,658	20,273	16,422	7,299	4,105	2,627	1,825	1,340
1.1	1,804,554	451,138	200,505	112,784	72,182	50,126	36,827	28,195	22,278	18,045	8,020	4,511	2,887	2,004	1,473
1.2	1,966,614	491,654	218,512	122,913	78,665	54,628	40,134	30,728	24,279	19,666	8,740	4,917	3,146	2,185	1,605
1.3	2,128,342	532,085	236,482	133,021	85,134	59,121	43,435	33,255	26,275	21,283	9,459	5,321	3,405	2,365	1,737
1.4	2,289,739	572,435	254,414	143,108	91,590	63,603	46,729	35,777	28,268	22,897	10,176	5,724	3,663	2,544	1,869
1.5	2,450,803	612,700	272,310	153,175	98,032	68,077	50,016	38,293	30,256	24,508	10,892	6,127	3,921	2,723	2,000
1.6	2,611,536	652,884	290,170	163,221	104,461	72,542	53,296	40,805	32,241	26,115	11,607	6,529	4,178	2,901	2,132
1.7	2,771,937	692,984	307,992	173,246	110,877	76,997	56,569	43,311	34,221	27,719	12,319	6,930	4,435	3,079	2,263
1.8	2,932,002	733,002	325,777	183,250	117,280	81,444	59,836	45,812	36,197	29,320	13,030	7,330	4,691	3,257	2,393
1.9	3,091,744	772,936	343,527	193,234	123,670	85,881	63,096	48,308	38,169	30,917	13,741	7,729	4,946	3,435	2,523
2.0	3,251,150	812,788	361,238	203,197	130,046	90,309	66,350	50,799	40,137	32,512	14,449	8,128	5,202	3,612	2,654
2.1	3,410,224	852,556	378,912	213,139	136,409	94,728	69,596	53,284	42,100	34,102	15,156	8,525	5,456	3,789	2,783
2.2	3,568,967	892,242	396,551	223,060	142,759	99,138	72,836	55,765	44,061	35,690	15,862	8,922	5,710	3,965	2,913
2.3	3,727,377	931,844	414,152	232,961	149,095	103,537	76,068	58,239	46,016	37,273	16,566	9,318	5,964	4,141	3,042
2.4	3,885,456	971,364	431,716	242,841	155,418	107,929	79,294	60,710	47,968	38,855	17,268	9,714	6,216	4,317	3,172
2.5	4,043,203	1,010,800	449,245	252,700	161,728	112,311	82,513	63,174	49,915	40,432	17,970	10,108	6,469	4,492	3,300
2.6	4,200,619	1,050,155	466,734	262,538	168,025	116,682	85,726	65,634	51,859	42,006	18,669	10,501	6,721	4,667	3,429
2.7	4,357,702	1,089,425	484,187	272,356	174,308	121,046	88,932	68,088	53,798	43,577	19,367	10,894	6,972	4,842	3,557
2.8	4,514,454	1,128,614	501,606	282,153	180,578	125,402	92,131	70,538	55,734	45,145	20,064	11,286	7,223	5,016	3,685
2.9	4,670,874	1,167,718	518,984	291,929	186,835	129,745	95,324	72,982	57,664	46,708	20,759	11,677	7,473	5,189	3,812
3.0	4,826,963	1,206,741	536,327	301,685	193,079	134,081	98,508	75,421	59,591	48,270	21,453	12,067	7,723	5,363	3,940
3.1	4,982,719	1,245,679	553,635	311,420	199,309	138,409	101,687	77,854	61,514	49,827	22,145	12,457	7,972	5,536	4,067
3.2	5,138,144	1,284,536	570,903	321,134	205,526	142,725	104,858	80,284	63,433	51,381	22,836	12,845	8,221	5,709	4,194
3.3	5,293,237	1,323,309	588,135	330,827	211,729	147,034	108,024	82,706	65,348	52,932	23,525	13,233	8,469	5,881	4,321
3.4	5,447,999	1,362,000	605,333	340,500	217,920	151,333	111,183	85,124	67,258	54,480	24,213	13,620	8,716	6,053	4,447
3.5	5,602,428	1,400,607	622,490	350,152	224,097	155,621	114,334	87,537	69,165	56,024	24,899	14,006	8,964	6,224	4,573
3.6	5,756,526	1,439,132	639,611	359,783	230,261	159,903	117,479	89,945	71,067	57,565	25,584	14,391	9,210	6,395	4,699
3.7	5,910,292	1,477,573	656,699	369,393	236,412	164,174	120,616	92,347	72,966	59,103	26,268	14,775	9,456	6,567	4,824
3.8	6,063,727	1,515,932	673,746	378,983	242,549	168,439	123,749	94,745	74,860	60,637	26,949	15,159	9,702	6,737	4,949
3.9	6,216,829	1,554,207	690,756	388,552	248,673	172,688	126,872	97,137	76,750	62,168	27,629	15,542	9,947	6,907	5,074
4.0	6,369,600	1,592,400	707,733	398,100	254,784	176,933	129,991	99,525	78,636	63,696	28,309	15,924	10,191	7,077	5,199

Don't forget that it is much more important whether the 1,000,000 list works than whether the 50,000 list works! The sheer economics involved proves that. You may decide to mail a larger test of the 1,000,000 names, just because you have set yourself stricter standards of accuracy, since a lot of your future advertising budget is going to be spent on the larger list.

Some useful guidelines

There is a useful rule of thumb for determining test results, and to determine whether test results are accurate or not. A properly conducted test, which produces 200 orders will be accurate to within plus or minus 30 orders. If you have fewer than 200 orders, treat your results with caution. This can be verified against the probability tables.

You will therefore get reasonably accurate front-end results with:

- A mailing of 5,000 pieces yielding four percent response or more
- A mailing of 10,000 pieces yielding two percent or more
- A mailing of 20,000 pieces yielding one percent or more

The 200 order response figure holds true for each list of each element tested. Any and every item you want to measure requires that 200 number to be valid.

Projecting your test results

Ideally, you should be able to project results on your roll-out by simple multiplication. In practice, however, your test will be somewhat more sophisticated and simple arithmetic will not give you accurate results.

Why? Assume that 1,000,000 potential names are split between eight lists.

1,000,000 NAMES, SPLIT BETWEEN EIGHT LISTS

List No. 1	300,000
List No. 2	250,000
List No. 3	100,000
List No. 4	100,000
List No. 5	75,000
List No. 6	75,000
List No. 7	50,000
List No. 8	50,000

The theory of probability shows that you expect a two percent response — a cross-section of 40,000 names out of the 1,000,000 total will be more than sufficient to give valid test results. This is based on limit of error between 1.86 and 2.14 percent at the 95 percent confidence level.

Common sense tells you, however, that each of these lists will produce a different level of response and a different quality of response. What you really need to know is the profitability of each one of the eight lists, which total your 1,000,000.

In order to do this, you need to mail a 5,000 name cross-section from each of the eight lists, for the same total test quantity, 40,000. You should notice that these tests of 5,000 names at two percent won't deliver the magic 200 replies for statistical validity. But we'll talk more about that later.

It becomes obvious that the overall percentage response on the 40,000 test is now not representative of the 1,000,000 universe. By selecting 5,000 names from each list, you have statistically accurate results by list. Each sample must now be weighted according to list size.

TABLE 8-5

PROJECTION OF ROLL-OUT RESULTS

	Test		Roll-out potential			
List	No. of names available (000)	No. of names selected (000)	Response	%	Projected response (000)	%
1	300	5	110	2.2	6.6	2.2
2	250	5	170	3.4	8.5	3.4
3	100	5	95	1.9	1.9	1.9
4	100	5	85	1.7	1.7	1.7
5	75	5	75	1.5	1.125	1.5
6	75	5	150	3.0	2.25	3.0
7	50	5	90	1.8	.9	1.8
8	50	5	50	1.0	.5	1.0
	1000	40	825	2.06	23.475	2.35

The 825 replies to the test give an average response of 2.06 percent. When the response is properly weighted by list size, that figure corrects to 2.35 percent. You can see that weighting your results by the roll-out potential of each list is an essential part of your test analysis.

You could have overcome the weighting problem by taking a cross-section of the total 1,000,000 names, but only by substantially increasing the size of your test. Unless, of course, you were prepared to sacrifice accuracy on the 50,000 name lists on which you would be mailing only 2,000 names per list. Either way, it's not a very sensible solution.

Of course, each list could have been further broken down into a large number of small groups by categories, such as, source, age, recency, and product purchased. That can become cumbersome and expensive. You must apply business judgment to determine how fine a breakdown of your 1,000,000 name universe you require.

How reliable are these test results?

Notice that although there are 825 total replies in the table, the number of replies for each 5,000 test segment is, in every case, below the 200 minimum guideline, which we discussed earlier. How valid then, can this test be? What conclusions can you safely draw from it? The answers are:

- The average response to the total 40,000 test is 825 (2.06 percent). You can therefore have a high degree of confidence in that 2.06 percent figure. At the 95 percent confidence level, the limit of error will be +-0.14 percent. The range is therefore between 1.92 and 2.20 percent. (Check your tables to ensure the accuracy of this data.)

- You have weighted the results according to total potential list size. Here you are on somewhat weaker statistical ground. You have projected from some pretty small figures. It would not take too long to put limits on the best, the worst, and an average pulling list.

TABLE 8-6

List	Names used	Response	%	Limits of error	% Response range
2	5,000	170	3.4	+-0.5	2.9-3.9
8	5,000	50	1.0	+-0.3	0.7-1.3
3	5,000	95	1.9	+-0.4	1.5-2.3

These are fairly wide ranges. You can calculate the limits of error for every list — and you should.

The roll-out

Your product profit and loss calculation shows the percentage response you need to make a profit. If that figure is one percent, then you are obviously on solid ground mailing all lists with the possible exception of List 8. If you need a two percent response to show a profit, then you would probably limit your roll-out to a large volume on Lists 1, 2, and 6, and a smaller re-test of Lists 3, 4, and 7. The remaining lists would be, for the time being, eliminated. Your test has given you the precise data. Now it's up to you to determine how aggressive you want to be.

Take a look at the big lists — this is where the action is. The first two lists give you a projected 15,100 responses out of the total potential of 23,475. That is nearly two-thirds of your potential future business and accounts for 55 percent of your maximum potential advertising budget (550,000 pieces out of the total 1,000,000). If your limits of error are acceptable on these, then you are on firm ground and can proceed accordingly.

You must now make your own decisions in line with the test data and the marketing philosophy of your own firm.

Remember:

· Be sure to keep a record of test names mailed and, if you are renting lists, ask your list supplier to keep a record.

· These names should not be mailed again as part of your roll-out, because they will no longer perform as they did in the test.

· These names have already been exposed to your offer and you already have the cream of the crop.

· If you have a winning promotion, you may want to consider re-mailing the test names only under controlled conditions and separately keyed. This can give you an indication of repeat mailings one or two seasons later. But this should be done only under controlled conditions, and the subsequent mailing should be separately keyed and tracked.

▶ Multi-phase roll-outs or step testing

Because of uncertainties in the marketplace and high risks in jumping from a 40,000 test to a major mailing of 1,000,000 pieces, it is more often done in two, three, and sometimes four mailings. There are a number of advantages to this, and some disadvantages.

Advantages

The greatest advantage is minimising the risk. By going from a 50,000 test to a 250,000 modified roll-out, followed by appropriate sized mailings, you hedge your bets. The 250,000 modified roll-out gives you a chance to confirm your test results without having spent your total budget. You can then add tests of additional lists, and re-test the marginal lists from your first test, as part of your 250,000 modified roll-out mailing.

You have the advantage, especially on longer-term programs, such as continuity programs or cross-selling to existing customers, that you can review back-end performance before you become too deeply committed.

Disadvantages

On the other hand, you will obviously be sacrificing sales and profits by spreading your roll-out over a number of seasons. Inflation will increase costs. You will be incurring higher printing and perhaps higher product costs because of your smaller quantity mailings. You will also be moving further and further away from the time period of your original test, and you must be sure to keep a close eye on any possible changes (for better or for worse) in the market acceptance of your product.

On balance, you should promote as aggressively as you can afford in order to strike while the iron is hot, but never to the point of risking large sums of money on relatively unproven product.

▶ Slippage

Experience dictates that there is almost always slippage — a discrepancy — between test results and volume mailings. Some of this is undoubtedly the result of duplication between mailing lists on the volume mailing.

The ideal is to ensure that your test names are truly representative of the total lists, no better and no worse. The recommended procedure is to downgrade all test response percentages by a correction factor of 20, and make your list selection accordingly. You can always re-test the marginal lists later.

▶ Measurement of profitability

In measuring the results of your test, the key figure is your projected bottom line profit that you will make on the roll-out. This can be measured in three ways:

1. As a percentage of sales

2. As a percentage return on investment

3. In absolute dollars

Of course, you must have a clear idea of your profit objectives before you analyse your test results.

Let us examine a cookbook test mailing, and assume you take a cross-section of test names and come up with results, which translate into a simplified volume product profit and loss.

Corporate criteria

1. Your company has minimum profit objectives

2. 10 percent on net sales

3. 25 percent on money invested

4. A minimum contribution of $25,000 based on the internal decision that anything less than $25,000 will cost too much in management time and setup to justify the effort involved.

TABLE 8-7

PROFIT AND LOSS STATEMENT

Mailing quantity	1,000,000
Percent response	2.5
Number of orders	25,000
Sales revenue at $20 a book	$ 500,000
Product cost (delivered) at $10 a book	$ 250,000
Promotion costs at $200/M	$ 200,000
Profit margin	$50,000
Profit margin as percentage of sales	10
Profit margin as percentage of investment	25

Results

1. You have a marginally successful product

2. Proceed with caution from test to roll-out

Note that your profit must be large enough in absolute terms to make the effort worthwhile. It must also be large enough as a percentage of sales and as a return on capital. Mailings that have a higher advertising cost in relation to sales are more risky than those with a lower profit margin as a percentage of investment.

Analysing test results for profitability

A detailed analysis of test results shows that not all lists within the 1,000,000 total were equally profitable. A breakdown of test results by list gives the significant differences in profitability as shown in the next table (Table 8-8).

The overall result of the test, when projected to the 1,000,000 mailing, shows a $50,000 profit. Based on that number alone, you might decide to proceed to your volume mailing, even though results were not quite as good as you had hoped.

TABLE 8-8

$20 COOKBOOK
PROJECTED ANALYSIS OF PROFITABILITY FOR DIFFERENT PROMOTION QUANTITIES BASED ON TEST RESULTS

	Mailing quantity				
	250M best	250M next best	250M next best	250M next best	1,000M universe
Response	10,000	7,500	5,000	2,500	25,000
Percent response	4	3	2	1	2.5
Revenue @ $20/book	$200,000	$150,000	$100,000	$ 50,000	$500,000
Less:					
Product cost @$10 delivered	$100,000	$ 75,000	$ 50,000	$25,000	$250,000
Promotion cost $200/M	$ 50,000	$ 50,000	$ 50,000	$50,000	$200,000
Profit margin	$ 50,000	$ 25,000	$ 0	($25,000)	$50,000
Profit margin as a percentage of sales	25	17	0	(50)	10
Profit as a percentage of promotion cost investment	100	50	0	(50)	25

A more detailed look reveals:

1. The best quartile of 250,000 names will provide $50,000 profit

2. The second best quartile of 250,000 names will provide $25,000 profit

3. The third best quartile of 250,000 names will provide only a break even

4. The fourth quartile of 250,000 names will provide a $25,000 loss

5. The projected roll-out will produce $50,000 profit

This detailed test analysis shows the fourth quartile of 250,000 names should not be mailed. The third best quartile of 250,000 names do not meet the 10 percent of sales and 25 percent of investment criteria previously set and probably should not be mailed! This shows the importance of profitability by list.

Marginal cost analysis

It was said earlier that the third best quartile of 250,000 names in the example should probably not be mailed. You may ask why, when you have no profit, and a nil return on your money invested: why consider taking a risk with no apparent gain?

The answer lies in marginal cost analysis. You should know, when buying larger quantities of printing, you can get a better price. When you buy 750,000 four-colour brochures, the extra cost of the third or marginal quartile of 250,000 will be significantly less than that of the first two quartiles at 250,000 each. Assume the following in-the-mail costs for a package of different quantities:

TABLE 8-9

MARGINAL COST ANALYSIS

| | Average in-the-mail cost | | Marginal in-the-mail cost | |
	Total cost	Average cost/M	Total cost	Marginal cost/M
250M	$60,000	$ 240	$60,000	$ 240
500M	110,000	220	50,000	200
750M	156,000	208	46,000	184
1000M	200,000	200	44,000	176

Results

- The marginal cost on printing each of the 250,000 lots has dramatically changed your marginal cost per thousand in the mail

- It costs $240/M to mail only 250,000 names

- That cost drops to $184/M on the third group of 250,000 names

Before doing your new profit and loss, take the marginal cost of product into account. For simplicity, assume that the cost of fulfilled product is $11.50 per unit on the first 10,000 units and $9 per unit thereafter. See the profit and loss statement to give you new profit and loss calculations with marginal costing.

Your new marginal profit and loss calculations based on your test results shows that:

1. You should mail the first 500,000 names

2. You should consider mailing the third group of 250,000

3. The second group of 250,000 names produces more absolute profits and a higher percentage profit than the first 250,000

▶ Summary

Testing is an exact theoretical science. Testing is essential. The data it provides is invaluable. Do not bypass this most important element of your success. Let's summarise some basic principles of testing:

1. Your sample size and quality must be representative of the universe.

2. All elements in the roll-out must be identical to those of the test.

3. Comparative testing requires that every component, except the piece being tested, remain identical.

4. Roll-out decisions must be based on test results that have been adjusted for seasonality and market conditions.

5. Your test size must be large enough to give you the level of confidence you require to move forward. Too large a sample wastes money and with too small a sample, your results will not be statistically valid.

6. Sample size is determined by reference to the theory of probability after deciding on an acceptable confidence level and acceptable limits of error.

7. When projecting the results of your test, it is important to take into account the differences in properties of various lists that make up your test universe. Your test should be done with a cross-section of each list and the results weighted according to the size of each list.

8. A record should always be kept of the test names, to control repeat mailings.

9. It is often advantageous, and less risky, to conduct the roll-out in more than one phase of mailings.

10. The prime consideration in all decisions relating to testing and subsequent roll-out is the bottom line — profitability. Profitability is measured by a combination of: (1) percentage of sales; (2) percentage of ROI; and (3) absolute dollars.

The answer to the most-asked question: what response rate do you think I'll get?

It's a fallacy that the average direct mail response rate is two percent. Each program requires a different response rate to be considered successful. A lead generation program for computer hardware worth $200,000 a sale needs a different response rate than a sales lead for a $50,000 luxury car or a $25 magazine subscription. Testing will set your benckmarks for response rates and will be driven largely by the expenditures involved in your program design (ROI).

CREATIVE

9

CREATIVE

Today's sophisticated consumers want to receive information that is relevant to their needs and is presented in a way with which they can identify. Part of a consumer's ability to identify with a product lies in how it is presented. And that screams: *make sure your creative product is the best it can be.* Don't underestimate the power of consumers. They can to say "no" to your offer if the creative does not get their attention.

Throughout this book, there is constant reference to the creative product and its importance to your success. The creative product has evolved over the years, but the basic principles of what works and what doesn't work remains the same. The relevancy to the consumer is still the driving force behind success. The selling techniques, originally developed for direct mail, are being successfully applied to television, print ads, telemarketing, and most of today's traditional media, but with that one key difference — response. The best way to get response is to deliver the right message to the right audience with the right creative.

You'd be surprised to learn that not everyone can write a letter. And not everyone knows how to sell over the phone. Many of us write letters and use the phone daily, but how many of us are measured on that performance? There is a real skill and training that goes into our creative product. I am thrilled that three of the best creative minds in our business, not only know how to write letters and telemarketing scripts, but how to apply their direct marketing skills to every direct marketing media around today. Their passion about the creative product they produce and the skills they look for in the creative people they hire, make for great reading and great learning for us all.

▶ The gospel according to Fransi Weinstein

Fransi Weinstein is senior vice-president, creative director at BBDO Response.

When I was asked to contribute to the creative section of this book, I was thrilled. It has nothing to do with getting my 15 minutes of fame. It's because 10 or 15 years ago, there probably wouldn't have been a creative section in a book about direct marketing. At least not one that talked about *great* creative. Direct marketers were into the list and the offer and the call to action. What *wasn't* discussed a lot, were ideas and brands.

But that's all changing, I'm happy to say. And the industry is better for it. Just look at how we've grown — direct marketing is, in fact, the only sector of the communications industry experiencing double-digit growth. And a lot of that growth can be attributed to mainstream clients who needed to be sure that the brands they've spent millions of dollars and many, many years building, would be safe in our hands.

Don't get me wrong. With all the privacy issues we're facing, talking to the *right* people (list) is more important than ever. We'll always have to come up with compelling ways (offer) to overcome inertia. And if we don't ask for the order (call to action), we won't get it.

What I'm talking about, and what this particular section is all about is *how* you do it.

So what *do* I think makes great creative, great? Well, interestingly enough, the subject was the topic of last year's BBDO management meeting. And you know what? After spending two and a half days looking at and talking about both good *and* bad advertising, I'm more convinced than ever that whether you're discussing 30-second awareness or two-minute DRTV commercials, billboards, or FSIs, print (direct or otherwise), mail, point-of-purchase material, or press kits, the same principles apply:

- First and foremost, make sure the strategy's nailed down. You can't do great creative if the strategy's wrong, or weak, or incomplete. Period.

- You need an idea. This doesn't mean it needs to be complicated. On the contrary, the best ideas are always the simplest. They're usually obvious, too. For example, when you look at a piece of work and say, after hitting yourself on the side of the head, why didn't I think of that?

- This idea needs to be appropriate for the brand. In other words, if you're selling an $80,000 car or a $15,000 cruise, or even mutual funds, it doesn't matter that you've always wanted to create a brochure that looks and reads like a comic book. Save it for the *right* client, or you'll turn what *could* be a good idea into a bad one.

> An idea doesn't need to be complicated. On the contrary, the best ideas are always the simplest.

- You also need to respect your target audience. A great ad man by the name of David Ogilvy once said: "the consumer is not a moron." He's right.

- Remember. You're telling a story. Now that "story" could be three *really* carefully chosen words on a billboard, or a six-page letter, but it's still a story — a story that gets consumers' attention. Engages them. Holds their interest. Amuses them. Or scares them. Or shocks them. Or saddens them. But *never* bores or disappoints them.

- By its very nature, "out of the box thinking" (which, if you think about it, is what we're talking about here), often takes a risk. Calculated, but a risk nonetheless. So, presuming it's on-strategy, on-brand, etc., you need to be brave enough to show it to the client. And the client needs to be brave enough to approve it.

- If you're the one doing the evaluating, you need to be able to recognise great work. I know, because inevitably, those are the times when I say to myself: gee, I wish I'd thought of that. And it doesn't matter whether it's work I'm approving, a TV commercial I see at home, an ad that pops out at me while reading a magazine or newspaper, or a billboard I happen to drive past.

Speaking of which, what better time to talk about those of us — the creatives — who *do* come up with all those ideas. Other than talent, here's what I think it takes to be a great writer or great art director. Let's just call it Fransi's Top Ten List:

1. Be curious. You should be curious about life and about people (or more to the point, consumers) and what makes them tick. What they're afraid of? What they dream about? Get into their heads. You need to know your customers and prospects, and understand what they're going through to do a *convincing* job of selling.

2. Be a trend watcher and spotter. In fashion. In movies. In books. Art. Architecture. Cars. Design. Food. Pets. Health. Wealth. Computers. Commercials. Ads. TV shows. DJs. Music. Travel destinations. You name it. You want to keep your eye on it. They all have an affect on what you do and how you do it. If you don't keep up, your work will look out of date.

3. Know, and I mean *know,* the product or service you're selling. Again, you can't talk about something with which you're not familiar. At least not if you want consumers to believe or trust you. Which they must, if they're going to buy from you — sight unseen.

4. Be passionate. About your work. About the business. About your assignments. It shows. And everyone, from your colleagues to your clients, get off on it. Being blasé is *not* a good thing.

5. If you think advertising is art, it's not. There *is* an art to doing it well. But our work doesn't hang on museum walls. Nor is it intended to. So get over it.

6. Become a craftsman. Do it. And do it again. And again. Edit ruthlessly (yes, art directors, too). Refine. Polish. Perfect. Think of your work as a fine piece of mahogany. How many sandings, buffings, and polishings does it take to bring out its richness? Unless, of course, you're prepared to settle for pressed wood — in which case, don't come to me looking for a job.

7. Learn to move on. Sometimes you've got a great idea, but for one reason or another it's just not right. Pin it to your wall and worship it. Keep it under your pillow. Put it in a creative bring-forward file, because someday, it might work for someone. But for now, you need to start over. One-trick ponies don't make it in our business.

8. Become comfortable presenting. *Nobody* sells work better than the people who create it. Practice by presenting to your colleagues. Ask for feedback and training if necessary. Rehearse in front of a mirror (no, I'm not kidding) before the presentation. And before you know it, you'll find *your* style.

9. This is not an industry for the faint of heart. If you can't stand criticism, if you give up easily, if you have no sense of humour, then you should seriously consider a different line of work. As glamorous, as exciting, as easy as it looks from the outside, let me assure you that on the inside, it's damn hard work. If you love it, and can handle it, there's nothing like it. And like your favourite Timex, you need to be able to "take a licking and keep on ticking."

10. Be relentless in your pursuit of excellence. No matter how experienced you are, no matter how senior you may be, no matter how talented you are, you can always be better. And smarter. Always.

There you have it. What *I* think. I also think I'm one of the luckiest people alive to be working in this industry. It's stimulating, constantly changing, evolving, and growing beyond anyone's wildest dreams. What more could anyone ask for?

Lead generation direct mail sample

Client: General Motors of Canada
Product: Automobiles
Campaign: Chevrolet Venture 1997 launch
Agency: MacLaren McCann Direct

Creative Director: Kirk Fischer
Copywriter: Rick Muldoon
Art Director: Kirk Fischer, Lynn Sproatt

The objective of this campaign was to announce the launch of the Chevy Venture, an all-new entrant in the expanding mini-van market, and to generate qualified leads.

The audience was college-educated parents of active young children, current owners of GM vehicles, and prospects from outside lists.

The main creative element of the direct mail campaign was a unique Venture activity centre, containing; a page of stickers that allowed customers to *"Build their own Venture"* by sticking their choice of wheel trim, seating configuration, and interior trim onto a Venture side-view illustration.

A box of crayons (selected to match available Venture exterior colors) was also included so customers could colour their vehicle. A Walt Disney World Sweepstakes was offered to prompt completion of a purchase intent survey, and the return of the crayon-colour Venture illustration and option/feature sticker sheets.

The interactive packages involved the entire family in the selection and buying process. The stickers highlighted the numerous options and flexible features of the vehicle, while the Disney sweepstakes acknowledged the vehicle's family positioning. The response rate exceeded projections by over 350 percent.

▶ Bob Sabloff's secrets for success

Bob Sabloff started his own direct marketing creative and consulting business in 1974. Prior to that he was the vice-president and consumer sales director of Reader's Digest Canada from 1968-1974. From 1964-68, he was executive vice-president of Grey Canada. Sabloff is a direct marketing educator, and is known for his practical how-to approach to solving problems.

There's an easy way to recognise good creative — it works. That is, it generates the desired number of orders at an affordable cost. It also produces the kind of customers who will become repeat buyers.

In other words, in direct marketing it's not creative if it doesn't sell. No amount of industry awards or praise from peers is as important as the bottom line results from an in-the-market test.

The problem is: how do you go about writing and designing the creative materials that will prove successful?

Here are my 7 secrets for success:

1. **Know your prospect.** You must know who you're writing to. Are they your current customers or prospects who've never bought from you before? Research on current customers should tell you a lot about the kind of people who are most likely to buy. Also, you should know who's on the mailing list you used. Who reads the publication the ads are running in? The more you know about your prospects, the easier it will be to sell them.

2. **Know your product.** You must find out as much as you can about what you're selling and what it will do for the reader. Make a list of all the product features and translate them into reader benefits. Then list these benefits in order of importance to your reader. Again, customer research will help.

3. **Sell the benefits.** Concentrate on promoting the reader benefits. Imagine that the prospect is opening your mailing piece and saying: I wonder what's in this for me? Don't allow the company's enthusiasm for the wonderful features of the product get in the way of telling readers how it will improve their life.

4. **Make an offer that's hard to refuse.** You must offer readers something important in return for responding. There are over 50 different kinds of offers to choose from. If you can, test several different offers to find out which has the greatest appeal to your readers.

There's an easy way to recognise good creative — it works. That is, it generates the desired number of orders at an affordable cost.

5. **Make it easy to understand.** Write to an individual and make it friendly. Use simple everyday words, short sentences, and short paragraphs. Use active words. Make it interesting and believable.

6. **Make it easy to read.** Good design makes for easy reading. Use easy-to-read typefaces and make the type large enough. Avoid type over half-tones or type on deep coloured stock. Don't use body copy blocks in reverse type. Photos should be clean, sharp, and show the product in use.

7. **Ask for the order.** Ask for the order now. Tell the reader what you want him or her to do to place an order. Make the order form look important and large enough to complete easily. Make it easy to respond by providing an 800 number or a postage-paid reply card or envelope.

As a freelancer, I work alone mostly, consulting from time-to-time with a design associate and my client. When I've gathered all the information I need about the prospect and the product, I'm ready to start creating.

I turn on my Mac and start writing a sales conversation with my prospect — just as if I'm standing in that person's living room or office. Opening the dialogue, like a sales person with a foot in the door, I realise I've only got a few seconds to capture that person's interest and to make that person want to hear more. Often, I'll start off by selling the most important benefit and making an offer that's hard to refuse.

As I continue, I keep thinking about possible objections my reader may have to buying. So I try to answer these objections by listing all the other benefits of the product or service. These may include saving money, getting healthier, investing smarter, winning praise, being more successful, attaining greater popularity, becoming more financially secure, getting promoted, having more fun, getting a better job, etc. Here, it's important to back up the benefits with proof, testimonials, and endorsements.

This process continues through all the elements of the mailing. I do my best to keep the copy interesting, believable, and motivational. Also repeating the basic offer and providing a guarantee of satisfaction. I'll ask the reader to pick up the phone or to mail the order form at various places throughout the mailing, not just at the end.

These creative guidelines have helped in the preparation of many of our most successful direct response ads and packages. I'm sure they'll continue to work in the future.

I urge you to steal these secrets, which I've been using for years. Why not? I did.

▶ David Taylor's Dos and Don'ts

David (Dave) Taylor is president of TCP Direct Inc. His knowledge is extensive and invaluable. One of Dave's passions and strengths is his commitment to training. It wasn't difficult to get him to share his secrets in this book.

Great creative is usually not the product of momentary inspiration. Like so many things in life, great creative can usually be attributed to 90 percent perspiration and 10 percent inspiration. No one is born an art director or a copywriter. These professionals learned their craft, usually through an informal apprenticeship system. Graduating from apprentice to journeyman to master, takes a long time.

Along the way, the pros learn the tricks, the techniques, the skills, and devices that work well. And in the process, they usually make their share of mistakes as well.

Here are just a handful of pointers to help you recognise great creative, punch-up good creative, and avoid spending money on long shots with little chance of success.

The dos

1. Do write to one. Avoid the word we — talk you.

2. Do remember that your old grammar teacher won't be marking your work. Contractions are okay. Dashes are too. All sentences don't need a noun and a verb. You *can* begin a sentence with "and" or "but" and you *can* end a sentence with a preposition.

3. Do remember that you, your boss, and your boss' wife are not necessarily representative of the audience to which you are writing.

4. Do use short words. Short sentences. Short paragraphs — your ad or direct mail package is not a platform to display your erudition. Arbitrarily split your larger paragraphs into two smaller ones if you have to. Remember. What you write shouldn't just be easy to read — it should look easy to read.

5. Do remember that the strongest words in a copywriter's arsenal are still free and new. But remember too that consumers are skeptical. If there are strings attached be forthcoming, e.g., "Free with your paid subscription" or "free with purchase."

6. Do look at what you've written and ask yourself: do I really need the first two or three paragraphs? All too often they are equivalent to a

> Great creative is usually not the product of momentary inspiration. Like so many things in life, great creative can usually be attributed to 90 percent perspiration and 10 percent inspiration.

pitcher warming up in the bull pen and your letter or ad may be stronger without them.

7. Do put your copy aside when you have finished and take a fresh look at it the following day. The odds are, no matter how good your first draft is, you'll find ways to make it better.

8. Do translate product features and characteristics into user benefits. Your reader doesn't want to know that the footprint of your new computer terminal is 15 inches by 13 inches. Tell your reader instead that it takes no more space on his or her desk or credenza than a letter tray.

9. Do keep your offer simple. The more choices a prospect has to make, the more likely he or she is to procrastinate. For example, in publishing, the strongest offer you can make is normally all credit with no choice of subscription term. Ask the reader to choose between "cash with order" or "bill me later" and you'll reduce response. Ask your reader to decide between one year or three years and you'll reduce response further.

10. Do remember that long copy usually out pulls short copy. Use enough copy to do the job effectively then stop.

    The key to success is not length or brevity. It is the ability of your copy to grasp the reader's attention and hold it. This means you have to make your letter look easy to read. You can do this with Johnson boxes, indented paragraphs, bullet points, margin notes, underlining, or highlighting.

11. Do stay abreast of technology. In direct mail, for instance, the computer has allowed us to re-establish one-on-one communications with our prospects and customers. The days of "Dear Canadian Executive" and "Dear Friend" are over. Address prospects by name and, in the case of customers, we know what they buy, how often, and for how much, we know their titles (Mr., Miss, Mrs., Ms., Dr., etc.). Any marketer who does not take advantage of this data and addresses customers as "friends" or "customers" instead of as individuals, is still living in the dark ages.

12. Do make your package fit your product, service, or cause. In fundraising, for instance, you would not send a letter to your donors on an expensive paper like Byronic Text asking for a $20 donation — they would think you spend their money on fancy promotions.

13. Do consider involvement devices such as scratch-offs, stickers, decals, tokens, etc. While most of these devices add to the cost of a package, the increased response they generate can, frequently, more than offset any cost increase.

14. Do use testimonials — prospects will believe real users a great deal more readily than they will believe you. Remember too, if you are using testimonials, you should, wherever possible, attribute them to the customer, using full name, geographic location, and, if possible, include a photo.

15. Do use both sides of an envelope for your creative message. No matter how you look at it, you have to pay for both sides to be printed. Why not make the envelope work twice as hard for you by using the front and back portions for creative.

The don'ts

1. Don't write to a formula, but do pick one of the copy formulas you like and use it to review your work to make sure it's going to be effective.

2. Don't typeset your letter — a letter should look like a piece of personal or business correspondence. How often do you send a letter to your aunt out to be typeset?

3. Do not use "showroom" shots. In your brochure, use "product-in-use" shots wherever possible.

4. Always caption photos — just as you read a newspaper or magazine and look at the photos, then the descriptions — that's how your reader goes through your brochure. A photo without a caption is a missed opportunity.

5. Don't use reverse type of greater length than three or five words.

6. Don't use sans-serif type for long blocks of copy. There is a reason why almost every newspaper and magazine uses serif type (serif type has little feet that lead the eye across the line) — serif typefaces are easier to read than sans-serif faces.

7. Never, never send a direct mail package that does not include a letter. In fact, in many cases, two letters are better than one — your main "sell" letter and what is called a "publisher's" or "lift" letter. That this technique should work defies logic. After all, you took your best shot in your main letter and the lift letter largely says: "if you don't believe the person who signed the main letter, then believe me." Nevertheless, it almost always boosts response.

8. Do not use all capital letters in a headline of more than four or five words — use uppercase and lowercase. Similarly, do not use a period after a headline. The purpose of a headline is to lead the reader into the copy. You don't want the reader to stop after he or she has read your headline, you want him or her to read on, almost without interruption.

9. Do not end a page of a letter copy at the end of a sentence. You want to force the reader to turn the page. So, break the last sentence on the page in the middle. For instance:

> *She strode across the room, wrapped her arms*
> *around him and....*

10. For your first direct mail effort, do not test one of the more exotic direct mail formats — formats like Zipvelopes, one-piece mailers, double postcards, etc. *Test a Classic direct mail* package instead (outgoing envelope, two or four page letter, separate brochure, separate order form, and a postage-paid reply envelope). Then, once you have established a benchmark, test the less expensive format against it.

11. Don't use illustrations if photos are possible. A photo is more believable and allows your prospect to better visualise himself or herself using and benefiting from your product or service.

12. Don't ever do a direct mail campaign with only one package or one offer. Learn something from every mailing. Test different headlines, different copy appeals (for example, comfort, self-esteem, avarice, etc.), different prices, different offers, even different paper colours.

▶ A few of my own tips for art directors

- Work in partnership with your copywriter

- Design the response form first. Good direct response advertising is built around the response mechanism.

- Choose an easy-to-read typeface, whether it's for seniors or Generation X.

- Great design, isn't always the most colourful. Don't overuse colour, make it efficient.

▶ Conclusion

Our roots

The key, I believe, to understanding the creative process and its rationale, is to go back to what I identify as its roots. The basic style and format of good direct response copy and layout can be found in our daily newspaper. Study it the next time you read the front page. Look at the headlines: always in uppercase and lowercase, in a good size typeface, always bold, and never incorporating a period at the end of the headline. The lead story never finishes on the front page. Always, it is continued on the inside pages. This involvement device is called a page-turner and is used to get you inside the newspaper. Every photo is captioned. There is a contents box on the front cover.

Our aim should be to have our consumers look forward to reading our solicitations just as they look forward to reading their morning paper. These same techniques are what you should be looking for when approving good, response-oriented creative.

If your envelope of a direct-mail package never gets opened, *it won't sell.* If your one-page ad has no stopping power, *it will never get noticed* and you won't get a response. If your TV commercial doesn't get attention and repeat the phone number often enough, *your phones won't ring*. Simple things to say, but difficult in their execution. Direct response creative is not easy.

My friend and associate, Geoffrey Bailey says: "The older I get, the better I get at direct marketing. It's a game of patience and detail. It's a game of craftsmanship. Frankly, it's not really about being creative at all. Direct mail, classic direct mail, is about being sensible and tactful and reassuring and not pressing so hard that you're a turn off. It's that simple. And that hard."

Our aim should be to have our consumers look forward to reading our solicitations just as they look forward to reading their morning paper.

DIRECT MAIL

10

Direct mail has always been the most popular "secret weapon" in the direct marketer's arsenal. This popularity has been largely based on the endless testing possibilities (with telemarketing placing a close second). But for today's marketers, there are some additional reasons, other than the testing application, behind the popularity of direct mail.

With the importance of and focus on the consumer, and as a consequence the customer database, the characteristics of direct mail give the marketer a distinct competitive edge.

▶ The characteristics of direct mail

Direct mail is personal and builds customer relationships. It delivers the opportunity for your product or service to be invited into your customer's or potential customer's home or place of business. I liken it to the door-to-door salesperson finally being invited into someone's home and having the opportunity to address the prospect personally. That salesperson knows, if she can just get her foot in the door and demonstrate the product's benefits, she can close the sale. But once inside that door, she must be sure the offer is relevant to the customer needs. In addition, she has the opportunity to position the company well and build the company's brand — all with the intent to close the sale right then and there. Whatever the customer's choice, you want to make a good first and lasting impression. Think of your direct mail as the salesperson who has been invited into your customer's home and craft your package and its contents with a personal tone and ensure your offer is relevant to the customer's immediate needs.

Direct mail is targeted. It gives you the opportunity to target both your audience and your offer. By segmenting your customer file, you may choose to make different customers, different offers. It is not a broad net that is thrown out to the masses. It is very targeted and offer-specific. This specificity gives you the unique ability to read results on a segment-by-segment basis and treat each customer as a segment individual.

The consumer gets involved. The minute the recipient decides to open the envelope, he or she is involved — reviewing the contents, deciding whether or not to go further into the package for details. Once the envelope is opened, it's up to you to deliver your message in the most effective way possible.

There are no competing messages. If you're using a direct mail package, once the envelope is opened, you have no competition, no competitive messages trying to grab the customer's attention. So, your first job is to keep the recipient interested in your offer. This may be the only opportunity you have to make your first impression. Make it the best message you've got. Tell the whole story. Make it interesting. Make it informative. Make it relevant. Take advantage of the moment and ask for the order over and over again.

Contrary to popular belief, direct mail is not produced overnight. It can take up to 16 weeks from the strategy to the mailing. It is not cheap. It is efficient. It reaches a tightly defined audience without any waste. That is the efficiency. It is personal, involving, targeted, and offer-specific. The basis of accessing this efficiency requires an understanding and application of the basic economics of successful direct marketing.

Success in direct mail is a multi-pronged venture — selecting the right audience (Chapter 7), applying your customer knowledge and segmentation efforts (Chapter 17), targeting your offer (Chapter 8), and delivering the consumer message with the best and most appropriate creative (Chapter 9) to represent both your product and your company. But your success will also depend on the appropriateness of the format you choose, the costs you incur, and the tests you incorporate into each mailing effort.

▶ Choosing a format

There are two types of direct mail:

1) Addressed direct mail

2) Unaddressed direct mail, which is often referred to as "householder" direct mail

There are many format choices for direct mail. Some of these formats are examined here. Taking a look at all of these formats may lead you to believe that the decision is more difficult than it really is.

All marketing programs should have a predetermined measurement of success. That is, which parameters determine whether a campaign is successful or not. A large portion of direct mail success is measured by a return on investment (ROI) calculation. This ROI can be the driving force behind your choice of format, with a focus on how much you can afford to spend to accomplish your stated objectives and your allowable cost per order (CPO). Also heavily weighted in this decision is any direct mail format results you may have collected from previous campaigns.

1) Addressed direct mail

The Classic package

The Classic direct mail package is exactly that — a classic. It should be the starting point for your direct mail campaign. If you are using an existing direct mail package that is not the Classic, consider including the Classic as a testing variable in your next format test matrix. The Classic has the most history across the most products and services. It has been researched the most and has been responsible for more direct mail successes than any other format in Canada. Let's review the contents of a Classic package.

Basic components

The Classic direct mail package consists of an outer envelope, a letter, a brochure, an order form, and a reply envelope.

This should be your foundation for building response. Based on these components, you can build a solid foundation for response. But now you must consider affordability. And affordability is based on what you can afford to spend to acquire a new customer, retain an existing customer, encourage existing customers to spend more with you, or win-back a lost customer.

Direct mail is easily misused by those not performing this single calculation of allowable costs. Assuming your costs and return justifies using direct mail, let's now look at the individual components of the Classic direct mail package.

The outer envelope

If your envelope never gets opened, it won't make the sale.

- Is your outer envelope personalised, label addressed, or a window envelope?

- What size is your outer envelope?

- Will you use a standard-size outer envelope, such as a 6 x 9, or a No. 10?

- Will you introduce an odd size or shape of envelope?

- Can your product and margins justify a 9 x 12 size outer envelope?

- Is your outer envelope design strong enough to break through the mailbox clutter and get noticed immediately?

Tip 1: If you are using an oversized envelope, make sure you know the consequences both in increased costs and glamour. Will it fit properly into the mailbox, or does the mail carrier have to fold it? What will it look like folded?

Tip 2: In business-to-business marketing, find out who is opening the envelope. Does the entire package, including the outer envelope, get to the recipient, or is it opened by a gatekeeper? Who must the outer envelope appeal to?

Not only must these decisions be made based on costs, they must also be based on market research — what your audience will respond to best and what represents your product/service best. Don't forget to include in your considerations what your competition is mailing.

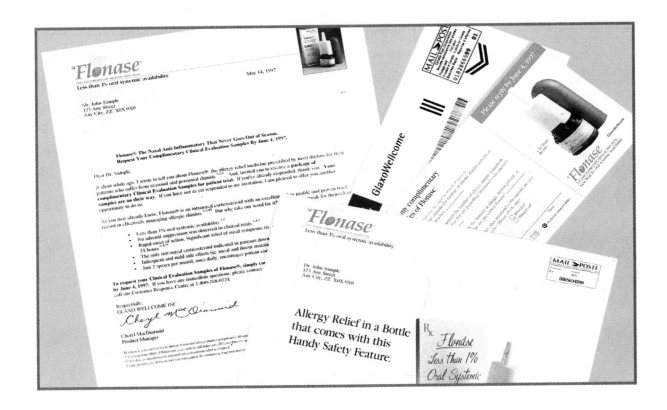

Classic direct mail sample

Client: Glaxo Wellcome
Product: Allergy relief medicine
Campaign: Flonase acquisition mailer
Agency: OgilvyOne Worldwide

Creative Director: Pete McLeod
Copywriter: Helen Prokos
Art Director: Gerry DeRose
Photographer: Guy McCrum

Flonase is the nasal corticosteroid most frequently prescribed by Canadian physicians, yet with five major players vying for market share, Glaxo Wellcome, its manufacturer, felt that the need to defend and increase its share of market was a top priority.

Hoping to increase the prescription rate of Flonase by physicians who had already recommended the product, Glaxo Wellcome chose to embark on a database segmentation program to gain a better understanding of its audience's needs and behaviours.

Using prescription-habit surveys to identify unique segments of its user base, Glaxo Wellcome identified 25 subgroups, which were subsequently targeted with "tailored" messages in a direct mail acquisition campaign that offered respondents four free samples of Flonase.

The program achieved an unprecedented response rate that exceeded the performance of past programs of its type by as much as 82 percent.

Tip 3: Make sure you respond to your competitor's offers. Getting your name on all your competitors' lists will assure you of an inside look at their strengths and weaknesses.

There are more decisions to make than personalisation and size of your outer envelope.

Colour

· How many colours should you print on your outer envelope?
· Should it be black and white? Black plus one colour?
· Can you afford a four-colour process outer envelope?
· Does your product/service need a four-colour envelope?

Tip 4: Once again, cost should guide your decision. But remember, a properly executed black-and-white envelope can do a great job of getting your package noticed.

Envelope copy

· How important is your logo to the front of the envelope?
· Does your outer envelope need teaser copy?
· Does it need a photo or an illustration, or should it be plain?
· Have you made the best use of the back and front of your envelope?
· Are you pre-printing a postal indicia?

Tip 5: In financial services, the logo plays an important role in getting the mail opened. If there is mail from your bank or insurance company, it almost certainly will be opened based on its implied importance.

Remember. Base each of these judgments on: allowable costs, your target audience profile, appropriateness for your product and company, and an understanding of what your competition is using.

Tip 6: Today's direct marketing community relies on the 6 x 9 window envelope or a No.10 outer envelope to set the standard for the Classic direct mail package results. Remember. If the envelope doesn't get opened, you have no chance of starting, or cementing the customer relationship.

Tip 7: The outer envelope is always worth testing, whether this is your first direct mail campaign or your one hundredth.

Your letter

The letter's primary objective is to begin, or cement, the relationship with the customer, in a personal way.

The letter is what defines direct mail as a personal medium. Use the first person throughout the content of the letter: I and you, not we and they. This private letter to your customer is what begins the relationship and eventually bonds your relationship with the customer. Don't neglect it. Your letter tells the whole story in words while your brochure tells the same story in pictures.

Getting attention immediately

· Does the Johnson box (see a sample of a Johnson box on the next page) communicate the message?

· Do you need to include a deadline date or reply date?

· Have you remembered to include a P.S. that is actionable by the customer?

Personalising your letter

· Is your letter personalised (Dear Mr. Smith)?

· Is it generic (Dear Sir/Madam)?

· What is the value of personalisation to your audience and to your product/service?

· Do costs allow you to personalise the letter?

· How much personalisation is needed for your message to have the greatest impact?

· Have you properly incorporated the personal tone of I and you and avoided the we and they trap?

Tip 8: If cost becomes the consideration with personalisation, and you can only afford to personalise one piece in your direct mail package, personalise your response device.

Tip 9: Personalising the response device requires a window envelope.

Tip 10: A personalised letter generally pulls higher response rates than a generic letter, because it reinforces the characteristics of a personal relationship.

Copy length

The second most asked question is "how long should the letter be?" (You'll find the most asked question in chapter 8.)

Sprint.
Canada

March 27, 1995

Marilyn Wells
401-44 Gerrard St W
Toronto, ON M5G 2K2   35   (5)

THE **Most** WORLDWIDE

Johnson Box →

Save 50% on every call to
the three numbers you talk to the most.
One in Canada, one in the U.S. and
one overseas. Plus 15% off on all
your other long distance calls.

Let's se

Plus, wi
number
number
also see
means t
It doesn

So, if yc
it's time
there wi
network
around
Sprint C

I invite
form in
(416) 48

I look f

Dear Marilyn Wells,

If you haven't yet switched to Sprint Canada for your long distance service, you're paying too much. It's that simple.

Because with Sprint Canada you get 50% off every call to the three numbers you talk to the most each month. One in Canada, one in the U.S. and one overseas. But your Sprint Canada savings don't stop there. You also save 15% on all your other long distance calls. That's why we call it The Most for the Least™.

These remarkable savings are yours 24 hours a day, seven days a week. You get savings on top of your local phone company's off-peak discounts. Call it a discount on top of a discount. For example, if you make a $20.00 call to someone in Canada on Sunday afternoon, your local phone company will discount the call by 60% to $8.00. With Sprint Canada, our 50% discount reduces this call to $4.00 – assuming that number was one of the three numbers you talked to the most that month.

To take advantage of The Most for the Least™, simply call 1-800-593-6678, or, if you prefer, complete and mail or fax the sign-up form below. Either way, you'll soon begin saving.

Over the past few months, you've heard a lot about other long distance suppliers promising savings. So how do you know Sprint Canada is offering the best savings? Let's see what an

(Over, please)

Sincerely,

David W. Hagan
President - Consumer Services Group

← *P.S.*

P.S. Remember, there are no restrictions on the times you call. You'll save 50% on every call to the three numbers you talk to for the most minutes each month, and 15% on all other long-distance calls, at any time of the day or week. And that's guaranteed forever. Reply today so you'll be assured quick activation.

GER3 (A)

An example of a Johnson box.

The answer to this question is: as long as it needs to be — that is, as long as is necessary to tell the whole story, be involving, and intriguing.

Look at your letter as the single piece that begins the relationship. You want it to let your customers know as much about your company, its products, your offer, your dedication to customer service, and your guarantee. Your letter also builds company and product trust and reliability. Don't skimp on the facts; this may be the only chance you get. Would you do business with someone you hardly knew? Chances are you will never have the opportunity to meet your customer face-to-face. They won't be doing plant tours or visiting your offices. Your company and product will be judged solely on your ability to communicate effectively in your letter.

A boring, unfocussed, unsatisfying four-page letter can be direct mail death. An interesting, factual, eight-page letter can make your response rates soar. One-page, two-page, four-page, eight-page — the choices are never ending. The story value, the involvement, and the benefits of your offer will be the key to unlock your decision.

Tip 11: Based on my personal experience, a factual, interesting, two-page letter that includes an actionable P.S. will yield higher response rates than a one-page letter without a P.S.

The signature

Spend some time deciding who should sign the letter. Who is this customer likely to have a relationship with in your company? What is the best title to support the relationship and your customer promise for the product/service being offered: president, sales manager, financial officer, customer service representative, or research and development contact? The title and signature can easily set the tone of your letter. What colour should you use for the signature?

Tip 12: In business-to-business marketing, the title of the signatory is often based on the titles of the targeted audience. The title must be one of believability and responsibility.

Tip 13: For consumer marketing, it is important to consider a name and title of a person that a consumer believes is accessible and knowledgeable.

Tip 14: Never use a phony title or fake name. If the potential signatory is not interested in answering customer phone calls or questions, you are not choosing the right signatory for customer communication.

Your order form or response form

Your order form supports the primary reason for direct mail: response.

- Is your order form clearly laid out?

- Have you made it easy for the customer to respond?

- Does it restate your offer clearly?

- Have you restated your commitment clearly?

- Is it personalised?

- If the order form is not personalised, have you left enough room for full name (and title), company name (if applicable), full address, phone number with area code, personal extension, and e-mail address?

- Have you left enough room for your customer to indicate any change of personal data, such as a new address or new title or to add an e-mail address?

- Which methods of payment are available?

- Is there enough room for all the credit card information — card number, expiry date, and signature?

- How many colours do you need on the response form?

- Does it need to be four-colour or will two-colour do the job? Is black-and-white the best choice?

- Does it need an involvement device for better response?

- What options are available for response: ordering a product, asking for more information, or just entering a sweepstake without ordering any product?

- Is there value in asking your prospect to return the order form even if he or she is not ordering the product, entering the sweepstakes, or looking for more information (these are referred to as "nos")?

- Are you including a questionnaire to begin your database collection? If so, are the questions clear and concise?

- Have you made your intentions clear as to the use of the survey information?

- Is there an incentive for completing the questionnaire?

- Are the return options clear? Return by mail, fax, or call our toll-free phone number.

- Is your guarantee clearly restated on the order form?

- Once the order form is returned, have you left the customer with all your company information needed to contact you later?

Tip 15: Write and design your order form first. When designing your response device, give it a test run. Have five to 10 people read it and fill it in. This will ensure that the offer is stated clearly and can stand on its own, separate from the other package components. Respondents should not need any other component of the package to understand your offer and their commitment. Remember. If you rent your mailing list to other users, you must obtain your customers' permission to pass on their name. Read the privacy code in the Appendix for clear guidelines.

Tip 16: If it is necessary for the customers to fill in their own name and address, make sure you have left enough room on the order form. A customer's handwriting, and your ability to understand it, will form the basis of your future relationship. You could risk the relationship if you were to spell your potentially best customer's name wrong.

Tip 17: Avoid using glossy stock for order forms. They are too hard to write on with a ballpoint pen.

Tip 18: If you are using colour on your order form, drop the colour out of any area in which the respondent needs to write.

Tip 19: Always make sure your full company name, address, and phone number are intact in the package once the order form is returned.

Your brochure

Your brochure tells the same story as your letter, only in pictures. Your letter tells the story. Your brochure visualises the story.

- What role will your brochure play?
- What size should it be?
- How many colours should it be to make the best impact?
- How will you show your product in use by the consumer?
- Are testimonials important to support your product claims?
- Will this brochure be used for any other medium or sales effort?
- Does the brochure complement the rest of the package?
- Does it give the full visual story based on your letter?

Tip 20: Some people love and respond to words. Some people love and respond to pictures. You will not know which of these attributes your target audience embraces. Everyone is different. Start out with a brochure in your Classic direct mail package and appeal to everyone.

Tip 21: The importance of the brochure telling the same story as the letter is based on direct marketing testing principles. Once you have established a response rate benchmark to the Classic package, you may want to look for ways to lower your costs. One way to lower costs is to eliminate your brochure. If your brochure tells a different story or your letter contains the expression "see the enclosed brochure for details," you will never be able to eliminate the brochure from the package.

Tip 22: Eliminating the brochure from the package supports a basic direct marketing testing principle: get the best response for the lowest cost.

Business reply envelopes (BRE)

The reply envelope deserves more attention than it gets. Make it an integral part of the package.

- Does your order form need to be returned in a BRE?
- If so, have you paid enough attention to its design?
- Does it reflect the image of the entire package?
- Should your BRE be returned to a specific person or department?
- Should your BRE carry a second offer?
- Does it need to be postage-paid?
- Should it also carry a change of address form?

Tip 23: Treat your BRE as the opportunity to extend the image of your campaign. Don't treat it as an off-the-shelf item that is left over from other mailings.

Tip 24: In consumer marketing, postage paid BREs will be returned earlier than BREs without pre-paid postage. This may not apply to business-to-business marketing where the company pays the postage through the mailroom. But in both cases, early returns can help your early order flow for reading test results faster, as well as bringing in early cash to support your overheads.

Tip 25: Since your company only pays for the postage that is used to return orders or a commitment to order in your BRE, this cost is well worth it. Postage paid also supports the convenience proposition so often tied to ordering by the mail.

▶ Classic direct mail sizes and costs

The unique characteristic of direct mail demands that you pay attention to every penny spent and demonstrate how incremental costs will yield incremental response rates. A large contributor to incremental response is in the format you choose and the tests you conduct. On the following pages we will look at the specifications and costs of two Classic packages (produced in one language only). Although neither size is restricted in its use, the

6 x 9 format is traditionally used for consumer marketing and the No.10 for business-to-business marketing.

Once the costs are established for the Classic package, we will then examine the cost impact on response, and add a publisher's lift memo to the overall package components as our first cost test. And in a second cost test, we will keep the publisher's lift memo, but eliminate the brochure.

FIGURE 10-1

CLASSIC DIRECT MAIL PACKAGE (6 X 9) SPECIFICATIONS

Component	Colours	Size	Folds
Outer window envelope	2/0 (black + 1 colour) 4/0 (4-colour process)	5 7/8 x 9	
Letter: personalised	2/0 & 4/0	8 1/2 x 11	5 1/2 x 8 1/2
Brochure	2/2 & 4/4	8 1/2 x 11	5 1/2 x 8 1/2
Order form: personalised and non-personalised	2/2 & 4/4	8 1/2 x 11	5 1/2 x 8 1/2
BRE	2/0	4 x 8 1/2	

Note: 4-colour process, both sides (expressed as 4/4) or 4 colour, one side (expressed as 4/0) and black plus one colour, both sides (expressed as 2/2) or black plus one colour, one side (expressed as 2/0) printing.

FIGURE 10-2

CLASSIC DIRECT MAIL PACKAGE (6 X 9)
COSTS

Component	5 7/8 x 9 window outer envelope Black + I colour (2/2 or 2/0)		5 7/8 x 9 window outer envelope 4-colour process (4/4 or 4/0)	
Quantity	10,000	100,000	10,000	100,000
A. Printing				
Outer envelope	$2,750	$11,200	$3,300	$12,100
Letter	1,900	4,300	2,500	5,000
Brochure	2,550	5,450	3,700	6,700
Order form				
Personalised1	3,998	9,100	5,500	11,500
Non-personalised2	3,100	7,900	4,300	9,900
BRE	750	4,500	750*	4,500*
A. Sub-total:				
Printing: personalised1	$11,948	$34,500	$15,750	$39,800
Non-personalised2	11,050	33,350	14,550	38,200
B. Mail preparation				
Laser1	800	6,600	800.	6,600
Laser2	400	3,600	400	3,600
Lettershop1	1,230	9,900	1,230	9,900
Lettershop2	1,000	7,100	1,000	7,100
Data work1	2,900	5,300	2,900	5,300
Data work2	2,600	4,750	2,600	4,750
List rental**	1,250	12,500	1,250	12,500
Postage***	2,900	29,000	2,900	29,000
B. Sub-total:				
Personalised1	9,080	63,300	9,080	63,300
Non-personalised2	8,150	56,950	8,150	56,950
TOTAL A + B				
Personalised1	21,028	97,800	24,830	103,100
Personalised2	19,200	90,300	22,700	95,150

1, indicates personalised letter and response form, 2, indicates personalised letter only, *BRE not quoted in four-colour process, ** List rental based on total outside list rental calculated at $125 per thousand, *** Postage calculated at the bulk third class averaged rate of 0.29. The difference in personalised and non-personalised material is based on the grain of paper necessary for personalisation. Mail preparation is not affected by 2- or 4-colour process printing. All taxes are extra.

FIGURE 10-3

CLASSIC DIRECT MAIL PACKAGE NO. 10
SPECIFICATIONS

Component	Colours	Size	Folds
Outer window envelope	2/0 & 4/0	4 1/2 x 9 1/2	
Letter: personalised	2/0 & 4/0	8 1/2 x 11	3 5/8 x 8 1/2
Brochure	2/2 & 4/4	8 1/2 x 11	3 5/8 x 8 1/2
Order form: personalised and non-personalised	2/2 & 4/4	7 x 8 1/2	3 1/2 x 8 1/2
BRE	2/0	4 x 9	

Note: 4-colour process, both sides (expressed as 4/4) or 4-colour, one side (expressed as 4/0), and black plus one colour, both sides (expressed as 2/2) or black plus one colour, one side (expressed as 2/0) printing.

FIGURE 10-4

CLASSIC DIRECT MAIL PACKAGE NO. 10
COSTS

Component	No. 10 window 2/2 or 2/0		No. 10 window 4/4 or 4/0	
Quantity	10,000	100,000	10,000	100,000
A. Printing				
Outer envelope	$2,550	$7,100	$3,300	$8,000
Letter	2,500	5,000	3,000	5,800
Brochure	2,575	5,450	3,725	6,600
Order form:				
Personalised1	3,900	9,800	5,300	11,300
Non-personalised2	3,000	7,500	4,000	9,800
BRE	750	4,500	750*	4,500*
A. Sub-total:				
Printing - personalised1	$12,275	$31,850	$16,075	$36,200
Non-personalised2	11,375	29,550	14,775	34,700
B. Mail preparation				
Laser1	800	6,600	800	6,600
Laser2	400	3,600	400	3,600
Lettershop1	1,130	9,000	1,130	9,000
Lettershop2	900	7,100	900	7,100
Data work1	2,640	5,200	2,640	5,200
Data work2	2,500	4,700	2,500	4,700
List rental**	1,250	12,500	1,250	12,500
Postage***	2,900	29,000	2,900	29,000
B. Sub-total:				
Personalised1	8,720	62,300	8,720	62,300
Non-personalised2	7,950	56,900	7,950	56,900
TOTAL A + B				
Personalised1	20,995	94,150	24,795	98,500
Personalised2	19,325	86,450	22,725	91,600

1, indicates personalised letter and response form, 2, indicates personalised letter only, *BRE not quoted in 4-colour process, ** List rental based on total outside list rental calculated at $125 per thousand, *** Postage calculated at the bulk third class averaged rate of 0.29. The difference in personalised and non-personalised material is based on the grain of paper necessary for personalisation. Mail preparation is not affected by 2- or 4-colour process printing. All taxes are extra.

▶ The publisher's lift memo: a Classic direct mail package test insert

After you have tested the Classic package components, one way of testing for increased response rates is by adding a publisher's lift memo.

This piece got its name from its original use by book publishers for one more chance to convince the customer to say "yes" to the offer. Often the cover headline would read: "if you're still not convinced, read inside." And often it was taken one step further: "read this only if you've decided not to purchase." Publishers, and many other marketers, successfully use this technique today. As well, many marketers choose this format for drawing attention to a third party endorsement or to capture product testimonials from existing customers.

This piece is specially designed in a smaller format than the other pieces in the envelope to catch the customer's attention.

· At what stage are you ready to test a lift memo?
· Will it be a simple black-and-white printed piece?
· Does it need colour to stand out from the other pieces in the envelope?

Tip 26: Since the lift memo will increase your costs, test the Classic package first, benchmark your costs and response rates then use the lift memo as a test cell to determine incremental costs equal to incremental response.

FIGURE 10-5

PUBLISHER'S LIFT MEMO SPECIFICATIONS

Component	Colours	Size	Folds
Lift memo	2/2 & 4/4	5 1/2 x 8 1/2	2 3/4 x 4 1/4

Note: 4-colour, both sides (expressed as 4/4), 2-colour, both sides (expressed as 2/2).

FIGURE 10-6

PUBLISHER'S LIFT MEMO
COSTS

Component	6 x 9 window envelope Black + I colour (2/2)		6 x 9 window envelope 4-colour process (4/4)	
Quantity	10,000	100,000	10,000	100,000
Publisher's lift memo	$2,300	$4,000	$3,200	$5,100

The first test is based on adding the publisher's lift memo to the costs of the Classic direct mail 6 x 9 personalised1 package. This demonstration is based on mailing 10,000 pieces in either 2/2 or 10,000 pieces in 4/4. Remember. If your cost per piece mailed increases, it demands higher response rates to be successful.

Component	6 x 9 package		6 x 9 package	
	2/2	CPP	4/4	CPP
Classic personalised1	$21,028	$2.10	$24,830	$2.48
Lift memo cost	2,300		3,200	
C. Total cost	**$23,328**	**$2.33**	**$28,030**	**$2.80**

Personalised1 costs are brought forward from the printing and mailing calculations for the classic packages 6 x 9, quantity of 10,000 pieces, as indicated in Figure 10-2. CPP represents cost per piece calculations.

For the second test, review the cost implications for the same package (C) when the brochure is removed and the lift memo remains. If the costs decrease, so does the need for response.

Component	6 x 9 package		6 x 9 package	
	2/2	CPP	4/4	CPP
Total cost C:	$23,328	$2.33	$28,030	$2.80
Brochure cost	(2,550)		(5,500)	
D. Total cost	**$20,778**	**$2.08**	**$22,530**	**$2.25**

The self-mailer

The second format to be covered in this section is the self-mailer. When direct marketers spoke of self-mailers in the early 1980s, they referred to a mailing that was self-contained, an all-in-one direct mail package — hence the name. The definition still holds today. However, the possibilities and

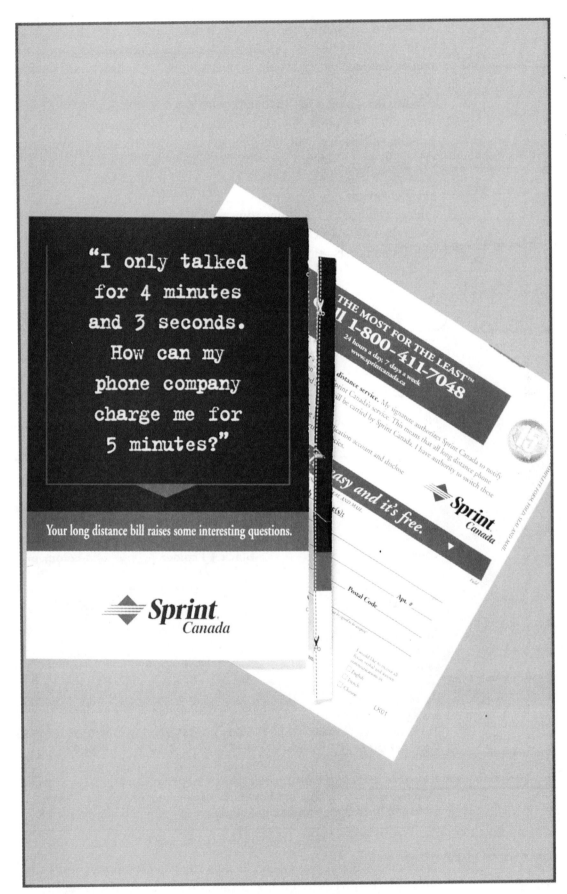

An example of a self-mailer.

formats of self mailers have changed dramatically. The change is a result of the innovative use of printing and on-line addressing equipment. A self-mailer can look like a brochure, a catalogue, or a direct mail package.

When designing a self-mailer, be sure to work with your production department, creative team, and your print suppliers at the concept stage. Today's printing and on-line equipment can do almost anything, but always for a price. Do your costings carefully, and seek the advice and guidance of your printers for exact page layouts. Even in a self mailer format, you should include a letter as part of your design. This is still the one piece that builds customer relationships. Traditionally, costs and response rates to self-mailers are lower than that of the Classic (personalised) direct mail package. However, the reduction in costs may not be worth the reduction in response.

FIGURE 10-7

SELF-MAILER SPECIFICATIONS

Component	Colours	Size	Folds
Personalised self mailer	2/2 & 4/4	7 3/4 x 19 1/2	5 x 7 3/4

Note: 4-colour process, both sides (expressed as 4/4) and black plus one colour, both sides (expressed as 2/2).

FIGURE 10-8

SELF-MAILER COSTS

Component	Black + I colour 2/2		4-colour process 4/4	
Quantity	10,000	100,000	10,000	100,000
Self-mailer: personalised	$ 2,800	$7,000	$ 3,500	$ 8,300
Data work	2,000	3,600	2,000	3,600
Laser	250	1,800	250	1,800
Lettershop	250	1,400	250	1,400
List rental*	1,250	12,500	1,250	12,500
Postage **	2,900	29,000	2,900	29,000
Total costs: self-mailer	**$9,450**	**$55,300**	**$10,150**	**$56,600**
Cost per piece (CPP)	**0.95**	**0.55**	**$1.02**	**0.57**

*List rental based on the total mailing of outside lists calculated at $125 per thousand.
**Postage is calculated based on bulk third class averaged rate of 0.29. Printing costs are based on a good quality matte coated stock.

Although your cost per piece is attractive and tempting, compared to your cost per piece for a 6 x 9, personalised Classic package, the possible reduction in response rates and ROI may not meet your objectives. Traditionally, if your Classic package pulls three percent, your self-mailer may only pull an up-front response of .08 percent.

If you are a large and consistent mailer, once you have set your response/ROI benchmarks with the Classic combination, the self-mailer may be worth testing to a segment of your list.

2. Unaddressed or householder direct mail

Unaddressed direct mail is just that, unaddressed and delivered to the household. Although Canada Post mailing guidelines for unaddressed direct mail (see sample on following page) are similar to addressed direct mail, the cost of distribution differs. Be sure to check with your Canada Post representative prior to finalising design and print quantities.

When using this mailing option, outside list rental is replaced with demographic data related to neighbourhoods and the people who live in those neighbourhoods. You may select distribution as targeted as delivery to one side of the street and not the other. This data is available through Canada Post and should be planned and tested carefully.

Traditionally, unaddressed direct mail responds lower than addressed mail. Without the personalisation of addressed direct mail, your mailing may not be the best start to building a customer relationship than otherwise expected. But because there are no laser costs, data work, and list rental costs to incur, the cost per piece will be lower.

▶ Co-operative mailings (co-ops)

There are two types of co-op mailings: consumer and business-to-business. A co-op is best described as a number of different offers from different companies contained within one outer envelope and delivered to selected households (see sample on page 147).

Co-ops may look like Classic direct mail, but response rates are dramatically lower. Participation costs are less than Classic solo direct mail — lower response rates and lower costs. There is success to be found and you should experiment with regional tests prior to a commitment to the full circulation.

Tip 1: The envelope is delivered unaddressed to selected homes or businesses, and does not carry noticeable postage, but there is a charge for distribution.

Tip 2: Co-ops are owned by independent businesses. They use Canada Post distribution based on selected postal walks by FSA or LDU, or by private companies on the basis of a demographic or psychographic criteria.

An example of unaddressed householder.

An example of a sample of a co-op mailing.

Tip 3: Participating companies either print their own insert material or the co-op mailer can print them.

Tip 4: Participants are charged on a cost-per-thousand (CPM) basis for each insertion and this cost goes toward the cost of producing the carrier envelope, insertion costs, and postage costs.

Tip 5: Traditionally, response rates fall below the personalised Classic direct mail package as well as falling below the rates expected for unaddressed solo direct mail efforts.

Research in the late 1970s by O.E. McIntrye Ltd., showed that prospects had a higher recall of a co-op package if it contained a large number of inserts. The research, which was based on a test of 20 inserts versus five inserts, also found that the number of coupons redeemed in a 20-pack was not significantly greater than that of those redeemed in a five-pack. This suggests that somewhere in between there is a successful combination. It would appear that the economics of the co-op mailer dictates 10 pieces are needed for the co-op owner to be profitable and this now is the most common and profitable (for the co-op owner) number of inserts used today.

This research also showed that the recipient was more likely to redeem coupons received through a co-op than those received through in-pack or on-pack offers, or in magazines and newspapers. This method of distribution is popular with packaged goods marketers for distribution of coupons to introduce new products and encourage product trial on existing brands.

There are a few techniques you should use when developing a co-op insert:

- Be offer-specific to avoid any consumer confusion. Communicate your sales message immediately, using bold headlines and simple layouts.

- Present your coupon first and your sales message second.

- Design with "the person who makes the decision" in mind. If your target is the "senior" or "grey" market, ensure your typeface is large enough for them to read and leave enough white space for your message to be telegraphic.

▶ Summary

1. Calculate your allowable costs before venturing into direct mail.

2. Direct mail is successfully used for customer acquisition, customer activation, customer retention, customer renewal, and winning back old or lapsed customers.

3. Choose a direct mail format that is not only cost-efficient, but addresses the needs of your target audience and supports your brand image.

4. Direct mail is personal and builds customer relationships. Use it properly.

5. Direct mail is targeted and gets the consumer involved the minute he or she opens the envelope.

6. Direct mail measurement of success is based on your ROI and not merely on a response rate.

7. Addressed direct mail will out-pull unaddressed direct mail.

8. The Classic package should be your standard for benchmarking ROI and response rates.

9. Your outer envelope must be intriguing and relevant in order for your target audience to open it.

10. The letter is the key component to building customer relationships.

11. Write and design your order form first. If you have a choice, personalise the order form in addition to personalising the letter.

12. Include a postage pre-paid BRE in all your consumer mailings.

13. A publisher's lift memo may increase your response rates.

14. Self-mailers traditionally carry less response than the Classic package.

15. Unaddressed (householder) mailings are distributed to selected households and businesses based on neighbourhood demographics, not individual customer behaviour.

16. Co-op mailings can be an efficient distribution method to drive retail traffic.

17. Examine what your competition is doing. Get on your competitor's mailing list.

18. For long-term success, plan all aspects of your mail campaign from test to roll-out, up-front.

19. Ensure you build test scenarios into each direct mail package to ensure long-term success.

20. Build on your past test results every time you mail.

TELEMARKETING

11

When Alexander Graham Bell created the phone in 1874 in the town of Brantford, Ontario, he could scarcely have realised the impact telecommunications would have on subsequent generations: careers, technology, and the economy. A simple, direct way of keeping in touch with family and friends has not only opened up the lines of communication for marketers, but has also made Ontario one of the largest concentrations of call centre activity in North America, and home to two thirds of all call centres in Canada. The province currently has more than 3,100 call centres, employing up to 150,000 people in long-term, stable careers.

Whether you attract customers through direct response television, print advertising, or direct mail, the phone can be a key contributor to your customer knowledge, to understanding your customer needs, and to your company's bottom-line success. The marketing challenges for the telemarketer cover: taking orders, arranging for sales visits, gathering customer information, giving information about products or services, after sales support, selling more products to existing customers, and resolving customer objections. The telemarketer is your customer representative. As your company representative, make sure you devote enough attention and resources to this area to properly support your company image, product benefits, and your standards of customer service.

▶ What is telemarketing

In this chapter we will examine telemarketing as a direct marketing medium with all the inherent attributes of being customer focused, having a specific offer, incorporating testing techniques, and tracking and measureing your success. There are as many definitions and uses for telemarketing as there are for direct marketing.

Telemarketing has been defined as an interactive system of marketing that uses the phone in conjunction with a database and one or more other advertising media to effect a measurable response and/or transaction at any location. This definition leads us to some important components: marketing, database, measurable response, and/or transaction. The introduction and application of powerful phone technology offers marketers opportunities not found in any marketing medium other than the personal sales visit — the voice of your customer.

▶ Education

Canadian Direct Marketing News reported in February 1998 that Centennial College in Toronto was introducing a call centre program in its curriculum. The college and the private sector partnered to provide an up-to-the-minute training program for Ontario's rapidly growing call centre industry. Some 400 students will graduate from the program each year.

Centennial's call centre is among the most technologically advanced, with hardware, software, furniture, and design supplied by corporate partners. A network computer system provides central control of the students' on-line activities, and prepares them for their future in advanced call centres.

"The industry has told us that it has a great need for trained, qualified staff," says Uwe Krebs, dean of Centennial College's School of Business. "Ontario already has a multilingual workforce and an excellent technical infrastructure. We are helping supply the trained staff."

Centennial College is one of a number of call centre programs available in Canada. Check with your local community college for program listings.

▶ The statistics

Based on the 1997 Ernst & Young survey on Canadians and call centres, I uncovered three sets of consumer statistics that represent the strongest support for incorporating a 1-800 (888) phone number into all your consumer and business-to-business communication pieces.

1. Purchases as a result of calling call centres

FIGURE 11-1

PURCHASES AS A RESULT OF CALLING CALL CENTRES

And how much would you say you have spent on this type of purchase over the last year?

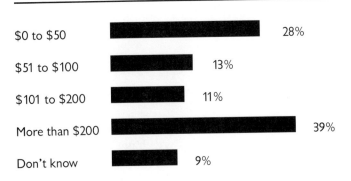

$0 to $50 — 28%

$51 to $100 — 13%

$101 to $200 — 11%

More than $200 — 39%

Don't know — 9%

Base: call to order/purchase a product or services: 339 (weighted)

Most likely to have spent more than $200 are:

- Residents of Saskatchewan/Manitoba (57%)
- Those without a high school diploma (50%)
- Men (48%)
- Those aged 35 to 54 (47%)
- Most affluent Canadians (47%)

Conclusion

By incorporating a 1-800 number into consumer offerings, you can reach more affluent Canadians (47 percent) willing to spend more than $200 (39 percent) over the phone.

2. Impact of quality of service

FIGURE 11-2

IMPACT OF QUALITY OF SERVICE

How much of an impact does the quality of service you receive when calling a 1-800 or 1-888 customer service number affect your future purchase decisions with the company?

Strong impact   47%

Slight impact   28%

No impact at all   25%

Base: call a customer service number: 1,379 (weighted)

The quality of service they receive when calling a 1-800 or 1-888 customer service number has a strong impact on the future purchase decisions of the following groups:

- Members of the higher income bracket (55%)
- Residents of British Columbia (54%), Ontario (54%), and the Atlantic Provinces (54%)
- University graduates (53%)
- Those aged 35 to 54 (51%)

Conclusion

With consumers in the higher income bracket (55 percent), the quality of your service and its affect on future relationships will have an impact on 75 percent of your callers (strong impact 47 percent, plus slight impact 28 percent).

3. Marketing calls based on past purchases

FIGURE 11-3

MARKETING CALLS BASED ON PAST PURCHASES

If a company knew from your past purchases that you were interested in certain products or services at certain times of the year, and they called to remind you about renewals or to tell you about new offerings, would you consider this to be a ...?

Good idea — 61%

Bad idea — 38%

Don't know — 1%

Base: all respondents: 1,504 (weighted)

Canadians most likely to consider these marketing calls a good idea include residents of the Atlantic Provinces (79%), those aged 18 to 34 (70%), and middle income earners (66%). Those most likely to consider these marketing calls a bad idea include Quebecers (47%), those over 55 (46%), and university graduates (42%).

Conclusion

Sixty-one percent of Canadians polled seem to agree that the phone is a great way to build customer relationships and therefore, good customer value.

Numbers like these confirm that the growth has indeed been dramatic. Telemarketing has taken its rightful place in contributing to today's marketing mix.

Telemarketing is more than phone selling. To understand telemarketing, you must first understand and embrace the principles and discipline of direct marketing: gathering customer information and turning that information into customer driven programs and services. Opening up the lines for a two-way dialogue with the customer is met head-on by a well-conceived strategy, well-trained telemarketers, and a clearly defined tracking and measurement system.

The phone, used to its full power as a direct marketing medium, can change the way we buy, sell, and service our customers. It can be a major element in an integrated marketing campaign.

▶ Getting started

What are the basics of telemarketing and how can they be applied to your business? Some of the answers will be found in this chapter.

Call centres employ telemarketers; telemarketers market on the phone. Stay up-to-date with the terminology. Once the terminology and technology are digested, you are ready to decide whether you'll develop and support an internal call centre or look for an external call centre.

How to Begin

1. Dedicate the necessary resources to define your needs: needs analysis

2. Define your expectations for a call centre and determine how they support your overall corporate strategy

3. Clarify and document your measurement of success

Whether you decide to use in-house resources or to outsource your requirements, you will find Dorothy Millman's insights on choosing the right call centre appropriate.

Dorothy is president of Phonettix Intelecom, one of Canada's largest outsource call centres and software developers, and this article is reprinted with the permission of *Canadian Direct Marketing News* (February 1998).

9 issues to consider in preparing your request for proposal (RFP)

With apologies to my husband, choosing an outsource call centre as part of a corporate marketing strategy, is not unlike choosing a spouse.

Both are about building a relationship. Both involve careful selection at the outset, then constant nurturing and attention. And both require each party to be flexible and responsive enough to adapt to change.

Selecting the right call centre is not easy, but not impossible. The key is approaching it with the mind set of a partnership.

Choosing a call centre is not just hiring a vendor where the relationship is one-way and the vendor simply supplies a client with services. Choosing a call centre partner means you have common goals and a keen understanding of each other's standards and expectations. You work together as a team. Like a marriage, the selection of a call centre doesn't end when the contract is signed — it is an ongoing relationship where communication is constant.

Writing a RFP is the crucial first step to choosing your partner. The RFP puts, in writing, what you want from your call centre. It's as important for clients as it is for the call centre to determining goals and expectations.

The RFP must provide enough information and sufficient time to return complete and accurate information. Your responsiveness to inquiries and careful evaluation of the submissions will complete the process.

But what issues should you address in the RFP? The following are some areas to consider.

1. Proven track record

Thoroughly investigate the prospective call centre. Ask for references of past clients and call them. Learn which companies currently work with the call centre and canvass them about their experiences. Better still, call a customer service number for the existing client of the call centre and witness firsthand how they handle inbound telemarketing campaigns.

Was the call centre representative (CCR) professional, courteous, and informative? Would you want that CCR involved in your program?

2. Open policy

Openness in an outsourced call centre relationship is akin to the trust in a marriage. How receptive is the call centre to open visits? How often? Does the call centre frown upon or encourage contact with CCRs?

Unlike some call centres, we encourage our clients to access our CCRs as focus groups since they have a keen sense of how a client's product or telemarketing campaign is succeeding or failing. Most call centres will allow a walk through of their call centre floor during the RFP process.

Listen for the call centre buzz and enthusiasm. Observe for positive CCRs who appear to be excellent listeners. They will be the ears and voice of your company if you choose them.

Open communications means that the outsourcer should welcome quarterly, semi-formal written reviews on any long-term project.

Openness in an outsourced call centre relationship is akin to the trust in a marriage.

3. Agent/management ratios

The ratio of supervisors to the front-line people on the phones is not a scientific calculation. Depending on the complexity of your message and requirements, the ratio varies.

The average campaign will be about a one to 12 ratio, but could go as low as one to four for campaigns involving business-to-business, high tech or high performance products or services that require greater flexibility, knowledge, and quick thinking by CCRs. Likewise, the ratio of management to agent could go as high as one to 20 in a straightforward teleadvertising campaign in which the CCR would simply read a one-minute script to targeted customers informing them about the sale of a product.

4. Staff turnover

Most call centres will try to tout their low turnover. Ask the call centre to provide you with hard numbers. Assess potential staff turnover yourself when touring the facility.

Does it appear to be a happy work environment? Does it have comfortable, attractive workstations? What do the lunchrooms look like? Are there posters or fliers about employee activities?

These mom and apple pie intangibles are often the best gauge of staff enthusiasm and turnover rates.

5. Training

How many hours/days/weeks of training will be conducted and who will cover the cost? Call centres should demonstrate a clear understanding of the client's product or service from the outset.

More importantly, the client should be involved early and often in the training process. In fact, you should be encouraged to participate.

6. Monitoring and coaching

How can you determine how the program is going? Do the scripts need changing? Who is allowed to call and observe, and when? Can you conduct off-premises monitoring? Will the call centre be responsive and act quickly to tweak and adjust a campaign?

7. Reporting

New programs may require frequent reporting, even hourly if necessary, for short-life campaigns. Reporting criteria on your RFP should not only involve frequency, but also your standard productivity and results categories with clear definitions of what these categories mean to you.

How will exception calls be handled? What is the correct party contact?

Providing results electronically is standard, but be sure to determine how the call centre plans to merge program data simply and efficiently at the back-end with your internal database.

8. Benchmarking

The standards you set for the success of your call centre program should be realistic. A good call centre will encourage members of the marketing team — CCRs, call centre management, advertising agency, senior client management — to help you determine performance objectives through benchmarking.

Vigorously question prospective call centres about how detailed their measurements and reporting will be to best determine if the call centre can do what is expected of it. This should involve measuring everything from CCRs communication skills (did they speak clearly and loud enough?) to benchmarking through predictive dialing reports to time service expectations.

9. Technology

Don't be lulled into a false sense of security with high-tech talk about megabits and switching equipment. The technology has to work for you and make your campaign better.

In other words, what is the functionality of the technology? Can it provide extremely detailed reporting, such as day part reporting and media reporting, as well as allow for direct marketers to use the information for database and loyalty marketing?

Is the call centre more than a simple call centre operation — a true communication centre? That is, can it handle other communications, such as Internet response? Can the reporting software work seamlessly with a fulfillment house? Does the call centre have predictive dialers and automatic call distributors?

The bottom line is the equipment must be capable of handling your needs and expectations.

Careful attention to selecting the right call centre partner will pay handsome dividends. Like a marriage, making the right decision at the outset will lead to short-term benefits.

Better still, it is the potential start of a long-term — and profitable — relationship. And just think, no in-laws to worry about.

Dorothy has given me permission to add a point of my own to this RFP process.

10. People you like

Do business with people you like — people who share your corporate values, share your commitment to success, and people you can share the glory with in successful programs and find solutions to the not so successful programs.

▶ Applications

The more high-priced your product, and the better its profit margins, the more likely telemarketing can fit into your marketing mix. All products, with the exception of low-cost items, which do not have a high enough margin to warrant the cost of a phone call, can be handled by telemarketers at some stage of the selling cycle. Generally, low-cost, low-margin, mass-appeal items, such as food, beverages, and household supplies are best promoted through other, mass-media campaigns.

Telemarketing works well on its own to resell, or upsell, a known or current product to a current customer base. It can also be used successfully to sell a new product, provided the product is not too complex. Although there are exceptions, the cost of the product and its profit margins should be your primary consideration. The cost should be low enough to take the risk away and make it easy for your customer to say yes.

The difficulty increases as you move to a new market with a current product. And, finally, when you have a new product to sell to a new market, it is best to use telemarketing in conjunction with other media. For example, you might send a letter and product information to establish awareness and a relationship with the prospect, then call. Or you might use the phone to qualify the prospect and generate interest, then send literature to interested prospects, and use telemarketing for follow-up. Every situation is unique and your's must be analysed to determine the best approach.

Some marketers assume, incorrectly, that telemarketing cannot come into play when the product is complex and expensive, the market select and sophisticated, or the selling cycle long. A review of the Ernst & Young survey on Canadians and call centres earlier in this chapter indicates that $200 and over is not unachievable. Remember. Every contact with the customer helps to further systematise and refine the selling process, thus making it more effective. The phone plays an important role both in your marketing mix and in your dedication to customer convenience and service.

▶ Outbound telemarketing

Outbound telemarketing (you initiate the call to the customer) is frequently used to service existing accounts, strengthen relationships, and cross-sell relevant products based on the customer's past purchase behaviour. The applications are enormous. Today, it is used by large mailers for acquisitions, and as a follow-up to solicit incremental response from current and past customers in all types of industries, and enjoys response rates of 300 to 500 times the initial mailing response. The phone can be extremely effective in reaching the procrastinators and fence-sitters.

▶ Inbound Telemarketing

Most inbound telemarketing programs use a toll-free service or 1-800 numbers initiated by the customer as a response to product offerings, requests for more information, generating leads either for a program or a sales force, or requesting more product or service information. The form of advertising that triggers the call is the primary medium, the phone playing a secondary, though important role.

Another growing use of inbound telemarketing, particularly with progressive, marketing-oriented companies, is the customer service operation, which reflects the awareness that it costs much less to keep an old customer happy than to find a new one. Companies who use the medium in this manner go out of their way to provide service, convenience, and information to customers and prospects alike.

Consumer

Consumer outbound telemarketing has continued to be on the rise in Canada. Magazine and book publishers have long used telemarketing for both renewal and continuity programs. In addition, telecommunications, cable, insurance, financial services, through to women's hosiery are enjoying the success of the phone.

Business-to-business

Telemarketing has followed the evolutionary pattern of direct mail. While consumer outbound telemarketing has continued to increase, it is the business-to-business market that will grow exponentially and present significant opportunities in the next decade.

The growth is inevitable. McGraw-Hill Research (U.S.) indicates that the average industrial personal sales call costs over $265. More importantly, 5.6 calls on average are required to close a sale. That's a whopping $1,484 investment in a final sale!

A business-to-business phone call cost can average $10 (including long distance). If telemarketing can reduce the number of face-to-face visits by your sales force and improve productivity, organisations must take this medium seriously and investigate the options.

> Consumer outbound telemarketing has continued to be on the rise in Canada. Magazine and book publishers have long used telemarketing for both renewal and continuity programs.

Developing your database

Part of taking telemarketing seriously as a marketing tool is to use it for the development of your database. Companies that market business-to-business rely all too frequently on the sales force to maintain customer contacts and records. Names are provided in every format imaginable, sometimes hand-written on pieces of paper, or on business cards. The quality of information gathered by salespeople is only as good as the representatives who prepare it. Organising and evaluating this information has been a massive, sensitive, and expensive task for most companies.

Fortunately, the phone is the ideal tool to verify your customer lists and update information with speed and accuracy. If you give your database priority within your organisation, you will stay competitive and maybe one step ahead of the competition. Telemarketing can be a powerful aid in maintaining your customer information.

▶ The elements of success

Scripting

Colin Taylor, president of Watts Communications Ltd., was kind enough to lay out a clear guideline for success in telemarketing for my last book. Upon review, much of the information is so important and relevant that I've included it again. The following comments originally appeared in *Sales & Marketing Management in Canada* (December 1989).

We must remember that telemarketing, by its nature, deals only with the spoken word — you cannot see your prospects, you cannot see their office or other items that may be competing for their attention. Within the first 10 seconds of the outbound telemarketing call, prospects will determine if this interests them, and if it does, they will listen, half-heartedly doodling or reading other things in front of them. And we must remember that people are by and large polite: they won't tell you that what you are saying is less interesting than the shopping list or the memo from the MIS department. They will allow you to carry on — but without them.

How can you expect to close a sale if you don't have their attention? Well, you can't.

Only if you have your prospects' attention, their interest, and their involvement can you expect to be able to make a sale.

So how can we do this? First, realise you have only 10 seconds to get their attention. Once you have their attention, you must do something with it: involve prospects in a conversation or you can lose their attention — and back they go to the memo or the shopping list.

It follows then that telemarketing, to be effective, must be a dialogue, a two-way conversation. This poses some interesting questions for those who must write telemarketing scripts.

The first question is how to write a presentation or script that will be effective when delivered via the spoken word rather than the written word. Secondly, we know that a prospect won't have a copy of the script to read along with. Life would be much easier if everyone we called knew the script. Then they could relax, doodle, read their mail, and know they don't have to pay attention until paragraph four, because that is where the script will be of interest to them. But they don't have the script, so they will decide in the first 10 seconds if they are going to pay attention or not.

The Hook

All good fiction writers know how to use a hook at the beginning of a story to get the reader's attention, and telemarketers must do the same

Mr. Smith, I'd like to talk to you today about how we can save you 74 percent on your operating expenses, without giving up anything. Would this be of interest to you?

There you have the hook. Who wouldn't be interested? But many telemarketers, and many who write telemarketing scripts, would leave this benefit statement buried in the middle of paragraph four, which is too late.

So we have the prospect's attention, now what?

Well, you could carry on with the presentation for the next five minutes, spurred on by the prospect's regular uh-huhs, and ask for the order — and be told no!

It is not enough just to get a prospect's attention. The caller must keep it, and while keeping it, he or she must remember that he or she is serving two masters: the prospect, whose attention span seems less than acceptable, and the client, who has given criteria and parameters for the call.

The easiest way to further this double end is to ask questions. The question-and-answer format allows the telemarketer to probe for additional information related to the prospect or his or her company. This detailing of the prospect's needs helps determine both how to sell the prospect and how to achieve your hidden agenda. For example, there is little benefit in selling to someone who cannot make or influence the decision.

So, you must qualify the buyer. Does he or she have the authority, alone or with others? Does he or she buy or just influence? If he or she influences, whom does he or she influence?

Also, it is important to realise, especially in business-to-business telemarketing, all companies are not the same. For example, the hook statement we used previously, "save 74 percent," may or may not be valid, and by means of probing questions, you can determine whether a given prospect should be enticed with a larger or smaller figure.

Keeping your prospect's attention

So, now that you have your prospect's attention and you have maintained his or she interest through the qualification, you're home free, right? Wrong. You must remember that your prospect has not given you his or her undivided attention. You must make sure you keep the prospect's attention throughout the presentation.

There are a number of ways to do this. For example, address your prospect by name. Using a person's name pulls him or her back, and he or she will listen intently to the next sentence.

Of course, he or she will begin to drift away once again, but you can't use the name in every sentence, because he or she will then tune out — too much of a good thing! So, you must proceed by using the name sporadically, asking questions to confirm understanding, allowing him or her to respond and expand upon his or her answers. Ideally, the last question you ask is the closing question, the prospect says yes, and you write the order.

So, all there is to writing telemarketing creative is to write a script that covers all of these points, allows for questions you can't anticipate, keeps the prospect's interest without sounding canned, too rehearsed or unpractised, and get your client to approve it. This is no small feat.

Ensuring quality scripting

The steps you should take to ensure good scripting are as follows:

1. Never lose sight of the fact that what you are writing will not be read, but spoken.

2. Write a conversation — a two-way communication.

3. Anticipate as many questions as possible, and script appropriate responses.

4. Provide stock responses for questions you can't anticipate.

5. Break your script down into segments of the call.

6. Determine the hook statement(s). Know the questions you will ask.

7. Anticipate objections. Plan how you will respond to each. There are basically three types of objections:

a) Price
b) Competition
c) Quality

If you follow the steps I have outlined, will you automatically have good creative? Perhaps, but it is not likely. Many people who write telemarketing presentations fall into common traps:

1. **The commercial script.** This kind of script sounds like a television commercial. It runs for five minutes without pause and offers the prospect no chance to respond.

2. **The letter script.** This script sounds like a letter being read out to the prospect — often it is a fine example of direct mail creative, chock-full of user benefits that are assumed, but never confirmed. These scripts are well-written, but in conversation, poor-sounding sentences. Again, they are like a monologue, often answering the prospect's questions without allowing him to ask.

In both cases, the prospect could likely go off for a coffee without the telemarketer even noticing.

Telemarketing as a process

In developing and writing phone presentations, remember that telemarketing is a process, not a commodity. In fact, telemarketing scripts must be permitted to evolve from the start of the call according to the prospect's responses and questions. Even though the full script might be five minutes long, a successful call might end up being only two minutes long, or as long as 10 minutes. Above all, if the prospect asks to buy during the introduction, don't make him or her wait — take the order.

Each aspect of a telemarketing call takes you another step through the process. A typical full presentation can be broken down into the following steps:

1. Introduction: explain who you are.

2. Qualification: find out whether you are speaking to the right person. What is the prospect or his or her firm all about? Probe.

3. Presentation: describe what you can do for the prospect — the benefits.

4. Close: ask for the order.

5. Handling objections: you should have anticipated most of the possible objections.

6. Close: take the order.

These six steps are probably the best script ever written. Think of them as stations along a railway line leading to your destination: a successful call.

Testing

Your testing approach is based on the role you have defined for telemarketing in your customer contact strategy. Based on the defined role, you should still test your way into each scenario.

Test results of telemarketing based on up-front responses, the quality of the offer, and the quality of the script can be determined quickly — every call, every hour, every day, every week. You can immediately make the necessary changes needed for better up-front response rates or better customer information and service. Here's a look at only two of your testing options:

Scenario 1

Test the incremental value of adding outbound telemarketing to cross-sell products to existing customers.

These results would be examined based on the cost of the call and number of products sold — compared to the cost and response rates of your previous method of cross-selling products to your customers.

Scenario 2

Test outbound telemarketing to existing customers who have received a direct mail package within the last five to seven days.

These results would be examined based on: incremental cost of the outbound phone call and incremental response rates, compared to the cost and response rate of the mailing alone. To accomplish this test, you must identify two distinct cells in your mailing and analysis. Methodology example only:

Total number of existing customers available for the offer	20,000
Test cell A receives mailing only	10,000
Test cell B receives mailing and phone follow-up	10,000

▶ Summary

The key to understanding telemarketing is to realise that it is part of the larger direct marketing process. You must approach it with a plan that has been carefully developed and examined. In planning you must consider four crucial elements:

1. The medium

2. The message

3. Your audience

4. Your offer

And, after this examination, keep in mind that telemarketing can be used for more than sales calls. Remember:

1. Listen to your customer and make adjustments quickly

2. Gather information and update the database

3. Provide customer information on products or services

4. Qualify or generate leads for your sales force

5. Sell a product or service directly to the customer

6. Deliver superior customer service

7. Build ongoing customer relationships

8. Sell more products and services to existing customers

9. Test your way to using telemarketing in your customer contact strategy. The results will be well worth the investment

10. Use statistics gathered from the call centre activities to plan future media programs focused on customer need

> The key to understanding telemarketing is to realise that it is part of the larger direct marketing process.

FUNDRAISING

12

BUILDING LOYALTY AND LIFETIME VALUE IN YOUR FUNDRAISING CAMPAIGN

By Anthony Lovell, president, Lovell & Company Inc.

▶ Overview of the sector

The charitable sector in Canada is surprisingly large. According to Revenue Canada, there were close to 75,000 registered charities from coast to coast in Canada in May of 1997. These organisations raise funds for a wide variety of initiatives in the public interest, including community centres, hospitals, medical research, social concerns, religious groups, the environment, international relief, and a wide variety of other causes.

Being a registered charity entitles the charity to issue tax receipts to its donors. In addition to these 75,000 registered charities, there are approximately 150,000 unregistered charities. Unregistered charities are "unregistered" because of the nature of the work they do — for example, organisations, such as Greenpeace, which engage primarily in advocacy and lobbying, are ineligible for registration.

The size and scope of this sector staggers most people. In fact, the sector generates $3.2 billion in revenue annually (source: Revenue Canada, 1994) in donations. And according to the Canadian Direct Marketing Association, charities raised $1.4 billion through direct marketing in 1996. By dollar volume, the not-for-profit sector is the fourth largest sector engaged in direct marketing.

At one time the charitable sector was run largely by volunteers who organised the fundraising drive and determined how the funds were distributed. However, this has changed dramatically over the past two decades. Professional management staff have been hired to increase the efficiency of organisations and to expand the charity's ability to raise funds. Many of these professionals have formally studied fundraising management and have deliberately chosen this field as their career.

As a result of this professionalisation of the sector, the level of competitiveness within the sector has increased significantly. In turn, the frequency that we as consumers and as business people are solicited, has also increased.

▶ Role of direct marketing in fundraising

There are a number of techniques that fundraisers have used over the course of time, from traditional bake sales and raffles to sophisticated infomercials and mega-lotteries. Each technique has its role for specific types of fundraising.

For soliciting gifts from individuals, the majority of fundraisers would agree that the most effective way to ask for a gift is through a peer-to-peer solicitation: a CEO solicits another CEO; a doctor solicits another doctor; a co-worker solicits another co-worker; and a neighbour solicits another neighbour.

Unfortunately it's not possible to solicit thousands or hundreds of thousands of people on a peer-to-peer basis unless the charity has a well-established network of volunteer canvassers. Two examples of this type of network are:

- Canadian Cancer Society's door-to-door campaign, which encourages neighbours to solicit neighbours

- United Way/Centraide's workplace campaigns where co-workers solicit each other

While this approach has been successful for these organisations, it also has its limitations:

- Building and coordinating the volunteer network is a massive job and may require significant staff and financial resources

- It's difficult to ensure that each person who is asked for a donation is asked consistently and effectively — while you may tell the solicitor about your organisation, and you may train them on how to ask for a gift, ultimately you are at the mercy of their "sales ability"

- Some door-to-door campaigns have become mired by the "pocket change" syndrome, where the average gift is extremely low because all that the canvasser receives is the change that's in the donor's pocket when he or she answers the door

The end result is that many charities will split their solicitation strategy into two parts: the peer-to-peer approach, which is reserved for the organisation's biggest donors; and the mass solicitation approach, which is used on everyone else.

Direct marketing techniques naturally lend themselves to the latter approach. The fundraiser is able to deliver a consistent message in a systematic manner to a group of prospects or donors at a time that best suits the organisation. By using a series of personalization techniques available to the direct marketer, the solicitation can simulate some of the advantages of the peer-to-peer technique. Telemarketing also has the advantage of allowing the caller to probe for and respond to objections the person might have.

▶ The importance of building strong, long-term relationships with your donors

It's common sense that the longer your relationship with a donor, and the stronger the relationship, the more revenues your organisation will raise over the course of time. The overall objective of the best fundraising direct marketing programs is to build the long-term revenues for the organisation

The longer your relationship with a donor, and the stronger the relationship, the more revenues your organization will raise over the course of time.

by increasing the "lifetime value" of each donor. "Lifetime value" refers to the cumulative amount contributed by a donor to an organisation.

Virtually all fundraisers who use direct marketing techniques will acknowledge that the lifetime value of the donor is vital to the success of the program. After all, these days it usually costs more than a dollar to raise the first dollar you receive from a new donor.

Direct marketing fundraising is not a "cash cow" or an instant way to generate huge revenues. A number of organisations have — at one point or another — flirted with direct mail or telemarketing. Unfortunately, some have abandoned it after reviewing the net cost of initial entry into the market, without regard for the longer-term potential. It's important to take the long view as you develop your direct marketing program because the economies of direct marketing are working in your favor.

If you encourage donors to renew their support, year after year, then you can amortize the initial cost of acquisition over this period. It may cost your organisation — for the sake of argument — $50 to acquire a new donor, but if that donor contributes $40 per year for five years for a total of $200, then you have had a substantial return on investment.

Donor loyalty becomes a significant factor for most direct marketing fundraisers. Another critical factor is your ability to increase the donor's average gift. For example, if you can increase the donor's gift in the example above by $5 per year for each of the five years, then that donor will have contributed a total of $250. And if you can get a second gift from some of your donors, then you can also boost the overall average gift. Increases of this sort add up, whether you have a donor base of 2,000, 20,000, or 200,000 donors.

Given the importance of increasing the lifetime value of the donor base by building donor loyalty and raising the average gift, the best-run direct marketing campaigns usually have at their heart well-constructed plans for dealing with donors at the various stages of involvement with the organisation, and the various stages of loyalty.

Throughout the remainder of this chapter, we'll explore the different direct marketing strategies and techniques that fundraisers incorporate into their plans.

▶ Description of the direct marketing cycle for fundraising

As donors become involved with your organisation, they go through a series of stages:

· Initially, they need to find out about the organisation, and the work it does.

- They need to feel strongly enough about the work, and feel positive enough about the organisation to decide to support it by making a donation.

- Next, they need to make a decision that they'd support the charity a second time.

- After that, they need to make a decision to support the charity year after year.

What we've just described is the relationship cycle between an individual and an organisation: developing interest, increasing interest, and building loyalty.

In terms of a direct marketing cycle:

1. The "acquisition" strategy acquires new donors.

2. The "conversion" strategy converts first-time donors to regular donors.

3. The "renewal" strategy obtains gifts from active donors (donors who have given within the last cycle — usually the last 12 months).

In addition to the donor cycle, there are two other phases:

4. The "reactivation" strategy obtains gifts from inactive donors (donors who did not give in the last cycle, but did give in the cycle before that — usually donors who last gave between 12 and 24 months ago).

5. The "recovery" strategy obtains gifts from lapsed donors (donors who have not given for more than two cycles — usually donors who last gave prior to the last 24 month period).

1. The acquisition strategy

Before we examine how to reach prospective donors, let's look at who the most likely prospects are.

Based on the donor file of most organisations across the country, you'd find a fairly consistent demographic profile of a direct marketing donor:

- They are older (usually 60 years or older, with a significant number in their seventies and eighties).

- There are more female donors than male donors.

- They are financially comfortable.

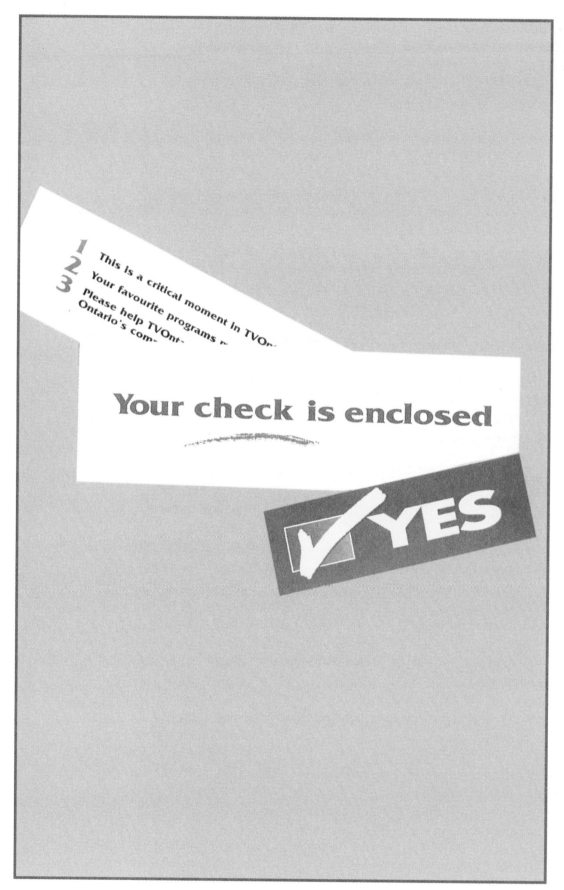

An example of an unaddressed fundraising package.

While the latter trait is understandable — after all, most people won't give money if they don't have it — people are frequently puzzled by the first two traits — age and sex.

Age

Whether it's because older people have lived through harder times, or now have the disposable income that allows them to help others, the age pattern is a strong trend from charity-to-charity. Organisations that have managed to build a younger donor base have succeeded frequently for two reasons: first, there has been a grassroots movement that has mobilized younger supporters and donors; and second, the organisation has geared most or all of its overall marketing initiatives to the younger constituency.

Sex

With regard to the larger number of female donors, some fundraisers have suggested that it's because women are more receptive to solicitations. Others have suggested that women are more generous than men: and others still have suggested that this phenomenon occurs because women live longer than men, and any group of older donors will naturally skew to more women than men.

Regardless of the reasons for this demographic profile, you should be aware that this group is the most responsive to charitable solicitations. So, while you may have some poor 30-year-old males supporting the organisation, you should recognize that a new donor is likely to be older, female, and financially comfortable. Consequently, the messages you send should probably be geared toward this audience in a style and manner that's appropriate to this group. But before you suddenly shift your strategy and positioning, you should examine your own donor base to determine if your donors fit the typical profile.

How do you reach prospects?

Since you are trying to approach a group of prospective donors, you can proceed in two ways:

1. Deliver your promotion to them through a *broadly distributed medium* that is most likely to be seen by your prospects and invite them to respond back to it through a direct marketing channel (e.g., inbound phone or mail).

2. Deliver your promotion directly to a specific individual through a *selective medium* by building or acquiring a list of likely prospects.

FIGURE 12-1

1. Selecting broadly distributed media

Media in this category	Strengths for acquisition	Weaknesses for acquisition
Television: infomercials and/or direct response television (DRTV)	Can deliver powerful, consistent message to a broadly defined audience	Expensive to produce; expensive to purchase air-time; requires a secondary medium to take responses (local lines, toll-free lines, 1-900 lines, mail)
Radio	Can deliver highly focused messages; can saturate the audience in a community with the message; good for re-enforcing other direct marketing channels	Cost per response can be extremely high; requires a secondary medium to take responses (local lines, toll-free lines, 1-900 lines, mail)
Newspapers (including free-standing inserts)	Broad, consistent distribution of message to large audience	Low response rates; on-page advertising is competing with all other stories and ads for attention and is easily overlooked; requires a secondary medium to take responses (local lines, toll-free lines, 1-900 lines, mail)
Magazines (including free-standing inserts)	More focused audience than newspapers, particularly in specialty magazines	Low response rates; requires a secondary medium to take responses (local lines, toll-free lines, 1-900 lines, mail)
Transit ads	Builds awareness; reinforces other direct marketing channels	Negligible response rates; difficult to track as a medium; requires a secondary medium to take responses (local lines, toll-free lines, 1-900 lines, mail)

FIGURE 12-2

2. Selecting direct delivery media

Media in this category	Strengths for acquisition	Weaknesses for acquisition
Mail	Low cost per contact, high saturation potential, targetable, delivery of consistent message, trackable, tactile	Low response rate, can't change the message once its been launched, lists can be inaccurate or outdated, can get lost in the clutter, perception of junk, distrust of the medium, static (can't overcome new objectives — no interaction at time of delivery)
Outbound telemarketing	Low-to-moderate cost per contact, personalised feel, high saturation potential, targetable, can script and deliver a consistent message, callers can use their sales ability, can interact with prospect, can change script rapidly, trackable	Low-to-moderate response, nuisance factor, mistrust, reliant on caller's sales ability
Outbound Fax	Gets attention faster than mail, cheap way to deliver message, consistent message, trackable, tactile, can launch a campaign rapidly	Junk fax, passes through others' hands frequently, only for business-to-business
Internet	Novelty factor, inquiry made by user (inbound), low cost, enhances image, etc.	Novelty factor, concern over spamming (sending out unsolicited e-mail messages), users don't trust it for transactional security, limited audience, unproven medium, no one has yet found the magic formula

These response ranges are intended as rules of thumb. Remember each organization is different, and some will have greater success than others with the different media.

Regardless of the method of reaching the audience of prospective donors — broadly distributed medium or targeted approach based on lists — you'll need to remember that you are "selling" the organization. You will have to present your prospective donor with a compelling case, and make an effective "ask" if you are to convince people to respond right away.

2. Converting first-time donors

The hard work doesn't stop once you've acquired your new donors. In fact, one of the most challenging and important phases is the conversion of first-time donors into long-term donors.

The most obvious advantage of effectively converting a first-time donor into a long-term donor is that you will be building revenues for your organisation beyond the immediate campaign cycle. Also, given the economics of the acquisition program, it stands to reason that the more first-time donors you can convert into long-term donors, the faster you can amortise the cost of the acquisition program, and the faster your program can become profitable.

There are two stages you should be concerned about: the impression your new donors have immediately after they have made that first donation; and their receptivity when you approach them for the next donation.

Understanding how your first-time donor feels immediately after making the first gift:

It's not uncommon for first-time donors to be left with a bewildering series of questions once they have made that first gift through a direct response medium. After all, we've all heard the repeated warnings about mail-order scams and phone scams — so, it's not surprising that some new donors might wonder about the safety of their donation. They might wonder if it was delivered properly, and if the organisation was in fact legitimate (this is particularly true if your organisation doesn't have a high profile).

Other concerns they might have, include:

· Will this organisation spend my money wisely? (If your organisation has a high profile, your donors may wonder how much money is spent on advertising rather than on providing services.)

· Should they have given to a different organisation?

· Should they have just kept the money and used it for something else entirely different?

You can overcome a number of these concerns by providing a well-designed fulfillment package that welcomes the donor to your organisation and includes the donor's tax receipt. Keep in mind that we now live in an age where each of us has come to expect fairly fast service. If you provide the fulfillment package in a timely fashion, your donor will have greater confidence in your organisation. And conversely, if you provide the fulfillment package slowly, the donor may wonder about your organisation's effectiveness.

Approaching the donor for the second donation:

Something you said in your original appeal touched your new donors enough that they decided to contribute. As you approach them for a second gift, you need to review a number of issues:

- What message did the donor originally respond to? Why was this message so compelling for them?

- Did the donor intend to start a relationship with the organisation, or did he or she intend to simply help out once? (This is common when donors respond to an appeal that stresses the urgency of the cause or an emergency appeal.)

- What are the donor's current interests?

- What is the donor's current perception of your organisation now that he or she has become a contributor? Have you corresponded with the donor and kept him or her up-to-date on the work that you're doing or have you simply banked the money?

While there is nothing you can do to affect the donor's current financial position, you should also be aware that it may have changed for the better or the worse since the last donation was received.

Overcoming these potential barriers is a significant challenge for most organisations. As you attempt to convert your donors, you are in a situation where you have to reinforce with first-time donors that they made a smart decision the first-time around, and that they can make an even more important step by contributing a second time. You should review the issues that triggered the first donation, then overcome the obstacles.

Keep in mind, as you face the challenge of converting first-time donors to loyal, ongoing donors, that this is one of the most important phases of any direct marketing program, and it is well worth your time and effort to convert these donors effectively.

3. Renewing regular donors

A rule of thumb in direct marketing is that an individual's "recency" of doing business with an organisation is a strong predictor of future behaviour. This theory of recency is certainly true within the world of fundraising: the more recently an individual has donated, the more likely he or she is to donate again. Conversely, the longer the period of time since the last donation, the less likely it is that the donor will make another gift.

This correlation between the recency of a gift and the likelihood of another gift is one of the key reasons why it's so important to obtain regular donations from your core supporters. By renewing their support, you are both generating immediate revenues and increasing the likelihood of future revenues.

To renew this group's support, you'll have to make some key decisions:

- How many times should you attempt to renew the donor's support?
- How much time should lapse between each wave of the renewal cycle?
- What are the key renewal messages you will send to your donors at each stage?
- Which medium/media should you use?

How many times should you attempt to renew the donor's support?

Here you should have two concerns: first, how profitable is each renewal attempt? Usually the first several renewal attempts provide a strong return on investment, but this return on investment diminishes with each subsequent attempt. The following chart shows a hypothetical organisation's revenues, expenses, and return on investment to illustrate how the return on investment diminishes with each subsequent wave.

TABLE 12-1

Renewal Wave	Revenues	Expenses	Return on investment
First renewal	$100,000	$10,000	1,000%
Second renewal	$50,000	$8,000	625%
Third renewal	$30,000	$6,000	500%
Fourth renewal	$18,000	$5,000	360%
Fifth renewal	$8,000	$4,500	178%
Sixth renewal	$4,000	$4,000	100%

While the costs slowly decline, the revenues sharply decline with each subsequent renewal attempt. By the sixth wave, the revenues are at a break-even point, and it is likely that a seventh attempt would cost more than it raised.

But determining the economic break-even point is not the only criteria you should use to determine the number of renewal attempts that you make to your donors. The second concern you should have is subjective: how many attempts can you make without annoying your donor base?

Unlike product buyers, who are receiving tangible benefits when they place an order, donors are trying to help a cause. If the donor starts to perceive that his or her money is being used more for fundraising than for helping the cause, or that the organisation is too aggressive in the frequency of its fundraising approaches, then you run the risk of offending the donor.

Consequently you may have to trade off revenues for donor satisfaction. Is it worth more to you, in the longer term, to generate revenues for the current year, or to maintain good relations with your donors?

A number of strong arguments can be made for either side. Reasons to have more, rather than fewer, waves include:

· Each subsequent wave generates additional revenues, and these revenues are important to the organisation.

· If you let donors become inactive, then they will be doubly hard to reactivate. Every effort should be made to avoid allowing donors to lapse.

On the other hand, the reasons for fewer, rather than more, waves include:

· Some donors wait until the end of the calendar year before deciding who they will support — multiple solicitations will only serve to annoy them.

· The donor's economic circumstances or priorities may have changed during the current year. It's better to cut your losses this year, and wait until next when they may be more receptive.

· There are other issue-oriented solicitations coming up: if you can't renew the annual gift now, you may be able to persuade the donor to contribute to help on a specific issue.

Generally, successful organisations will send out between two and five renewal solicitations.

How much time should elapse between each renewal wave?

Your decision on how much time to let pass between each renewal wave should be based on two factors: first, how many other solicitations (either other renewal waves, or special issue solicitations) will you be undertaking over the year; and second, how long can you afford to wait while keeping costs down and cash flow up?

The number of solicitation waves are a factor because you'll need to build a schedule, and to do so, you'll have to know how many different initiatives will occur, when they'll happen, and so on. At the most basic level, you can simply divide the number of mailings by the number of weeks in the year to determine how far apart the mailings should be. For example:

- If you're planning on mailing three renewal waves, then you could space each mailing equally at approximately 17 weeks apart.

- If you add in a fourth mailing, then the space between mailings is reduced to 13 weeks.

But there are other issues to consider. For example:

- If that fourth mailing is a Christmas mailing, then you'll have to build your schedule in a way that ensures that the Christmas mailing has a reasonable chance of generating responses, and that other mailings aren't overlapping it.

You can use your past results to help you to determine how to keep costs down and cash flow up. Review the past results from your renewal waves to establish the average length of time between when the solicitation was sent out, and when you received all of the donations. Be wary as you do this calculation: many charities receive gifts from campaigns they ran three, four, or five years beforehand — these gifts should be regarded as anomalies. The answer you come up with should be somewhere in the range of 12 to 24 weeks. There are exceptions, of course, but this is a good rule of thumb.

Next, develop benchmarks to help you understand how quickly gifts come in. Find out what the average period is before you receive half of all the gifts from a particular wave; two thirds of the gifts; three quarters; etc. Armed with this information you must decide the optimal period between renewal waves.

- Remember. The lower the percent of all gifts in, the higher the cost of the next wave of solicitation.

- For example, if you know that you'll receive approximately 5,000 donations from the first wave, and you mail the next wave when you've received 50 percent then half your potential first-wave donors (2,500) will receive solicitations in addition to the non-respondents.

- If you wait until 75 percent of the expected donations are received, then you'll only be mailing out to 1,250 of the potential first wave donors. Both the cost and the annoyance factor bear consideration.

- Also remember that the longer you wait between the waves, the thinner your organisation's cash flow becomes: the initial torrent of gifts becomes a stream, then a trickle. If cash flow is an issue, then you may want to go out earlier rather than later.

What are the key renewal messages for your donors?

Donors are motivated to support organisations for different reasons, some of which include:

- A genuine desire to help

- To ensure that the service or facility will be there if they (or their friends or family) need it

- Because they, a family member, or a friend were helped

- To improve their own community

- To help people less fortunate than themselves

- Because they wanted the recognition

- To feel good

- Because of peer pressure from a friend or colleague

- To receive a tax benefit

Depending on why your donors support your organisation, you may choose to stress different messages. The key underlying theme, however, should be to show your donors how their support made a difference; how that gift ensured the continuation of services for friends and family alike; how that gift made a difference to an individual; and so on.

Based on the number of renewal waves you have planned, you may have the luxury of delivering an informative and low-key message in the first wave, and gradually increasing the urgency of the tone. On the other hand, if you only have two waves, then your first wave will have to be strong, and your second wave will have to stress the urgency of immediate support.

Choice of media for renewal

In the acquisition cycle you had a broader selection of effective media available than for the renewal cycle. This is true for a simple reason: you have already established a relationship with the donor. It is not a good use of your resources, for example, to try to renew your donors through mass media, since you can't ensure the delivery of your message directly to your donor.

The ability to communicate directly to your donors in a personal way is the primary factor that allows you to determine which medium is effective, and which is ineffective.

- For consumers, mail and phone are the most effective media. They deliver your message directly to your donor.

- For business-to-business approaches, you also have the fax machine at your disposal. However, with business-to-business approaches, you may have another factor to contend with: the gatekeeper — that is, the individual or the donations committee established to act as a buffer for the chief executive officer. Your challenge is to make your fax personal enough, compelling enough, or novel enough to ensure that even the most hardened gatekeeper will deliver it to your intended recipient.

- The Internet — though not widely used enough currently to be a consistent choice — may provide another channel of solicitation over the next few years.

4. Reactivating inactive donors

Donors who miss a single donation cycle are similar to first-time donors: they are less committed to the organisation than active donors. They may have decided not to donate during the previous campaign cycle for a variety of reasons, including:

- They are juggling financial priorities.

- They support a variety of organisations, and shift their support from time-to- time.

- They may have lost interest in your cause.

- They may no longer have confidence in your organisation's ability to fulfill its mission.

Just as you had to resell first-time donors, you may have to resell inactive donors about the work that your organisation does, and why they should continue with their support.

You should also consider the cost/benefit of the subsequent solicitations. Each time you solicit an inactive donor, your cost to reactivate the donor increases, and your chance to get another gift decreases. It may be worth your while to divide your inactive donors into segments, based on the amount of the last gift. This technique will help you focus your efforts on the most profitable segments of your donor base, while containing your costs.

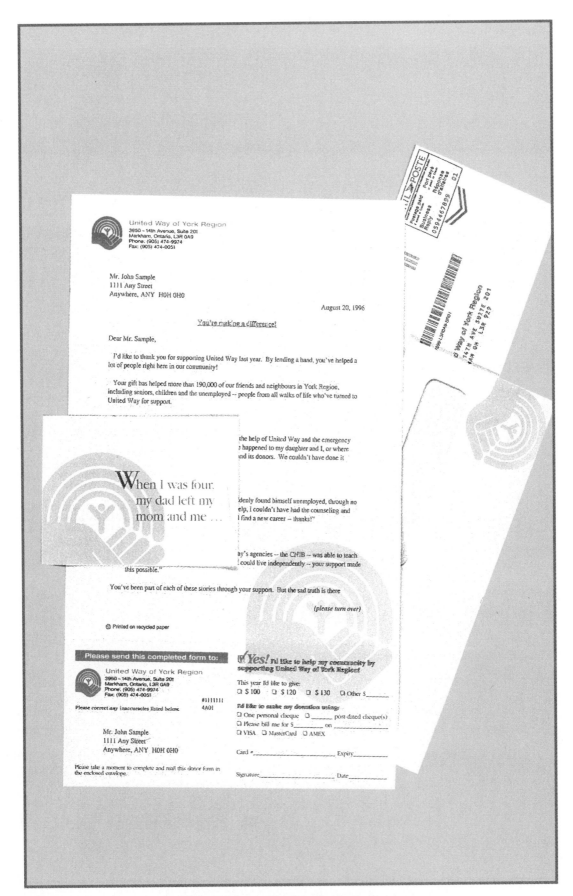

An example of a personalised fundraising package.

FIGURE 12-3

Example:

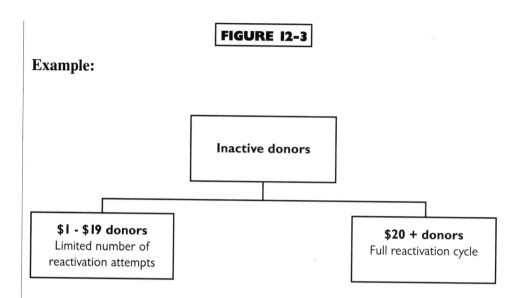

5. Recovering lapsed donors

Your chances of recovering donors decrease with each cycle they don't make a donation. To determine how to effectively recover a lapsed donor, start by looking at why a donor may have failed to support your organisation for the past two or more cycles. In addition to the reasons mentioned in the previous section on inactive donors, lapsed donors may have stopped giving because:

· Approximately 20 percent of the population moves each year, and if your solicitation hasn't been redirected, then it may simply never have reached the donor.

· They may have passed away. Remember that the average donor tends to be older.

· They may be upset by poor service they have received in the past.

· They may be displeased by a stance your organisation may have taken on an issue (or their perception of a stance your organisation has taken).

It's important to find out the reasons why your previously loyal donors have lapsed:

· First, so that you can respond to specific issues or to correct misconceptions

· Second, to determine if there are trends that should be investigated and addressed

· For example, if a significant number of donors were missed because they had moved, it might be a signal that you should be more aggressive in

Your chances of recovering donors decrease with each cycle they don't make a donation.

acquiring change of address information; or if donations were drying up because of a customer service issue, then you will need to identify and correct it.

To find out why your donors are lapsing, consider conducting a small survey. If you have phone numbers on your donor file, then you should probably start with a phone survey. You'll be able to update your list, to correct any address information, and to quiz donors on why they've stopped. And if the issue is a misperception about your organisation, then you can correct it on the spot. With a mail survey, the absence of a response could mean that either the donor never received it, or that the donor declined to respond to it. One of the strengths of a phone survey is that you'll know if the person has moved right away: either the phone will be out of service, or you can ask them if their address has changed. If there has been a change, you can capture the new information immediately.

The tone of lapsed donor solicitations changes dramatically from organisation to organisation. Some charities treat a lapsed donor as they would an active donor, while others plead with lapsed donors to come back. The urgency and tone of your solicitation should at least partially be determined by the number of recovery attempts in your plan.

It's even more important with lapsed donors than it is with inactive donors to segment the file. Your segmentation strategy should be based in part on the amount of the last gift (e.g., last gave $1 to $25, $26 to $50, etc.); and on the basis of recency (e.g., the donor gave three years ago, four years ago, five years ago, etc.). You should use this segmentation model to examine your donor base of lapsed donors to determine the cost/benefit of soliciting each segment. While it may be costing you to do this comparison — for the sake of argument $0.80 to raise a dollar from lapsed donors — you may be spending five to 10 times this amount to acquire new donors. There is a temptation to cut out lapsed donors on the basis of recency, however, you should be more concerned with the profitability of each segment.

Example:

Your organisation has decided that it will send up to four waves of mail to recover lapsed donors. You have analysed the file, and have realised that it doesn't make sense to send out four waves to everyone, and that by reducing the total number of letters mailed, your organisation can save a significant amount on postage and printing.

During your analysis you discovered that lapsed donors respond differently for each year they are lapsed; and they respond differently, based on the amount of the last gift. Armed with this new information, your new lapsed donor strategy might look like Figure 12-4 on the following page.

> The tone of lapsed donor solicitations changes dramatically from organisation to organisation. Some charities treat a lapsed donor as they would an active donor, while others plead with lapsed donors to come back.

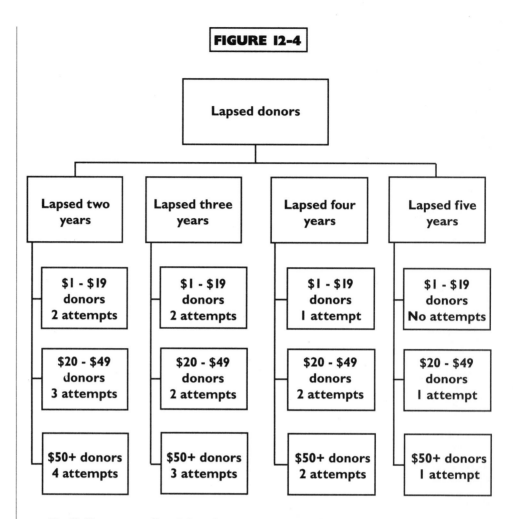

FIGURE 12-4

	Lapsed donors		
Lapsed two years	**Lapsed three years**	**Lapsed four years**	**Lapsed five years**
$1 - $19 donors 2 attempts	$1 - $19 donors 2 attempts	$1 - $19 donors 1 attempt	$1 - $19 donors No attempts
$20 - $49 donors 3 attempts	$20 - $49 donors 2 attempts	$20 - $49 donors 2 attempts	$20 - $49 donors 1 attempt
$50+ donors 4 attempts	$50+ donors 3 attempts	$50+ donors 2 attempts	$50+ donors 1 attempt

▶ Building profitable donor campaigns

While the donor cycle is the framework for a successful and systematic fundraising solicitation process, there are a number of techniques that you can employ to increase the revenues your organisation receives from its donors. These techniques include:

- Upgrading the level of support from your donors
- Building long-term giving programs
- Building effective segmentation models
- Building revenues through multiple gifts

Upgrading your donors

Increasing the size of the average donor gift is an important method of increasing the revenue your organisation receives. Determining how much to ask donors for — and how to ask them — is a perennial challenge that fundraisers face. There are many donors who are currently giving small amounts who can't afford to give any more; and there are many donors who are currently giving small amounts who can afford to give hundreds or thousands of dollars, but have never been asked.

There are three ways you can ask a donor for a gift:

1) Let them fill in a blank field after reviewing your material

Example:

I'd like to give $ _____

This technique has real limitations: donors are left baffled because they don't know what's appropriate or what's expected; and if you use it on renewing donors, you're likely to get a donation for less than the donor gave last year if they can't remember how much they previously gave.

2) Provide the donor with a pre-printed gift matrix

Example:

I'd like to give __ $35 __ $50 __ $75 __ Other $_____

The major advantage of this approach is that you can pre-print the matrix on a gift coupon. This technique is widely used in acquisition mailings, but it does have limitations for renewal programs. It doesn't make much sense, for example, to ask a $200 donor for $35, $50, or $75. And doing so may encourage some larger donors to downgrade, since you are creating the perception that the common gift level is between $35 and $75.

Issues you will have to consider when you use this technique are:

· Which amounts should you include in the matrix (e.g., $20, $40, $60 or $35, $50, $100)?

> You can best determine the answer to this question by examining your donor base to determine the most frequently contributed amounts, and by using them to build the matrix.

· How many amounts (e.g., three amounts — $25, $50, $75 — or four amounts — $25, $50, $75, $100)?

> You can best determine the answer to this question by testing the impact of three versus four amounts on the average gift.

· Should your matrix be listed in ascending or descending order (e.g., $30, $50, $70 or $70, $50, $30)?

> This tends to be a stylistic issue — you may choose to test it at one point or another, but there is a good chance that the difference will be negligible.

3) Use a variable matrix based on the donor's past history

Example:

If the donor's last gift was $50, the matrix could read: this year I'd like to give __ $60 __ $70 __ $80 __ Other $_____

If the donor's last gift was $80, the matrix could read: this year I'd like to give __ $90 __ $100 __ $110 __ Other $_____

While this technique has obvious limitations in an acquisition mailing, it has been used with a great deal of success within renewal programs by many organisations. The key decisions you have to make are:

· Should we increase the matrix based on a fixed amount or a percentage (e.g., should amounts increase by $10, $20, and $30, or 10 percent, 20 percent, and 30 percent)?

   On low-to-medium amounts the fixed amount method works well, however, asking a $500 donor for an increase to $510, $520, $530 isn't as effective as the percent method.

   If you use the percent method, remember that percent increases can provide unusual amounts that look computer-generated (e.g., a gift of $60 could end up with a matrix of $66, $72, $78). Round up the amount to the nearest $5 or $10.

This variable amount matrix method requires you to use a computer and a laser printer to generate the data and personalize it. This step pushes up your costs over a pre-printed version, but the increase in revenues will usually outstrip the increase in costs.

▶ Building long-term donors through long-term giving plans

In the last section we discussed how to increase the donor's average gift. Increasing the size of the average gift is one of the two ways to increase the donor's lifetime value. As mentioned earlier, lifetime value refers to the cumulative amount contributed by a donor to an organisation. In addition to increasing the size of the gift, one of the goals of a direct marketing fundraiser is to increase the total number of contributions every donor makes.

Two techniques that a number of organisations have used very successfully to extend the number of contributions a donor makes are:

· Fixed pledges over several years
· Pre-authorized payment plans

Fixed pledges

This payment plan is most commonly used by capital and equipment campaigns. Donors are told they can make a substantial contribution, and they can pay for it in manageable instalments each year, over a number of years. Donating $2,000 to a university might seem intimidating for many people, but learning that you could give $100 every three months for the next five years can make it a lot more palatable.

While fixed pledges do build up the donor's lifetime value, they can inadvertently create the impression that the donor's obligation and involvement are finished at the end of that pledge. Another disadvantage is that if someone is committed to donate, say $250 per year for the next four years, it is virtually impossible to upgrade the amount of each year's instalment. This is not such an issue on large gifts, but when donors are contributing small amounts each year, it can be a real limitation.

If you are setting up a fixed pledge program, consider how you will convert donors to the next gift once the term of the current gift comes due. With the right solution, you can have an extremely successful series of campaigns.

Pre-authorized payment plans

Donors who use pre-authorized payment plans (PAPP) typically give a higher average gift than those who make one-time gifts.

The most common PAPP has been the pre-authorized chequing plan. Each month a relatively small amount comes out of the donor's bank account. Over the course of time, this small amount adds up to a significant contribution. More recently, charities have used this type of initiative with credit cards: each month a small, manageable amount is charged to the donor's credit card.

Where the fixed pledge is usually promoted as a method of making a big gift in manageable instalments, the PAPP is usually promoted as a convenient way to make easy payments that add up to a significant amount.

While the term of a PAPP may be fixed (e.g., the donor agrees to have the amounts charged or withdrawn for a single year), in many cases it is open-ended or apparently perpetual. Until the donor asks for the donation to stop, closes the account, or passes away, the donation will continue. The rollover that's required at the end of a fixed pledge isn't an issue.

Upgrading, if handled properly, can also provide charities with additional revenues. After all, the jump from $5 to $6 per month is easy for the donor to make.

► Building segments

Taking the time to divide your donor base into segments, and to analyse the results of the various segments can provide you with invaluable information on what to do, and in some cases, what not to do!

With this information you can develop strategies on how to retain a specific segment, how to increase the support from another, and so on.

Some segmentation strategies you may wish to consider include:

Segmenting by recency of gift — As already discussed, recency of gift is a strong predictor of future donations. You can establish benchmarks for each of the segments you develop, and devise methods for improving the performance of each segment.

Segmenting by amount of gift — This form of segmentation can be used to evaluate the effectiveness of an approach on a cost/benefit basis; and it can be used to maximise return on investment while minimising costs. Donors can be segmented by gift ranges, and the likelihood of future donations can be benchmarked and monitored. In addition, you can study patterns of donor upgrades and downgrades, and develop strategies for the appropriate segments.

Segmenting by frequency of donation — Donors who contribute more frequently are more likely to continue to support your organisation: is there a pattern that you can determine through segmentation? What strategies can you develop to increase the likelihood of additional gifts?

Segmenting by geographic location — Some areas have poor response rates, while others have very strong patterns.

► Building revenues through multiple gifts

In addition to the annual gift you receive from donors, you can solicit additional gifts from them through "special appeals." Special appeals may focus on a specific project your organisation is working on, a capital campaign, or an emergency relief appeal.

As you develop the concept for your special appeal, you should review the suitability of the issue as a fundraising appeal:

- Is it easy to communicate the issue to your donors, or does it require a very lengthy or technical explanation?

- Does the issue have a media profile, or are you explaining the issue to your donors from scratch?

- Is your organisation's stance clear and easy to define?

- Can you show your audience why it's important that they support you on this issue, and how that support will help?

- Will you be able to show people who support this issue the progress you've made at some reasonable future time?

You should think about how the timing of this special appeal will affect your renewal cycle. However, once you determine the right issue, and you integrate it with your renewal cycle, you have the potential to raise significant additional revenues from your donor base.

▶ The future of direct marketing and fundraising

The level of professionalism within fundraising has brought about significant changes within the not-for-profit sector over the last few years. And with the desire for governments to trim expenditures, the role of the not-for-profit sector will continue to grow, at least for the next several years.

However, just as the last few years have been characterised as more competitive, the next few years will see even stronger competition in the mailbox, over the phone, and in the news media. Concurrently, the databases that fundraisers have been building are becoming more sophisticated: the emphasis is now shifting from acquiring new donors to maintaining existing donors, and increasing the organisation's share of wallet.

In the longer term, the more time and energy a fundraiser spends now toward building strong relationships with the donor base, the more secure the future of the organisation in the years to come.

QUEBEC MARKET

13

Quebec's population makes up 25 percent of the Canadian household statistics, according to Statistics Canada. There are some 2,500,000 households housing approximately 7,300,000 people. Of these, there are some 600,000 people who identify themselves as English speaking. Therefore, our primary marketing opportunity exists in a universe of over 6,500,000 French-speaking individuals. Forty-five percent of the families in Quebec are either single-parent or reconstructed families, and 60 percent of the women have a job outside the home.

The key direct marketing benefits of convenience and saving time are as appropriate for this market as they are for the rest of Canada. But the key statistic that will drive your marketing efforts is that nearly 90 percent of the Quebec population is French speaking. We should, of course, acknowledge that Quebec is not the only province in Canada with a French-speaking target audience. There are others. But for the purposes of simplification, let's identify our audience as Quebec.

There are legal issues involved in doing business in Quebec — issues that dictate language, how your offer can be positioned, the use of premiums, and what type of response mechanisms are permitted in your mailings or response-generated advertising. The province also has strong regulations on advertising geared to children. Before venturing into Quebec, look into the legalities of doing business in the province as well as the guidelines for how you must construct your offer. Local direct marketing agencies and consultants can be a great resource.

If there was no question of law, only a question of marketing techniques, would you market to a French-speaking province in English? I think not. Marketing in Quebec is not just a matter of developing a direct mail campaign or response-generated ad in another language. It must be a commitment to advertise, service, and fulfill in French. I urge you to revisit the chapters on Opportunity Evaluation and The Marketing Plan as you look at the particular opportunities in Quebec. Tie these two chapters together with research, followed by in-the-mail testing, and you'll have your formula for evaluation.

There are some specific areas we will deal with, in this chapter, but none is more important, in my opinion, than the commitment that you and your company must make to this marketplace. As mentioned before, it is not just a matter of advertising in another language. It is a matter of involvement. The following list presents what I believe is the minimum commitment your company must make to this market:

- **Research**

It must be conducted by a research group with its finger on the pulse of the province.

- **Direct mail testing or on-page advertising testing**

This is not an exercise in translation. It is an adaptation best suited to talents that reside in Quebec. You must choose a consultant or a direct marketing agency that services and understands this market.

- **Fulfillment**

Your commitment must not only be to the sale of your product in French, but also to all materials and follow-up programs in French.

- **Customer service**

It goes without saying that you must ensure your customer service representatives are well versed in the language and the culture.

- **Telemarketing**

Many marketers today are using the phone for solicitations as well as customer service and follow-up. Many call centres offer excellent service in French. Be sure you choose one that has experience in the market.

Media

You must also consider the opportunities and differences in the available media.

Advertisers discovered long ago that they should rely heavily on Québécois entertainers and themes to sell products. The classic example is Pepsi-Cola, which outsells Coke by a margin of two to one in Quebec. A decade ago, the cola company dropped Michael Jackson in favour of Quebec comedian Claude Meunier, the creator and star of La Petite Vie. Mr. Meunier's colourful characters strike a chord with Quebecers. Stories like this are endless.

Lists

When considering a direct mail program consult your list broker about the availability of lists. Qualified mailing lists for the province may contain in the range of 300,000 names. Although all segmentations may be available to you, the most critical selection will be language. There are strong language laws in Quebec that demand communication in the recipient's language of choice (makes sense to me). In a recent list usage study, Quebec ranks 25 percent higher on response rates. This is clearly a marketing opportunity if your campaign is specifically prepared for the market and culture.

Advertisers discovered long ago that they should rely heavily on Québécois entertainers and themes to sell products.

Telemarketing

This marketing medium may need more investigation before you decide to proceed. Based on the Ernst & Young survey on Canadians and call centres in March 1997, this market may not accept telemarketing as easily as the rest of the country. Although the numbers may indicate opportunity, I would suggest that you proceed with caution and plan your tests carefully.

FIGURE 13-1

FREQUENCY OF MARKETING CALLS
PAST 4 WEEKS

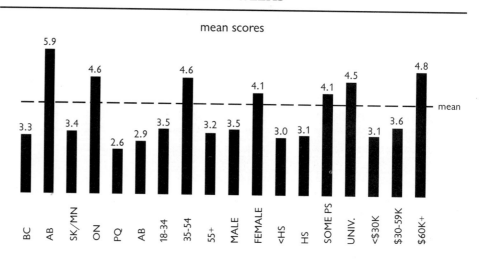

Base: all respondents: 1,504 (weighted)

Some Canadians are receiving more marketing calls than others. The groups who have received the most calls over the last four weeks include Albertans (5.9), those aged 35 to 54 (4.6), university graduates (4.5), and those earning more than $60K (4.8). The smallest number of marketing calls have been received by residents of Quebec (2.6).

FIGURE 13-2

REACTION TO MARKETING CALLS

And generally, do you react to these calls by...?

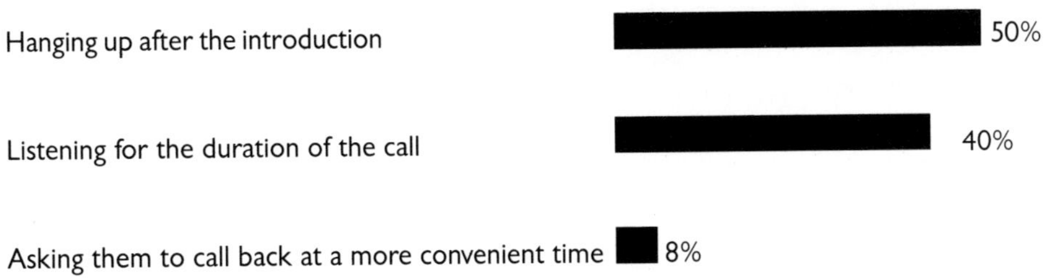

Hanging up after the introduction █████████████████ 50%

Listening for the duration of the call █████████████ 40%

Asking them to call back at a more convenient time ██ 8%

Base: have received marketing calls: 1,428 (weighted)

Of those who have received marketing calls from companies during either the last four weeks or the last year, fully one half (50%) generally react to these calls by hanging up after the introduction. However, there are two fifths (40%) who report listening for the duration of the call. There are fewer than one in 10 (8%) who ask the marketer to call back at a more convenient time.

In addition, in the Telemarketing chapter of this book, we reviewed Figure 11-3, Marketing Calls Based on Past Purchases (page 155) as an opportunity. If you look closely at the comments on Quebec, it reveals another story: 47 percent of Quebecers consider reminder/renewal phone calls a bad idea.

Media

When considering the available media, your choices include the traditional media options: newspapers, magazines, radio, television, and billboards. The circulation is certainly smaller than English Canada's numbers, but nonetheless well targeted. Still, there are other media opportunities in Quebec, and that is one of the key reasons for hiring local talent as a consultant prior to entering this market.

Yves Blain of FCB Direct, Montreal, says there are other media opportunities, such as investment and savings trade shows, where some 80,000 consumers gather information and resources to better plan their future. This may not be a viable alternative in other parts of the country, but financial service marketers should not overlook the opportunity to introduce or support their direct mail or print advertising campaigns in the Quebec market.

As Quebecers look for ways to invest in their future, mutual fund companies look for ways to interest them in their products. In a recent *Marketing Magazine* article on Quebec, Brian Gooding of Fidelity Investments, says that making a sale takes a bit longer because Quebecers like to know the person they're dealing with. "In Ontario, they'll buy over the phone from someone they've never met before, whereas in Quebec they want to meet face-to-face and they want to really know who the person is." When all is researched and analysed, the Ernst & Young survey on Canadians and call centres proves to be true, and Yves Blain seems to have a solid idea for marketing in Quebec.

▶ Creative considerations

There are some creative considerations for your product or service. If you are looking for a spokesperson, local Quebec personalities are highly supported, but you must consider the layout, the copy approach, and the appeal.

Layout

You will have to prove, by testing, whether the colours you choose are targeting the right audience or whether the emphasis on product and people is right. The visual aspect of your advertising or direct mail package is one of the hottest debated issues in the French market. But a few areas are beyond debate.

· Examine your photography carefully

Be people-sensitive. Blond hair and blue eyes are rare in Quebec's heritage. Ensure your models reflect the Quebec makeup of dark hair and dark eyes. Quebecers identify more readily with this image.

- **Examine the background of your photography carefully**

Don't try to sell your products or services with the CN Tower or the Calgary Stampede dominating the page or brochure.

- **Your guarantee should be far more prominent in your layouts**

Although guarantees should always be highlighted, many Quebecers are still skeptical about ordering by mail. Your guarantee can become one of the prime motivators of their trust.

Copy

As we review which copy approach works in the Quebec market, let's not forget the basic techniques that make all copy work — the right offer to the right audience.

Mark Morin, president of Strategies Marketing Direct, and author of many articles on the importance of the creative approach in Quebec, says:

> "The level of language used is important. The English language has two levels, formal and conversational. In French there are many levels, and from a corporate communications point of view, the tendency is to use a more sophisticated level — what we call international French.

> "But in many cases, that won't do as good a job in selling the product. You can't use anglicisms, you often can't use French from France, and you wouldn't necessarily use the same words to speak to the New Brunswick French customer as you would in Montreal.

> "An English Canadian relates more to rationality, but Quebecers relate better to appeals to their emotional motivations.

> "But don't let any of this scare you. If you've done your research and partnered with the right talent, some of the risks will be removed."

Let's look at some components of successful copy:

- Do not *translate* your English material — *adapt* it to appeal to this market segment.

- Do not use international French — use Quebec French, and make sure it is quality French. But don't write for snob appeal. For most products, snob appeal will not work.

Although guarantees should always be highlighted, many Quebecers are still skeptical about ordering by mail.

Multi-media with sweepstake offer sample

Client: Magazines Maclean Hunter Québec
Campaign: *L'actualité* Continuous Service Subscriptions
Agency: Pierre Nadeau Direct

Creative Director: Pierre Nadeau, Art Director
Copywriter: Charles Girard
Account Management: Pierre Savard

L'actualité is Quebec's public affairs magazine and the leading French-language consumer title in Canada. The celebration of the magazine's 20th anniversary in September 1996 became the focus of a successful year-long campaign to acquire new subscribers and promote its innovative continuous renewal concept: "L'abbonement-fidélité."

Educated consumers between the ages of 25 and 55, in the middle to high-income brackets were targeted. A special offer was built around a 20th anniversary contest, with draws for cash prizes scheduled to coincide with the publication of each of the 20 issues of *L'actualité* during its anniversary year. A commemorative long-distance calling card was also tested as a premium.

The 20th anniversary contest package beat the control both on outside prospect lists (by 33 percent) and on reactivation lists of previous subscribers (by 31 percent) and was used as the new control package during the whole anniversary year. Strong creative elements of the package were later successfully adapted to post-anniversary acquisition mailings.

- Ensure your quality French is done in a conversational, personal style. This is difficult to achieve in French, but it is a must to sell in this market.

- Have your letter signed by someone in your local Quebec office. This person should be the highest ranking francophone in your company, but make sure his or her title is relevant to your offer.

- Carefully research your selected spokesperson. Be sure you use local, respected talent.

- Put more emotion into your campaigns than you would in English Canada.

▶ Offers

Four words about offers — test and be selective.

Sweepstakes are a double-edged sword in Quebec. Francophones buy lottery tickets with a passion. But because legislation precludes linking participation to a transaction, you should expect a lot of entries from non-buyers and some from professional contest entrants.

Quebecers love premium-related offers (make sure you check the law on how to use them). Unfortunately, you'll find they attract a higher-than-average percentage of freeloaders who will gladly accept your free gift, but just as eagerly take advantage of your no-obligation, free trial period and promptly cancel when their time is up.

In summary, Quebec holds many opportunities for direct marketers. Remember. Language is not the only differentiating feature of Quebec. And while you're at it — don't forget the English-speaking population in Quebec.

SPACE ADVERTISING

14

Space advertising in publications is profitable for a wide range of products and services — from books to financial products to steak and potatoes. It has been tested on its own, with direct mail, with direct response television, and with direct mail and direct response television combined. It can play an important role in your marketing mix. However, success does not come about by accident. It is achieved by carefully planning and executing a well thought out marketing plan, properly integrating all media, and continuously testing. Should you be using space advertising in your media mix?

Whether you should be using space advertising or not can only be determined after sufficient testing. Let's find out how space advertising and direct marketing work together.

Space advertising regularly reaches mass audiences at a relatively low cost per reach. However, your message is one of the many that are vying for a reader's attention. Your challenge is to ensure that your creative and product get noticed and are responded to, generating a profitable cost per order.

When familiarising yourself with space advertising, you should have some handy reference material by your side: *Canadian Advertising Rates & Data* (CARD), the specific publication's rate card, each publication's media kit, and a recent sample of the magazine or newspaper. Armed with these references, you can now knowledgeably examine the opportunities in space advertising. In addition, you should always speak directly to the individual publications or your media planner if you are using a direct marketing agency.

In order to better understand these opportunities, this chapter will introduce you to on-page advertising and inserts.

▶ On-page advertising

On-page, or run-of-the-press (ROP) advertisements are not unlike those used by traditional advertisers — with some differences. Direct marketers include a response vehicle. This can be a coupon and/or a phone number, and sometimes both. The objective never changes — response and measurability. Your primary purpose will be to solicit a response at a profitable cost per order, or generate an inquiry or lead cost efficiently.

Research is underway that is based on the premise that the value of on-page advertising has a dual role: building image as well as generating response. I agree with this premise, but caution you to know and understand the costs of building image in this environment. The premise that every exposure the customer gets to your product builds image, is undeniable. But based on my philosophy as a marketer, I believe you must decide and assign a role to each and every vehicle in your marketing mix. Setting your objectives up-front is key to accepting this premise. Waiting for long-term response is not in the makeup of a direct marketer. Do not forfeit the opportunity of building image coupled with the demand for a response.

▶ Magazines

Within the magazine category, you will have many choices as well as several subdivisions and categories. Your challenge is to select the right magazine for your target audience and ensure it has a history of successful response-driven advertising. Magazines are not a homogeneous group; within this medium, there are several variables:

1. **Paid circulation magazines**

    (a) Mass distribution magazines

    - TV listings
    - General interest magazines
    - General information or newsmagazines

    (b) Vertical (special interest magazines)

    - Consumer magazines
    - Business magazines and trade magazines

2. **Controlled circulation magazines**

    - Consumer magazines
    - Business magazines, trade magazines

1. Paid circulation

This type of magazine is bought by consumers or businesses through subscriptions or at newsstands. This payment demonstrates the consumer's commitment to the magazine and its subject matter, and generally responds better than controlled-circulation magazines, which are distributed free of charge.

a) Mass distribution magazines

Paid circulation magazines, marketed through a combination of newsstand and subscription sales, generally have a larger circulation than either vertical or controlled circulation magazines.

Because mass distribution magazines reach such a large audience, they can be effective and cost efficient for direct response advertising if proper testing is conducted.

Because mass distribution magazines reach such a large audience, they can be effective and cost efficient for direct response advertising if proper testing is conducted.

There are several main categories of mass distribution paid circulation magazines of which you should be aware.

TV listings

Examples of this category are *TV Guide* and its French equivalent *TV Hebdo*. These magazines are directed toward the entire family and have relatively large circulations. This has always been fertile ground for direct marketers — both for response and formats. Unfortunately, response rates have been decreasing over the past few years due to the proliferation of, and improvement in, the editorial content of free TV listings that are distributed in local newspapers.

General interest magazines

This is a large group. The editorial content is usually general and varied, directed at a wide cross-section of readers. Not surprisingly, the general interest magazines that offer the strongest response rates are usually those with the highest circulation. You must test carefully when you have a large number of readers.

General information magazines and newsmagazines

General information or newsmagazines also work quite well. Magazines such as *Maclean's, L'actualité,* and *Time* offer high circulation and generally a higher demographic reader profile.

b) Vertical (special interest) magazines

Vertical magazines are also paid circulation magazines. Available through subscriptions and newsstands, they are aimed at a specific target audience with well-defined interests. They are divided into two magazine categories: consumer and business or trade.

Consumer magazines

There are over 500 magazines listed in CARD. The majority of the consumer magazines in this category cover a wide range of topics and interests. Because of their specialised content, they are referred to as vertical magazines. Many vertical magazines have a relatively small, though targeted, circulation. Consequently, such magazines can be an effective medium for the direct marketer, providing that the advertising material is carefully tailored to the audience.

Magazines covering photography and farming have enjoyed healthy response rates over the past few years. Farm publications in particular fit the criteria — primarily subscription based and distributed mainly to rural areas. These two factors can contribute to any publication's success for direct marketers. Incorporating the right offer and the right creative, however, are the key ingredients to make specialised publications work.

Business magazines/trade magazines

Business and trade publications make up their own specialised vertical category. The audience is clearly delineated: well educated, high income, and with an upscale profile. Some publications that match this criteria: *Canadian Business, Finance, Report on Business, The Lawyer's Weekly,* and *Le Devoir Economique.*

Business and trade paid circulation publications respond reasonably well (mid-range response rates), particularly for non-traditional products or services and high-ticket items.

2. Controlled circulation

A controlled circulation magazine is distributed free of charge, or as part of a package, either to the consumer or to the business community. In the consumer category, for example, you are able to select by household demographics or, in the business category, by type of business. There are additional selections available depending on the publication's ability to segment.

Consumer magazines

Magazines, such as *Western Living,* are distributed to the household by Canada Post. Other publications in this category may be left at a central location to be picked up by the consumer. *Tribute,* for example, is left in theatre lobbies for consumers to pick up. Some other controlled circulation magazines are sent to people who subscribe to a service. As part of their card privileges, members of the American Express Platinum Card receive a free copy of *Departures* magazine, for example. Another example is Pay TV subscribers who receive the monthly magazine *Primetime* in their monthly service price. Airline in-flight magazines such as *EnRoute* and *Revue* are also considered predominately controlled circulation.

Business magazines, trade magazines

Controlled circulation publications in this category are business and trade specific, and are mailed to people at their office. Some examples of these publications include: *Canadian Grocer, Small Business, Conventions & Meetings Canada, The Medical Post, Benefits Canada,* and *Food in Canada.*

These business and trade publications often provide a breakdown of their distribution by business title. Such breakdowns assist you in targeting your message to a specific audience.

Remember. Controlled circulation magazines, whether consumer or business, must be tested carefully. In the past, they have not generated a cost-efficient order for some consumer marketers. Yet, they can be successful in generating leads for business-related products.

▶ Newspapers

The newspaper media in Canada is divided into four main categories:

- Daily newspapers
- Business newspapers (weekly)
- Weeklies (including community) newspapers
- Newspaper supplements

Our newspaper industry enjoys wide circulation and can represent a large and profitable medium. Just as in the case of magazines, you must choose the appropriate newspaper based on the definition of your target audience.

Daily newspapers

There are currently 110 daily newspapers in Canada, and this number increases monthly. For example, Toronto has four major daily newspapers. Calgary and Edmonton have two dailies each. Quebec City, Ottawa, and Montreal have both English and French dailies.

Daily newspapers are an excellent, though potentially expensive, direct response medium. The most successful format for direct marketers is the pre-printed, supplied insert referred to as a free fall insert (FFI).

Business newspapers

There are several business newspapers in both English and French: *The Financial Post* and *Les Affaires*. *The Globe and Mail* publishes the *Report on Business* magazine, which appears as an insert in the newspaper 10 times a year.

Higher advertising costs in this group may be justified by potentially higher response rates. Because these business papers appeal to a more upscale audience, your objectives for the sale of higher ticket items may be accomplished more easily.

Weekly (including community) newspapers

There are 953 French and English local or community newspapers in Canada. They are generally distributed free of charge, much like controlled circulation magazines. The average circulation is 9.2 million copies. Direct marketers do not make high use of this vehicle because often the audience

Daily newspapers are an excellent, though potentially expensive, direct response medium.

is not as well defined, or as highly targeted, as that of controlled circulation publications.

Supplements

Many Canadian newspapers include a TV listing magazine as a supplement to their weekend distribution. These supplements can generate as much response as magazines, but not as high a response rate as FFIs. Nevertheless, these supplements can be cost-effective based on the lower cost per thousand. Before testing supplements, ensure the reader is your target audience.

As we continue through our print media section, let's stop here and review an important vehicle: the free fall insert as well as inserts in general. For a better understanding of the opportunity that inserts present, we'll review a description and various available formats.

▶ Inserts

An insert is distinct from an on-page ad or run-of-the-press (ROP), since an insert is usually printed separately and supplied to the publication for insertion. It is often printed on a different stock than the publication and is immediately noticeable in the newspaper or magazine.

Magazines and newspaper inserts

An insert is delivered by your printer to the selected publications for insertion. Some publications offer to print these for you. It is my experience that it is best to have control over this area with the co-operation of your printer.

Inserts are available in many sizes and formats. We are unable to give you all the specifications for each publication, but do check with each publication to ensure your piece fits their particular requirements.

There are four formats commonly referred to as inserts:

Free fall inserts

Some marketers refer to the free fall insert as a free standing insert (FSI), but since the insert is a loose piece that can fall on the ground when you pick up the newspaper, I stick to the original name of FFI. Once inserts have fallen to the ground, consumers must bend down to pick them up. This provides you with a big opportunity to grab their attention and get them to respond (see example on next page).

Since an insert is a supplied unit, it can be printed with any number of pages, any size, and virtually on any stock. Check with each publication

Once inserts have fallen to the ground, consumers must bend down to pick them up. This provides you with a big opportunity to grab their attention and get them to respond.

An example of free fall inserts.

for their FFI guidelines. Remember. You still must meet postal standards for the reply coupon.

Always submit a sample of your insert, in advance of printing, to the publication for approval. This can be accomplished at the mock-up or rough layout stage.

Centre card inserts

They are stitched to the centre of the magazine, rather than appearing loose in the publication.

Blow-ins

They are loose cards, usually in a small format, which are actually blown-into the magazine after it is printed. They appear loose in the publication and are printed on heavier stock. Because of their paper weight, blow-ins usually force a magazine to open at their exact page. A great way to get the consumer's attention.

Business reply cards

They can either be bound into the publication to complement an on-page ad, or can be loosely blown-in. Since this format is used to generate response, this small card's big job is to deliver your offer clearly and succinctly to the consumer.

Inserts are widely tested in direct marketing because they attract attention. Most sizes provide sufficient space to sell your product. And they supply the respondent with a vehicle, by way of a card or even an envelope, to which they can easily and quickly respond.

For all inserts that are stitched into the publication, you must observe specifications for trimming and live matter. If not, your insert may be chopped, inserted incorrectly, or worse, not inserted at all. When in doubt, it is best to supply the publication with 50 to 100 samples to run through its bindery equipment for testing.

▶ Testing opportunities in space advertising

In this section, we will examine a few of the many opportunities for testing in space advertising. Publishers recognise the importance of testing to direct marketers, and more and more testing options are becoming available. Always check with each publication, or your media planner, for the newest test options. Testing is constant and ever-evolving. Here are some for you to consider:

1. A/B splits
2. Regional splits
3. Partial circulation
4. On-page or ROP testing

1. A/B Splits

This is thought to be an accurate and reliable method of testing. An A/B split was conceived to give direct marketers the ability to test two different versions of creative, or an offer, or both at the same time. One portion of this test is referred to as Test A.

Test A can be your control piece (based on previous tests), which you use to gauge overall publication and offer success. Test B should be your new creative or new offer, which you want to test against your control offer. A perfect A/B split will ensure that every other person receives your test piece (Test B), while the remainder of the audience receives Test A.

For example, let's say we have two people living next door to each other on the same street: one will receive Test A, the other will receive Test B.

This form of testing eliminates bias — geographic, economic, or otherwise. The results from these tests can be read and analysed based strictly on the testing variables of creative or offer.

In order for magazines to accommodate this testing procedure, the material must be printed two-up. This printing method allows Test A and Test B to be properly distributed. A good example of publications that can accommodate this testing format are: *Reader's Digest, Selection du Reader's Digest, TV Guide,* and *TV Hebdo.*

It is still your responsibility to design and print your test inserts in the proper two-up position. Newspapers also accept A/B splits, but you should contact them for their own particular requirements and distribution limitations.

2. Regional splits

Regional splits are used to gauge how a particular region reacts to your offer. Caution is advised when using this split for testing your creative.

3. Partial circulation

This testing technique allows you to insert your test into carefully selected portions of the distribution (subscriber versus newsstand) and circulation. This test is often conducted when the circulation is so large that you cannot estimate response, and/or it is the first time testing this publication.

Some publications can charge a premium rate for partial circulation testing. For example, the regular rate for full distribution may be $45 per thousand. However, for the partial circulation test you may be quoted $50 per thousand. Remember. When analysing your test, it is important to project response and costs for the full distribution based on $45 per thousand.

4. On-page or ROP testing

As with inserts, some publications offer A/B splits on-page. Again, only certain publications lend themselves to this testing. You must contact the publication or your media planner to make arrangements and receive approval.

▶ Cost analysis for space

The sum total of all efforts within the direct marketing discipline comes down to two words — *measurable profits*. This is every bit as true of direct response space advertising as it is of direct mail or any other form of direct marketing.

The economics of direct marketing does not merely reflect advertising costs, it analyses all the costs involved in delivering the product or service to the customer. At the planning stage, compile all costs and prepare a profit and loss worksheet to establish the break-even point for a given selling price and offer.

The first stage of a hypothetical break-even profit and loss worksheet is displayed for your review. Remember. Account for every cost involved in filling an order for a product, including telemarketing, if your customers have the option to call your toll-free number.

The economics of direct marketing does not merely reflect advertising costs, it analyses all the costs involved in delivering the product or service to the customer.

- Assume you have selected a publication with a circulation of 100,000
- The space cost is $1,500 ($15 per thousand)

FIGURE 14-1

FIRST STAGE OF A SAMPLE PROFIT AND LOSS WORKSHEET

Selling price of product	$25.96	
Shipping and handling charges to the customer	2.04	
Gross sales per unit		**$28.00**
Total cost of product:		
Cost (landed) per unit	$5.30	
Handling, shipping carton, processing	.90	
Postage	.50	
Tax per unit	n/a	
Total unit cost		**$6.70**
Projected percentage of returns	10%	
Cost of returns plus postage and refurbishing	$2.00	
Chargeable cost of returned units (10% x $2)		.20
Estimated percentage of bad debt	10%	
Chargeable cost of bad debt (10% x gross sales)		2.80
Total variable cost		$9.70
Unit profit after deducting variable costs ($28 - $9.70)		**$18.30**
Less: returned units of 10%		1.83
Unit gross profit per order		$16.47
Overhead factor (10%)		2.80
Net profit per order/break-even cost per order		**$13.67**
Reasonable profit margin of 15%		2.05
Allowable break-even advertising cost per order (=15%)		**$11.62**

To arrive at the number of orders needed to break even, divide $13.67 into $1,500 to get 110 orders (1.1 orders per thousand).

Based on your product experience, now judge the probability of achieving this response from this publication — with this product, and this ad format and size. If the probability doesn't look encouraging, don't use it.

This profit and loss worksheet does not take into account the cost of creating and producing the ad. There are various methods of assessing this cost. Your company finance practices will guide you in your allocation.

1. Assess the total cost of ad origination to the first campaign in which it was used

2. Apply the preparation costs to general overhead figures

3. Amortise the ad cost over the anticipated life of the promotion.

▶ Conclusion

With both newspapers and magazines, space advertising opportunities are changing dramatically for the direct marketer. New publications are being introduced as quickly as the old fall by the wayside. Direct marketing agency media planners have dedicated their careers to understanding the nuances of each format and each publication. I encourage you to consult them prior to testing any space opportunities. By working closely together, you can develop new formats and new ways of segmentation to the mutual benefit of the marketing and publishing communities.

BROADCAST

15

Beyond direct mail, print media, and telemarketing, the broadcast medium offers direct marketers further advertising alternatives. Technological advances have expanded the broadcast media to include more than television and radio, but also cable TV, interactive buying, 24-hour home shopping networks, Internet, and e-mail or I-mail. Electronic media is one of the fastest-changing areas of our industry. At the time of writing this book, there are few secrets for success available. So, we will save that discussion for the next book.

This chapter concentrates on television and radio, and the opportunities they present. Understanding how to purchase this medium is best left to the expertise of a media planner specialist. This is one area I suggest you don't attempt to conquer alone.

▶ Television

Direct response commercials were vibrant even in the early fifties when direct response television (DRTV) was introduced by pitchmen. These pitchmen would, for 30 minutes — not 30 seconds — pitch products to the consumer. The 30-minute commercial was filled with eulogies to benefit and better your life and that of your family — plus, of course, a phone number for ordering.

The 30-minute pitchman is back in business. We see some of this longer programming in the area of fundraising with World Vision and the Toronto Humane Society; in exercise equipment; in healthcare for products, such as hair replacement and anti-ageing beauty products; in record clubs; and even in telecommunications and financial services.

There are also 30-minute programs dedicated to all kinds of products, such as: "Get Rich in Real Estate" and the Tony Robbins inspirational seminars for self-improvement. Today, we call this 30-minute format an infomercial. Infomercials run the full gamut of consumer lifestyle products and services.

The effectiveness of television as a direct response advertising medium is based on three factors:

1. Television is an extremely popular consumer medium and therefore provides wide coverage.

2. Television lends itself to products that require demonstration.

3. A well-designed television commercial uses a dynamic blend of audio and visual to appeal to your prospect's senses. Television can create awareness of, interest in, and a desire for a product using a combination of picture, sound, movement, and information — a mixture that no other medium can provide on its own.

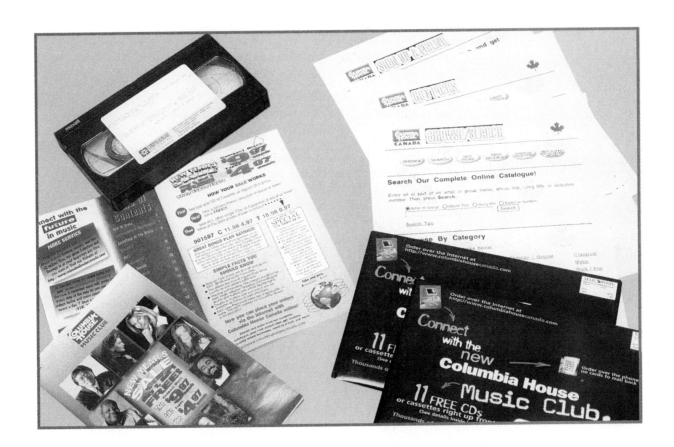

DRTV, Web banner, and monthly statement sample

Client: Columbia House Canada
Product: Music club

Campaign: Columbia House Canada Web site
Agency: In-house

In November 1996, Columbia House launched its English-language Music Club Web site, which allows visitors to browse the entire Columbia House catalogue, order selections, or join the club.

Additional site features include the ability for visitors to listen to sound clips, check out new releases, review lists of essential album collections, order or decline the selection of the month, and to change their address or listening preference.

With the intention of bringing added convenience to its members, Columbia House also set up a 24-hour-a-day interactive customer support phone system, which features an Automated Express Shopping Service that allows people to order selections by touch-tone phone.

Columbia House used a variety of media to promote its Web site, including 30-second TV spots, Web banner ads, a brochure inserted in all its monthly member mailings, and advertising in its monthly music magazine. Plus, all new prospect campaigns in print and direct mail now steer people to the Columbia House Web site for "thousands of more selections."

Results to date have exceeded all expectations, with more than 10 million hits in the first seven months of the site's existence, 425,000 customer transactions, and 45,000 e-mail messages from members.

While television is a potentially effective advertising medium for your direct response campaign, there are several considerations to keep in mind. The combination of product, price, offer, and creative will only be successful if you choose the proper stations, and obtain air-time at an affordable price. Either the product or services you are offering should appeal to a general audience, or your audience should be segmented by programming. The media buying techniques will make the primary difference. This is best left to the media specialist.

Like many other media, television is a highly specialised medium and requires its own type of creative. It is advisable to seek help from a professional direct marketing agency with DRTV credentials when creating your commercial. Here are some creative tips:

1. Product offer and benefits should appear in the first five seconds of the spot.

2. The toll-free number should be clear, bold, and reproduced on an uncluttered background in serif type.

3. Keep the toll-free number on the screen for as long as possible.

4. Keep the screen free of clutter by only showing shipping and handling charges and credit card options during the last frames.

5. Call to action should have impact: "call now to get…" or "order now and get…."

6. Mention price often throughout the script.

7. Give enough information to reduce call centre questions.

8. Make sure your company name is included in the call to action, but do not use your DRTV to build image alone — generate response.

The proven format for DRTV has been 120 seconds or two minutes in duration. Ninety to 100 seconds of this time is required merely to describe the product adequately and ensure a sale. The remaining 20 to 30 seconds is used for the tag (the presentation of the specific offer: the ordering address, phone number, and method of payment).

The 120-second format works, but it is more costly to buy and the availability has virtually dried up in the Canadian market. Most direct marketers are turning to a mix of 30-, 60-, and 90-second spots to accomplish their objectives. An effective media plan can give you 60- or 90-second spots in which you have time to build the product offering, rotated with 30-second spots for a more succinct offer that can be more frequently aired.

Television can be a profitable advertising medium in your direct marketing strategy, but it is an investment. So how do you get the most for your money when you've decided to create a television campaign?

Buying time

There are at least two ways to pay for television time: regular buys and a per inquiry (PI) buy.

1. Regular buys

Based on this method, the advertiser pays for a requested number of commercial spots — each 60 seconds, 90 seconds, or 120 seconds in length, to be run in a particular time slot such as 4 p.m. to 6 p.m.

The goal is to maximise your target audience. This can be expressed in gross rating points (GRPs), a unit that takes into account the size of the audience in that time slot and the length and frequency of the commercial. This method gives you more up-front data about the frequency, and the target audience. Buys, however, are an expensive means of securing DRTV time. An experienced DRTV media planner will have spent time with television media representatives and know the importance of being cost-efficient, while not sacrificing effectiveness, and have some incremental options for you to consider in this buying area.

2. Per inquiry (PI)

Using the PI method for buying, you pay a predetermined amount to the station for every response generated. Some stations will ask for a minimum guarantee up front, others may not ask for any guarantee up front. This may be an advantage, but you should be aware of some of the disadvantages:

a) You have little or no control over the placement of your advertisements. A campaign that has a chance to succeed in the 4 p.m. to 6 p.m. time slot may fail if the station runs it between 1 a.m. and 3 a.m.

b) PI availability is limited and sometimes difficult to obtain. Some stations make it their policy not to accept PI spots.

c) PI availability also varies seasonally. There may be some stations accepting PI between December and March, but very few during the fall period. This may affect your test and roll-out plans.

While PI has the added advantage of being an economical means of testing television, the stations that accept your PI may not be representative of your roll-out target audience. It is a good policy to test a couple of markets with buys, as a control for your PI test.

Remember. As in every direct marketing plan, no matter what the medium of choice is, you must plan your roll-out and then select the test from your roll-out plan. Do not test DRTV without establishing a clear roll-out criterion up front.

Seasonality

Costs as well as response rates can vary depending on the season. The optimum months for television response rates are:

1. The first quarter of the year, which seems to be the best performer
2. The third quarter, which comes in second-best

Depending on your product or service, the optimum time period for response rates may not always be the most appropriate or the most cost-efficient.

▶ The role of DRTV

DRTV can be used successfully in a number of combinations:

Lead generation

You can use DRTV to generate leads rather than orders. However, to qualify your leads, you'll need a fulfillment package to mail out as well as a phone follow-up at a specified date. These components will increase your costs. If your margins are high, don't hesitate to test this option.

Support of other media

DRTV is successfully used for introducing or supporting a direct mail campaign or a print campaign. It provides wide regional coverage in support of the other targeted media in your mix. Support commercials can be short — 10 or 15 seconds — just enough time to identify your product or service, and your key message — "look for this offer in your Saturday newspaper" or "look for your direct mail package, which will be delivered to your home on Wednesday." You can also use the spot to make the consumer aware of any incentives (sweepstakes, discounts, etc.). Some marketers include an extra box on the order form in the newspaper or direct mail, which allows consumers to tick a particular box if they see your commercial and get a special gift or a reduced price. This is one way of tracking overall results.

As a rule of thumb, if 40 percent or more of your broadcast audience is scheduled to receive your mailing or newspaper insert, consider television support for your program. Remember. Allocate your available budget accordingly.

1-800-519-2776
FOR RECIPES AND MORE

DRTV sample

Client: Robin Hood Multifoods
Product: Best For Bread Flour
Campaign: Baby Talk — Mom DRTV campaign
Agency: OgilvyOne Worldwide

Creative Direct or Associate Creative Director: Pete McLeod
Copywriter: Helen Prokos
Art Director: Steve Murray
Director (broadcast): Jeff Eamer
Agency Producer (broadcast): Lesley Ladd

Since consumer bread machines began taking off in popularity in 1993, the Canadian flour market has grown 27 percent. Recognizing the potential to increase sales volume by introducing a specialty flour that was formulated to bake higher, more even-textured bread, Robin Hood Multifoods launched its Best For Bread specialty flour line in Spring 1997.

In order to develop awareness and encourage trial of the product, general television advertising was aired for six weeks. Later, DRTV and IVR were added to the mix to extend awareness, increase usage, and begin to develop a long-term relationship with consumers.

The communication objectives were to position Robin Hood as a friendly bread-baking expert, convince customers that Best For Bread Flour is the best flour for their needs, and to develop a database of high-value bakers for future offers.

The strategy involved the national airing of 60- and 120-second DRTV commercials featuring a mother and her child baking bread in a warm, sunny kitchen. Incorporated in the spots were strong direct response principles, which encouraged viewers to respond if they wanted to obtain additional recipes and an opportunity to win a baker's prize pack.

Over the six-week campaign, total response was 200 percent above the objective. In fact, media had to be cut back in order to manage the overwhelming response.

Product sale

Many products and services are sold successfully from a DRTV spot. Remember. The combination of product, product benefits, a price point that includes uniqueness and value, and creative techniques are necessary.

Ordering options

The ordering options available in DRTV are a toll-free number and write-in ordering. When constructing a DRTV correctly, the largest percentage of your orders should be generated through a toll-free number.

The primary consideration here is payment. Make it easy for the customer to order and pay for your product. Ensure your call centre is capable of processing credit card orders and updating the database with ease.

▶ Radio

Radio is a potentially powerful medium. Of late, there have been some success stories coming out of radio use. For your marketing efforts, be sure to investigate radio stations that reflect your target audience and support your regional skew.

It is possible to buy radio air time on a more selective basis than television. Different radio stations cater to different audiences. Furthermore, every radio station divides its own air time into specific program segments. This allows you to segment and target specific groups of people to a much higher degree than is possible in television.

Radio is less expensive than television — air time is cheaper to buy and the commercials cost less to produce. Moreover, it is easier to revise or update radio scripts. It can also remain more current than television — shorter lead times and an easy production process.

It is only recently that marketers talk about success with radio. When you are considering this medium, be sure you know how to capitalise on its strengths and weaknesses.

1. Direct response commercials traditionally tell long stories about product benefits. However, radio stations do not generally accept commercials that are over 90 seconds in length, and some even have a limit of 60 seconds. This means a shorter, snappier spot is what you need. Creative plays an important role in delivering the message in a short period of time.

2. Radio is an auditory medium. It may be ideal as a support medium (refer to DRTV), but it is ill-suited for demonstrating products — the key word being demonstrate.

3. Radio does not make the ordering process easy. Much of our radio listening is secondary to other activities, such as eating, shaving, and driving. Talk radio has increased our listening ability, but the consumer does not transfer this attention to commercials. Remembering phone numbers to call for a product cannot be likened to listening to your favourite talk show.

Despite these drawbacks, radio can be a valuable support medium for your campaign. The key to success is to get the listener's attention and deliver your message quickly.

▶ Conclusion

Broadcast offers some exciting media options:

· Careful media selection, testing, and roll-out can be profitable if your product is suited to the chosen medium.

· DRTV is becoming far more sophisticated, but that doesn't necessarily mean more responsive.

· It is essential to hire professional help: a DRTV media specialist and specialised creative.

· Television and radio are increasing in importance. Evaluate them separately. Don't underestimate what they can bring to your marketing mix.

OTHER MEDIA

16

All media opportunities should be considered when formulating your marketing plan. This section deals with three: free rides, take-ones, and catalogues, which represent additional options for your direct marketing plan. The importance of these options depends largely on your product or service and your target audience.

▶ Free ride

A free ride is defined as any promotion that is carried by another at little or no cost. Costs of a free ride are lower, as are your response rates. Remember. Calculate a return on investment (ROI) to make sure these options meet your response objectives.

Option I: Statement stuffers

By far the most significant type of free ride is the statement stuffer. There is a strong rationale for this type of promotion. Since you are sending your customer an invoice or statement, why not offer another product or service at the same time? The purchase has arrived, and for the most part, this is the time of high customer satisfaction. Now is a good time to offer another product to a satisfied customer.

The most successful statement stuffer contains an offer that requires customers to simply tick a box or detach the order flap, write in their name and account number, and return the new order along with the next scheduled payment.

In all cases, the promotion piece is considered an abbreviated brochure or product letter. Why abbreviated? Statements are mailed by weight cost, and if your insert increases the weight, extra postage may be required. Since the essence of a free ride is postage savings, you should ensure the inclusion of a statement insert does not increase your postage. But if the insert increases the postage cost marginally, it still may be worth consideration.

Segment your audience carefully. The prime purpose of the statement is to collect payment. Don't include a statement insert to a customer who consistently pays late or may well be a credit risk if he or she makes an additional purchase.

Remember. All invoices included with the product shipment or first bills should carry also a stuffer.

Package Inserts

Including promotional pieces with product shipments is another economical way to get your sales message to satisfied customers. This promotional piece may even be for the same product, but with an offer for a friend.

What better time to recommend a purchase to a friend than when you are in receipt of your own product!

Package inserts can also be bought from other mailers. Many companies offer their product shipments as a carrier for another company's product. Costs for these inserts are calculated based on cost-per-thousand. Your direct marketing agency or list broker will have an up-to-date list of candidates for your product.

You are able to select demographic and previous purchase behaviour, just as you would when renting a mailing list. Size and weight constraints are imposed according to the overall dimensions of the product being shipped. Size and weight of your piece must be an integral part of your up-front production planning.

Promotion piggybacks

You can sometimes improve the overall profitability of your promotion by including an alternate offer inside your mailing package. This can be done in a number of ways:

1. The offer can be a separate piece of promotional material within your direct mail package. This, however, must be carefully planned. Two brochures about different products and two separate order cards can confuse your prospect, and your response rate can drop rather than increase.

2. If you offer a "Yes" and "No" reply for your product, you may want to insert your extra offer inside the no reply envelope. In this way, you will not interrupt the buying decision of your customers, but rather influence only the leads.

3. You can test insert an extra tick box on your order form for an additional product. Choose an inexpensive product that requires little description.

Remember. Free rides can be very profitable. Do not clutter up your original offer and cause confusion for the customer. Always test the effect of a free ride on the carrying product.

▶ Take-ones

You will find most take-ones peering at you from atop the counter space in retail outlets, airline counters, banks, and movie theatres. Take-ones can be used for credit card offerings, financial information, as well as the distribution of general consumer information.

Shell Canada displays take-ones in its stations across Canada, encouraging customers to apply for a Shell credit card. And Holt Renfrew displays

You can sometimes improve the overall profitability of your promotion by including an alternate offer inside your mailing package.

take-ones for credit cards, gift certificates, and catalogues. Most banks and trust companies display racks of take-one material with information on everything from RSPs to mortgages.

A take-one display is sometimes made up of two parts: a plastic holder and a backer card. The backer card is considered a miniature poster within the plastic holder and acts as an attention-grabbing technique to stop consumers and entice them into taking one. The backer card must be clear and arresting — you have only six seconds to convey the sales message to the right target audience. Examine a few displays. Has the creative challenge been met?

▶ Catalogues

Technically, catalogues are not an autonomous medium, but rather a specific use of direct mail. Mail-order catalogues can be defined as catalogues sent through the mail to customers or prospects, who can order either by mail or by phone. Mail-order catalogues are also defined by the method of delivery — the mail. We must not forget about electronic catalogues, such as Canadian Home Shopping Network and CD-ROMs offered by many business-to-business marketers. Categorising catalogues is difficult. A non-exhaustive list could include:

- Retail store catalogues including business-to-business

- Catalogues produced by oil companies, credit card companies, and airlines to support their loyalty programs

- Specialist or vertical interest catalogues

- Seasonal catalogues, garden supplies, Christmas gift baskets, etc.

Catalogue cost analysis

As we have discovered throughout the entire direct marketing process, analyses of costs and results are important to your success and growth. Catalogues present a unique situation.

Because a catalogue or multi-item promotion piece is made up of various products, it's necessary to determine the contribution to profit from each product. You must also evaluate every page or fraction of a page, just as if each unit was a separate advertising medium.

If your catalogue is made up of 48 pages and costs $80,000, and of these 48 pages, five are dedicated to your covers and your order form, then each full page costs $1,837 ($80,000 divided by 43) and each half-page is worth $918.50. Because your covers and order form do not generate product sales, the balance of the catalogue must meet the cost difference.

Just as in any other direct marketing calculation, this space cost must be added to your cost of goods, shipping, and overhead. Based on this type of analysis, cataloguers determine the proper life span of a product and the proper space size that should be allocated.

Success in Cataloguing

Despite the abundant market opportunities, starting a mail-order catalogue business in Canada is complex, expensive, and risky. Catalogues require creative techniques that walk the consumer through the pages, directly to the order device. This is not an easy task. Many catalogues have failed because their creators did not do enough research to better understand consumer attitudes about catalogues or creative presentation techniques.

There have been some success stories and some dismal failures. Most cataloguers would agree with the old rule in the mail order business — 40 percent of your profit comes from selecting the right merchandise. Then add to that rule, service, service, and more service. Omit solid customer research and insight, and you can quickly be on shaky ground.

The most recent catalogue survey was conducted by Kubas Consultants and AC Nielsen in February 1997 and reported in CDMA's 1997/98 *Annual Fact Book*. The highlights of this survey are:

- 46 percent of consumers have ordered goods from a mail-order catalogue. This was up from 44 percent in 1996.

- Shopping by mail-order catalogue was highest in Edmonton at 53 percent and lowest in Montreal at 44 percent.

- Females, at 52 percent, were also more likely to have used mail-order catalogues than males, at 40 percent.

- Fifty-nine percent of consumers had at least one mail-order catalogue, up from 55 percent.

- The overall average per household was 1.3 catalogues.

- There was an average of 2.2 mail order catalogues in homes of respondents who reported at least one catalogue in the household.

- Overall, 60 percent of consumers were at least "a little" interested in shopping by mail-order catalogue, and 23 percent were "quite" or "extremely" interested.

Consumer catalogues face real challenges in today's market. As this book goes to press, American Express Canada Inc., the winner of many catalogue awards for excellence, has announced it will not continue its catalogue business.

Business-to-business cataloguers seem to be in a better position to offer their products and services to a group of businesses that are willing to accept catalogues as the replacement for the sales call of yesterday. For this group, the catalogue may be all it was meant to be — provide good products at a reasonable price and deliver real value and convenience. In the time-starved business world, the catalogue delivers the goods.

While all agree that the opportunities in catalogues are plentiful, it is the detail that may kill you and your profits. With the spillover of U.S. based catalogues, the Canadian cataloguer is facing strong competition. Do your homework, hire a direct marketing professional if you don't have the knowledge yourself, and get ready for your experience in mail-order catalogues.

BUILDING CUSTOMER RELATIONSHIPS

17

In preparation for this chapter, it is important that two key ideas be brought forward from chapter 1, The Nature of Direct Marketing. Upon review of the chapter, two key differences are highlighted that set direct marketing apart from other marketing disciplines: its ability to build customer relationships, and to apply a calculation for determining the lifetime value of your customers.

In A.T. Kearney's survey of CEOs, customer relationships have become the top priority, higher even than shareholder value and globalisation. In many Canadian boardrooms you can hear the questions: who is our customer? How many different relationships do we have with our customers? How loyal are our customers? What do we know about our customer's needs and behaviour? What are we doing to keep our customers? What do our customers know about us?

The business issue is the customer — not all customers are created equal. The marketing challenge is loyalty — identifying the right prospect, turning that prospect into a profitable customer, turning the profitable customer into a friend, and treating that customer as a friend for life. What you know about your customer is crucial. What you know about your relationship with them is crucial to your success.

If you're going to keep your best customers, your marketing strategy must include retention — keeping the right customers, winning back profitable customers, and identifying those customers not worth nurturing.

Although a customer database plays an important role in identifying and applying your newfound customer knowledge, this chapter is not about the construction of a customer database. The cost of the design and construction of a customer database is within the reach of most budgets and can take on many different forms — from a simple filing system to a PC-based system all the way up to mainframes — databases must be evaluated based on individual business needs and unique business applications. This chapter focuses on finding the right customers and building relationships with them for life — *relationship marketing*.

If we liken building relationships to our own life, we soon discover that we spend a lifetime building relationships in our own personal and business lives, so what makes us think that we can build relationships with our customers overnight? We can't. It takes time and patience. A commitment must be made to know customers as individuals based on their purchase patterns, behaviour, and more important, understand their expectations of us and our products.

▶ Identifying your best customers

Your best customers can be defined and segmented based on a formula of recency, frequency, and monetary value (RFM) — what customers are currently buying (R), buying repeatedly (F), and who is spending the most money (M). This formula, in combination with profiling techniques discussed in this chapter, will assist you in identifying your best customers and finding new and equally valuable customers (lifetime value) with whom you should build a relationship with for the long-term.

Relationship marketing is centered around 4 pillars:

1. Being customer focused in all your activities

2. Opening up the lines of communication for a two-way customer dialogue

3. Information and data-driven communications based on a customer file or a customer database

4. Success based on the application of customer segmentation, knowledge, and customer insight

1. Customer focused in all your activities

These two words — customer focused — have been bantered around as if any company could switch from a product focus to a customer focus overnight — it is not that easy. Being customer focused can mean turning your workplace upside down. It affects your company, its systems, and your people.

It starts at the planning stage in preparation for your marketing plan. Instead of setting objectives based on the number of products to be sold, you now move to measuring profit based on customer loyalty.

FIGURE 17-1

Customer focus process	Product focus process
Target market	Product specifications
Customer needs	Product features
Value of product to each segment	One offer for everyone
Profit through customer loyalty	**Profit through product sales volume**

This model often moves a company to redefine the roles and responsibilities of each member of its marketing team — dedicating a team to acquire profitable new customers and win back lost customers, and a second team devoted to retention of existing customers and building customer relationships, and rewarding loyal customers.

Employee incentives and rewards are therefore calculated according to retention rates of best or loyal customers and acquisition or win back of potentially profitable customers.

2. Opening up the lines of communication for a two-way customer dialogue

We must talk to our customers, listen to our customers, and respond to our customers — a truly interactive relationship.

Staying accessible to customers is not as easy as we may first think. How often do you take customer phone calls? How often does your customer service department meet with the marketing department to share your customers' concerns, complaints, and compliments? In order to set the course for the customer-focused organisation, you must experience customers first-hand. And customers must experience you and your corporate values first-hand. The customer must speak with someone who is empowered to make decisions, put forward solutions, and save or enhance the relationship.

An important component in opening up the lines of communication can also be customer research — research that confirms a customer's decision to buy the right product, from the right supplier, for the right price. These results should provide insight into understanding customer expectations before and after the purchase decision.

With the influx of large, successful loyalty programs designed to acknowledge your most loyal customer, the need for open communication becomes more important. Assigning a dedicated phone number, fax number, and address for your best customers is instrumental in defining the importance of the relationship. Your best, most loyal customers should not be getting a busy signal or be put on hold. Every communication, including fax and e-mail should be customer friendly, and should be acknowledged quickly.

3. Information and data-driven communications based on a customer file or a customer database

If you have not yet developed a customer file or database, you may wonder how to get started. Customer information may be found in various places in your company. It could be in your sales force files, in your finance department where your present customers are billed, in your customer service department where your customers call in for service or information, on warranty cards, and on the coupons that have been filled in by your customers in response to a recent offer (unfortunately, you may find those under someone's desk). Scour your office for the names of your customers.

Once you have located your customer names, develop a plan before entering them into a customer file or on a customer database.

First, analyse your needs. Second, decide how you are going to use customer information. Third, identify what you need to know about your customers in order for your customer information-driven communications plan to be successful. And that's what you have at this stage, customer information. You don't need a lot of information to start, you just need the right information.

An example of identifying what customer information was necessary to collect is demonstrated by Gerber (Canada) Inc. in the four outer envelopes on the next page. The needs analysis indicated that, based on the Gerber product line of baby food, the food was formulated according to the age of the baby. It therefore became important to collect the child's date of birth. The database based all its age calculations on date of birth and the appropriate package arrived in the mother's home in time to encourage purchase of the next age group — the congratulations package was sent on the birth of the child; the four months package just before the child turned four months; the eight months package just before the child turned eight months; and the 12 months package, just before the child turned 12 months.

For Gerber the date of birth calculation was based on months, yours may be based on years, but the same principle applies. This date of birth data formed the foundation for the creative brief that produced these award-winning and relevant communications.

Some customer information you may want to gather if you are marketing to consumers at home, includes: customer full name, full address, phone number, fax number, e-mail address, the original source of the order, product(s) purchased, purchase date for each product, and the price paid for the products. It is also important to track any special offers the customer may have responded to, such as a free 10 day trial, 50 percent off sale, or a full-price product offer.

If you are marketing to businesses, you may want to consider collecting: company name, full address, name and title of the person who ordered, name and title of person paying the bill, type of business (SIC), size of company, company phone number, direct-dial phone number(s), fax number, e-mail address, the original source of the order, product(s) purchased, date of each purchase. You may also want to note any special offers that may have generated the order. Remember. Determine what information you need and are going to use before you begin constructing your customer file or customer database. Too much information can make your customer file difficult to manage and analyse.

Whether you have a lot of customer information, or a little, there are some successful techniques you can use to enhance your existing customer information.

Outside databases, such as Dun & Bradstreet or Canadian Business List are available for rent and can be used to overlay appropriate data on your business files. Once again, don't enhance any data you won't use either for

An example of building relationships at different lifestages.

profiling your customers or building relevant product offerings and communications.

Large consumer databases are also available for enhancing customer information. Ask your list broker for list recommendations that are appropriate for your needs and customer files.

When budget permits, my personal preference for both business and consumer data enhancement methods is a personal survey delivered directly to the customer to secure the required additional information. I prefer this method because it is a good way to show customers your commitment to building a relationship with them and opening up a two-way dialogue. If packaged and introduced properly to your customer base, the information gathered from the survey becomes personal, relevant, and valuable. But once you ask customers for information, make sure you use the information for offering relevant products using their preferred channel of communication and respecting their privacy. It's not what information you use — it's how you use it.

In summary, your customer file or database should store customer characteristics, purchase behaviour, promotional history, and response patterns.

4. Success based on the application of customer segmentation, knowledge, and customer insight

Once you have gathered your customer information, your success in building relationships will come from how you apply the information.

An independent women's fashion retailer started a customer file about five years ago. On the customer file, it documented the customer's full name and address, in which primary fashion season the customer made most of her purchases, the designer name she purchased, and the colour family she most often purchased. Today, as the new season arrives, the customer receives a small hand-written card from one of the owners with actual material swatches in her favourite colour range. These colour swatches would not have been the foundation for communication if the decision to collect and use the data were not made up-front in the planning stages.

Staff at Canadian Pacific Hotels always recognise me at the front desk, know the date of my last stay, and when I arrive in the room, there's a personal hand-written note from the manager welcoming me back to the hotel. Believe me, I wouldn't stay anywhere else. That's what building customer relationships is all about — delivering the unexpected with ease and grace.

Once you know more about your customers, the customer expects you to use that information in a personal, non-intrusive way.

Multi-media sample

Client: Amex Canada
Product: Credit Card
Campaign: American Express/Air Miles credit card launch
Agency: OgilvyOne Worldwide

Creative Director: Pete McLeod
Copywriters: Pete McLeod, Colin Cunningham
Art Director: Steve Murray
Photographer: Graham French (photography),
Michael Fellini (digital imaging)
Director (broadcast): Clay Staub
Agency Producer (broadcast): Donna Hefferman

With the new no-fee credit card it had developed with Air Miles, Amex Canada was hoping to appeal to a broader customer base than that of affluent business travellers, the American Express card's traditional stronghold. The challenge was to make the new card stand out in an intensely competitive and mature Canadian marketplace.

To meet that objective, the launch campaign was targeted exclusively to active Air Miles collectors — people who would be more likely to be enticed by the prospect of using a credit card to earn additional Air Miles. Research had indicated that the ability to "double dip" would be a compelling reason for many targeted prospects to apply for such a card.

Using an integrated multi-media approach that included direct mail, awareness TV, DRTV, ESIs, take-ones, and statement inserts, the American Express/Air Miles launch campaign led to the most successful product introduction in the history of American Express in Canada.

242

Many large investment firms and financial institutions have massive customer files. Those files contain customer behaviour, products purchased and when those products were purchased. How they analyse and apply the information may be the difference between offering relevant programs to complement the customer's existing holdings and the invasion of a customer's privacy.

Here's an example of how large files may segment based on the information already held to determine the most relevant offers:

FIGURE 17-2

Segments	Holdings	Action or offer
Age: 68+	RSPs	Conversion to RIFs
Credit	Credit card, car loans	• Eliminate from card and car loan acquisition efforts • Offer credit card protection plan • Offer new car loan prior to existing loan expiration
Affluent, 45+ ages	Investments	• Begin to educate this group on your benefits and offerings for RSP investments • Offer like products with similar risk factors that should be of interest
First-time homeowners	Mortgage	• Extend credit offerings, such as renovation loans or credit card application

In applying customer knowledge, be driven by behaviour for each segment and apply that knowledge to support or identify business-building ideas.

▶ Identifying customer segments

Throughout this chapter we have discussed customer segments. But how do you start identifying important customer segments? Here is an outline of my approach and expectations when setting out to identify customer segments.

1. **Identify the problem**: Know what customer information you have, what customer information you are missing, and what you will do with the information once you have it.

2. **Apply the tools:** Apply RFM and LTV to determine broad actionable customer profitability segments. You do not want to create segments that you cannot action in your communications plan. Know which customers are profitable today and which customers can be profitable in the future. Apply profiling and modelling techniques to each of these broad segments, which will yield segments appropriate to your needs and opportunities.

3. **Measure the effect of the solution:** Put in place a predetermined measurement of success. That can be increasing product holdings of existing customers or maybe acquiring new customers that match the profile of your existing best customers.

And once you have identified actionable segments, you should have a clear description of what your existing customers look like and the business opportunities they present. I have always liked a visual portrayal of my customers so that, other than the words that go with each segment, I know how they may look if I met them face-to-face.

promote to customers in a one-to-one manner. This implies that the discrimination of customers based on some performance expectation occurs prior to the promotion. The discrimination of customers allows the development of more targeted lists and more appropriate offers based on a better understanding of the target. The use of statistics and predictive modelling are advanced tools for creating targeted lists.

A case study

This increased emphasis on building customer relationships is best demonstrated through an example of a credit card company. In the 1980s, a major marketing objective was acquisition; a focus on acquiring new customers. Minimal attention was devoted to the increasing cost of acquiring credit card customers. As a result, the cost per new customer acquired doubled: $100 to $200. Besides the increasing cost of acquiring new customers, the company experienced the erosion of its customer base from a credit-worthiness standpoint.

This erosion was caused by the surge in credit losses caused by these new credit cards. It became clear that both acquisition costs and the credit loss costs of new cards needed to be significantly reduced. Reducing both these costs dictated that the selection of prospect names had to be more targeted. However, in order to be more targeted, data at the individual level was required. Although some level of customer data was available in an ad hoc manner from previous mail tapes, it was certainly not comprehensive enough to track the full promotion history of prospects for the last couple of years.

Recognising that the targeting exercise could be facilitated with individual customer data, an organisation should focus its efforts on the development of a prospect history database.

The predictive models, which are developed using information from the database, now had access to the promotion history of the prospect. The database not only included the frequency of promotions to a given prospect, but the type of promotion. From this data, it was quickly realised that the overall targeting strategy would be significantly enhanced just by segmenting prospects into new and previous names. Predictive models were then developed for prospects within each segment. At first, models were developed for the maximisation of gross response.

Although this approach doubled overall response rates, it did not help in the reduction of overall credit losses from the new card member segment. This information led the company to adopt a strategy whereby prospects were selected by their potential profitability. In order to implement this strategy, a series of models was built that optimised response and spending, but minimised credit losses and voluntary attrition. These profitability models resulted in ROI improvements of approximately 50 percent.

2. Technology

The second factor in the growth of predictive modelling is technology. In the 1960s, only a handful of companies had the resources to apply these techniques. These organisations had assembled customer databases that could more fully capitalise on the techniques. Their system for data capture were entirely mainframe. Statistical programs and routines were written in FORTRAN or PASCAL within these mainframe systems. Although this required a tremendous amount of resources, this was easily justified by the fact that direct marketing was the key revenue generator. Technology has been able to change the playing field by making data and these statistical techniques more accessible to organisations with lesser resources. For example, regression routines can be run against a 500,000 customer record database with each record comprising 500 bytes entirely on a PC. The entire cost of the PC, plus appropriate software is $5,000 today.

3. People

The third factor for predictive modelling's growth is people. More people are becoming trained in this area as more organisations employ predictive modelling as one of their key business strategies. At the same time, the universities and colleges are also establishing new courses in this area. Many of the direct marketing courses and seminars include predictive modelling as an important subject. Despite the growth in competency within this area, the demand for predictive modelling far exceeds the available personnel. This is not surprising since once an organisation first experiences the successful results of predictive modelling, other business applications arise. With modelling-related projects growing exponentially, hiring new personnel or outsourcing become the two alternatives in meeting work requirements.

If an organisation decides to staff up in this area, some key criteria should be considered when evaluating candidates. Many organisations assume that the best candidate in this area is a PhD in statistics. Although one definitely needs to have a solid foundation in statistics, it is by no means the overriding criteria. The most successful candidates are those with the business practitioner's insights into successfully applying these techniques within a business environment. For example, when studying regression analysis at university, most case studies are dealing with R^2 of .70 or higher. In building direct marketing response models, typical R^2 range from .01 to .1. The academic with the PhD in statistics might focus on the R^2 as the true measure of the model's power. The direct marketing practitioner, while also looking at the R^2, will look at other reports to evaluate the power of the model. Through these reports, the practitioner gains insight into how effective these models would perform if they had been applied against a validation sample. We will see examples of these reports later in the chapter. There are numerous other business insights that are required for a model to be successful. This will become readily apparent later on in this chapter when we discuss the entire modelling process.

▶ Uses for predictive modelling

Predictive modelling generates the target group of customers for a given promotion. Products are offered to those customers who are most interested in the product. At the same time, customers with no interest in a given product are not bombarded with endless promotions. The result is a happy customer who has a much stronger attachment to your organisation. The types of models that can generate targeted groups depend on the type of marketing promotion.

- Acquisition models are developed to identify prospects who are most likely to become customers.

- Retention campaigns use models that identify customers who are most likely to cancel.

- Cross-sell models identify customers most likely to purchase another product from the same organisation.

All these models are campaign specific and are intended to optimise the desired customer behaviour in a given campaign. Meanwhile, LTV or profitability models are more generic since they can be applied to any campaign based on the intended objective of targeting high-potential, high-value customers.

4 steps to successful predictive modelling

We've reviewed predictive modelling as a complement of both business and technical skills. But why is this? The modelling process is not just using the appropriate statistical technique to lift performance. In fact, the statistical component of the modelling process represents one of the four major steps that are required for a model to yield successful results. These four major steps in a modelling project are as follows:

1. Problem identification
2. Creation of the analytical data environment
3. Identification of data mining tools
4. Implementation and tracking

1. The problem identification stage

The most important step is the problem identification stage. The other steps in the process become irrelevant if this first step is not done correctly. The analyst must have the insight to identify the problem, which is required for modelling. Often enough, an organisation assumes that the problem is identified. However, in the information gathering process, an analyst with excellent business skills may either identify the problem, which is of a more urgent priority, or be more specific concerning its details. One organisation may want to develop lifetime value models as a way of retaining its best customers. In discussions with the organisation, the analyst realises that customer defection has doubled in the past year. Clearly, lifetime value models allow us to focus our retention efforts on our best customers. But it may not directly address the critical business problem of defection. In this particular case, two kinds of models could be developed.

Reactivation models could be developed for defectors who are most likely to reactivate; while defection models could be developed for those customers who are high-risk defectors. Retention strategies can be developed to deal with the individual customer defection and when the same customer is at risk of defection.

Overlaying the current value of the customer along with the risk of defection further enhances the decision-making process. The following matrix demonstrates the different types of marketing approaches that could be employed if one could segment by value as well as likelihood to defect.

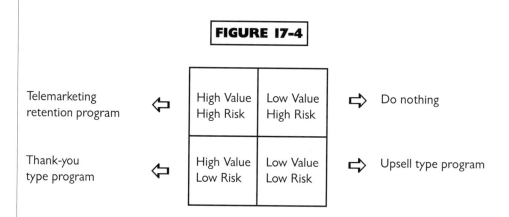

FIGURE 17-4

Another example that further demonstrates the importance of this stage can be seen in the financial institution that is trying to convert more of its regular card members into gold card members. Without asking the appropriate questions, the analyst would simply develop a model that predicts the likelihood of a regular card member becoming a gold card member. However, previous learning by the financial institution reveals regular card members spending less than $100 per month are unprofitable as gold card members.

This would indicate to the analyst that the relevant universe for building a gold card conversion model is regular card members spending more than $100 per month.

Both these examples reinforce the importance of effective information gathering when defining a problem. The information gathering process aside, the analyst must have a broad understanding of the current data environment. This understanding identifies key limitations in the development of any given model. These limitations could then help redefine the business problem such that a more appropriate selection tool be developed. If a company's marketing objective is to increase new customers, this is accomplished but at a more cost-effective rate. The solution for this organisation may be to develop acquisition models using geo-demographic overlays as a source of data in identifying those customers who are most likely to respond.

The key piece of data that is required to build an acquisition model comes from previous campaign history or data from a prior mailing that flags mailed prospects as responders and non-responders. But the analyst discovers that there is no previous campaign history to access. The company does track where its current customers live. Based on this knowledge, the analyst could recommend that the optimum solution, given the current data environment, is to provide a list of postal codes ranked by customer penetration rate.

Although the overall objective of the analysis is increased cost effectiveness of new customer acquisition, the problem definition needs to reflect the fact that customer penetration analysis is the preferred targeting technique.

Remember. This stage is the most critical in the entire modelling process. Both the gathering of information from key stakeholders in the project as well as a broad assessment of the data environment are crucial in identifying the business problem. At this stage, the required analytical skills are more practically oriented to the business needs rather than academically oriented toward achieving the best statistical solution. With the problem identified, the next major stage in the process is the creation of the analytical environment.

2. The creation of the analytical file

Some pundits refer to this stage as the data cleansing or hygiene stage. We believe that the title above best describes this stage of the process. Essentially, data needs to be organized in a manner that allows as many meaningful variables to be created as possible. More potential variables increase the likelihood that a better model can be built. This is the part of the process that causes models to yield significantly different performance levels. As most analysts have access to a wider variety of canned programmed statistical routines, the information that is fed into the model changes the performance levels of different models.

The next step is for the analyst to decide which information to include within the statistical routines.

The first task in the creation of the analytical file is to determine which source files will provide the necessary information. For most companies, we consider a customer master file, which contains customer demographics, such as name, address, start date, age, household size, etc., and a customer transaction file, containing the purchase history of the customer.

In other cases, prior promotion history may be available on a separate file. Although source files may vary from project to project, the key point is that the source file identification will be used in the analytical file extraction process. Once the source files are identified, the analyst then conducts a frequency distribution on all fields within the source file. This routine allows the analyst to exclude variables that either have a large percentage of missing values or variables that contain the same value for most of the records.

In this case (Table 17-1), the product type variables would not be considered as most of the values (95 percent) are missing.

TABLE 17-1

Product type	% of file
A	2%
B	1%
C	2%
missing	95%

Other insights provided by frequency distribution reports are how to create new variables by manipulating fields together.

FIGURE 17-5

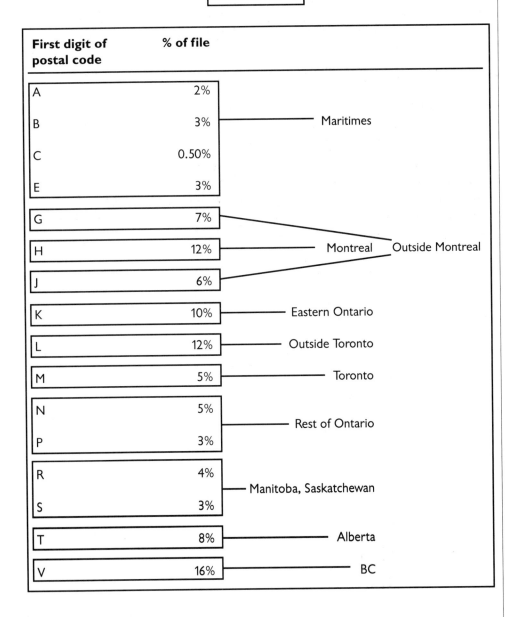

First digit of postal code	% of file	
A	2%	
B	3%	Maritimes
C	0.50%	
E	3%	
G	7%	
H	12%	Montreal / Outside Montreal
J	6%	
K	10%	Eastern Ontario
L	12%	Outside Toronto
M	5%	Toronto
N	5%	
P	3%	Rest of Ontario
R	4%	
S	3%	Manitoba, Saskatchewan
T	8%	Alberta
V	16%	BC

The above figure illustrates how an analyst can combine values of the first digit of a postal code into regional variables. Each of these above regional variables would be coded as a dummy variable (e.g.,"1" if the customer resides in the region and "0" if the customer does not reside in the region). Table 17-2 on the following page is another example of how an analyst can combine fields into other variables.

FIGURE 17-6

Gender	% of file	
Male	25%	— reported gender
Female	20%	
Missing	55%	

In the above case, another dummy variable has been created: reported gender. This field represents all customers who have reported their gender to the company.

Once the variables have been created, either directly from the source files or manufactured as a result of information from the frequency distribution, exploratory data analysis (EDA) reports are produced for the variables. These reports demonstrate if there is a relationship between a given variable and the variable we are trying to predict. By splitting a given variable into meaningful intervals, we can then ascertain whether or not there is a relationship with the given variable and the predicted variable. Let's take a look at a couple of examples.

The next example (17-2) is of variables, which we are considering for a response model.

TABLE 17-2

PERFORMANCE OF VARIABLES IN PAST CAMPAIGN

Tenure in years	% of customers	Response rate	Response index
under 1	25%	2%	57
1-2	25%	3%	86
2-4	25%	4%	114
5+	25%	5%	143
average	100%	3.5%	100

In the above case, there is a positive relationship between tenure and response rate. In other words, higher tenure customers are more likely to respond.

The response index is calculated as the response rate of the interval divided by the average response rate. For instance, the response rate index of the under one year tenure group is calculated as (2%/3.5%) x 100 or 57.

The tenure variable would represent a strong possibility as a potential model variable and its weight or coefficient would be positive.

TABLE 17-3

Age	% of customers	Response rate	Response index
under 25	25%	6%	171
25-35	25%	4.5%	128
35-50	25%	2.5%	71
50+	25%	1%	28
average	100%	3.5%	100

In 17-3 above, the relationship between age and response is negative, implying that younger customers are more likely to respond. By plotting the response indexes, one can see that the age variable produces a steeper trend line than the tenure variable. This steeper trend line would indicate, from a preliminary standpoint prior to any statistical analysis, that age is a more powerful variable than tenure. The weight or coefficient of this variable in the equation would be negative.

TABLE 17-4

Household size	% of customers	Response rate	Response index
1 person	25%	4%	114
2 persons	25%	3%	86
3 persons	25%	4%	114
4+ persons	25%	3%	86
Average	100%	3.5%	100

In the above case, we can see that no clear trend, either positive or negative, is occurring within this variable. As a result, we would expect this variable not make it into the final model equation.

These kinds of reports would be produced for all potential model variables that are on the analytical file. They are extremely useful since they can provide background information to the marketer as to why or why not a variable was included in the model. This type of information is more readily understandable to non-statisticians. However, the analyst will use information from these reports along with the statistical information in building the models. From these reports, the analyst can create further variables, such as categorical variables based on the index values. For instance, a new indexed age variable could be created with four possible categories of values for all customers: 171, 128, 71, 28.

Indexed variables have been shown to be more predictive than leaving the variable with its current range of continuous values.

The statistical information which the analyst uses in building the model is the subject of the next discussion.

3. Identification of the data mining tools

At this point in the modelling exercise, the analyst should have a feel for those variables that have a strong impact on the predicted variable. However, with the recent explosion of data mining software, a variety of statistical techniques now provide some science in the selection of variables for these models. Tools, such as chi-square activation interaction device (CHAID), neural net techniques, and different types of regression routines, are applied against the data in the analytical file.

As mentioned previously, the data and variables that are input to these routines are critical to understanding the output produced by these routines. Black box software solutions, which require minimal data involvement by the analyst, should be considered with extreme caution. These point and click solutions represent additional tools in the data analyst's tool kit. But they are not a replacement for the analyst whose expertise is invaluable. This expertise consists of interpreting the data to be considered within the model, a solid understanding of the statistical routines, and application of these routines to demonstrate the model's effectiveness.

Before actually applying the statistical modelling routines, correlation analysis is conducted on all the variables in the analytical file. This technique allows the analyst to both quantify and prioritise the significance of each variable from a statistical standpoint. Each variable is evaluated against the predicted variable or objective function. The two key numbers to focus on within the correlation analysis routine are the correlation coefficient and its confidence level. The report is produced in a manner that ranks the variables by their correlation coefficient value.

At the end of this process, we can then understand those key customer characteristics or independent variables that most impact the predicted variable, assuming that there is no relationship between the independent variables. An example of this report with six variables and their impact on response rate is listed below. In the report, the variable name is indicated with the correlation coefficient and statistical level of confidence.

FIGURE 17-7

Age	Tenure	# of products purchased
-.0673	+.0550	+.0450
99.5%	98%	97%

# of promotions since last purchase	Income	Household Size
-.0310	-.0045	+.0010
96%	50%	20%

From the 17-7 report, four variables (age, tenure, number of products purchased, and number of promotions since last purchase) are statistically significant while the other two (income and household size) are not. The sign of the correlation coefficient indicates whether the variable has a positive or negative impact on response. For instance, age and number of promotions since last purchase have a negative impact on response; while tenure and number of products purchased yield positive impacts on response rate. From these reports, one can identify the key variables that should be considered within the statistical modelling routines.

At this point in the process, one could ask why we can't simply use the results of the correlation analysis to identify key segments from the above variables as our final model. The reason is that there is always going to be some relationship or influence between the potential model variables. The correlation analysis reports do not account for this interrelationship otherwise known as multicollinearity. For example, two variables, such as tenure and age, exhibit a strong impact on the predicted variable response rate, with age being the stronger of the two variables. A high negative correlation also exists between age and tenure since both variables exhibit the opposite impact on response. In this case, it would be highly likely that only one variable of the two, namely age, would be in the final model equation. The statistical modelling routines account for both this model variable interrelationship as well as the impact on response in the determination of the final model variables

As mentioned earlier, there are a number of routines that can be used. The most appropriate technique is the one that yields the best performance when applied to a validation sample. Before discussing how we analyse modelling results through its application to a validation sample, it is important to have a basic understanding of the most frequently used statistical routines. In building predictive models, the underlying statistical objective is to maximise explained variation and minimise unexplained variation. For example, in a linear regression, if one were to plot the predicted results versus the actual results, a perfect model would yield a straight line. In other words, the variation of the predicted variable is 100 percent explained by the model equation. As this plotted line becomes bumpier, the model's explained variation decreases. The statistical reference for this explained variation is R^2.

Two regression techniques are most commonly used for direct marketing predictive models. Linear regression, as its name states, assumes that there is a linear relationship between the modelling equation and the dependent variable. The values of the dependent variable are continuous. For example, using this technique in a probability-type model, such as response or defection, yields predicted model score values that can be below "0" and above "1".

The regression technique that does yield a probability-type function is called logistic regression. The actual possible range of predicted model value scores, although continuous, is confined to values between "0" and "1". Keep in mind that the use of one technique over another is not in its ability to predict accurate predicted scores or point estimates but to enhance performance lift as demonstrated when applied within a validation sample. Once a model is produced from either of these two routines, a report should be produced that lists the final model variables, its impact on response and the strength within the equation. Table 17-5 is the same response model example, which was used in the correlation analysis.

TABLE 17-5

Variable	Impact on response	Strength within equation
Age	negative	50%
# of products purchased	positive	40%
# of promotions since last purchase	negative	20%

FIGURE 17-8

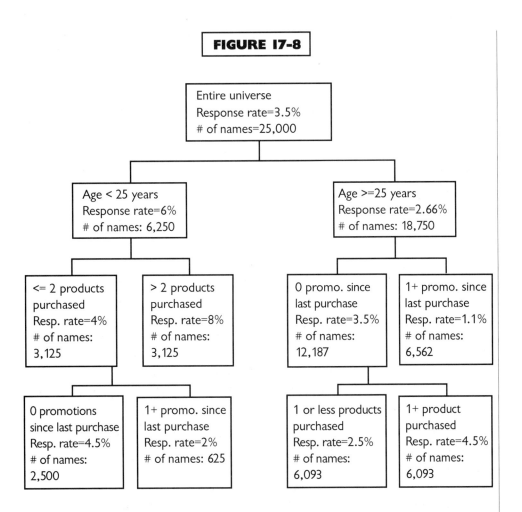

CHAID is another statistical routine used to develop predictive models. It is different from regression in that the output of the routine is not an equation but an algorithm.

The output of CHAID is a tree-like diagram with the nodes of each branch representing a segment. The actual statistics employed in CHAID are chi-square estimates of all possible variable combinations. Only those combinations that are above a certain statistical threshold (confidence level) and have a certain minimum sample size are indicated on the output report. The analyst or user can control both the confidence levels and minimum sample sizes when using this routine. This allows for more flexibility when exploring different possible models. Using the same response model example as we've seen earlier, Figure 17-8 illustrates what CHAID output would look like.

From the CHAID output, the following segments might be selected:

SEGMENT 1:   < 25 years old and purchased two or more products

SEGMENT 2:   < 25 years old and purchase less than two products and have received zero promotions since last purchase

SEGMENT 3:   >= 25 years old and have received zero promotions since last purchase and have bought one or more products.

As you can see, the actual model is a series of statements rather than an equation with coefficients or weights for each variable.

Other routines that have become more widely used in the last few years are neural net models. These models are highly complex routines that attempt to mimic the patterns and processes of neurons within the brain. Mathematically, the routine identifies nodes or distinct data patterns that best explain the variation of the predicted variables. The nature of the routine represents a series of nodes connected to each other in the form of a net. These nodes are constantly adjusted for the routine to minimise the unexplained error and maximise the explained error. In marketing-related applications, this can be quite serious in leading to erroneous assumptions as the routine has been known to overstate the actual model's effectiveness. This is because the true unexplained variation of the modelled output or random error becomes explained by the neural net routine. As a result, a huge emphasis is placed on the analyst to properly calibrate these neural net models such that these models are not overstated. Application of the routines against a validation sample allows the analyst to fine-tune the model until optimum results are achieved. The validation sample is even more critical within a neural net routine.

Now that we've discussed some of the techniques and methodology in developing models, we need to understand how to best demonstrate the model's effectiveness.

This demonstration acts as a benchmark when building models. As the analyst attempts to improve the model, he or she needs a report that represents the results of applying the model to a validation sample. This report should also easily be interpreted by marketers and used as a decision-support tool in the selection of names. On the following page is an example of the type of report that should be used in validating models. Another name for this report is the gains chart.

TABLE 17-6

GAINS CHART FOR A RESPONSE MODEL
APPLICATION OF THE MODEL TO THE VALIDATION SAMPLE

% of list (ranked by model score)	Validation mail quantity	Cum resp. rate	Interval response rate	Interval response rate lift	Cum % of all responders	Cumulative ROI	
0-10%	2500	2.20%	2.20%	220	22%	65%	
10%-20%	5000	2.00%	1.80%	180	40%	50%	
20%-30%	7500	1.80%	1.40%	140	54%	35%	
30%-40%	10000	1.63%	1.10%	110	65%	22%	List efficiency break-even point
40%-50%	**12500**	**1.50%**	**1.00%**	**100**	**75%**	**13%** →	
50%-60%	15000	1.40%	0.90%	90	84%	5%	
60%-70%	17500	1.30%	0.70%	70	91%	-3%	
70%-80%	20000	1.20%	0.50%	50	96%	-10%	
80%-90%	22500	1.10%	0.30%	30	99%	-18%	
80%-100%	25000	1.00%	0.10%	10	100%	-25%	

Assumption: Revenue is $60, which is the card fee.

No incremental spend is included in the revenue number.

Cost of 1 mail piece is $.80

The gains chart

The results of the gains chart on the opposite page represent how the model would have performed if it had been applied against a validation sample. The model's performance can be evaluated by analysing the interval response rate lift at each decile. The response rate lift is simply the interval response rate divided by the average response rate with no modelling (one percent). Stronger models will have higher response rate lifts at the top of the gains chart with lower response rate lifts at the bottom. By plotting the response rate lifts at each decile of the gains chart, we can then produce a Lorenz curve. The analyst's objective in building predictive models is to make this Lorenz curve as steep as possible. In assessing other models or even other techniques, the analyst can always use the resulting Lorenz curves to determine the best model or technique.

As a marketing tool in selecting names, the gains chart is invaluable. A number of columns can be used for decision-making by the marketer. The cumulative response rate column indicates the expected response rate performance at a given percentage of the list. Although in this example, we are assuming an overall response rate of one percent without modelling, the marketer can produce different versions of this gains chart with different overall response rate scenarios. For example, if the overall response rate with no modelling is two percent, then the cumulative response rates at each decile doubles. Remember. The model's deliverable is response rate lift not response rate. Given this understanding, the marketer can employ sensitivity analysis to see the impact of the model at different response rate scenarios.

Besides the cumulative response rate results, decisions concerning the selection of names can also be made from an ROI or list efficiency standpoint. Using ROI, the cut off for selecting names might be at 20 percent of the list if the company ROI threshold is 50 percent or higher. The list efficiency break-even point occurs at 50 percent of the list. This is the point in the list where the response rate lift falls below 100. Below this point, the interval response rates are below the overall response rate average of one percent.

As you can see, this report is flexible in providing the necessary information given the marketer's objective. With the model developed and validated through the results of the gains chart, the modelling exercise is still not finished. Powerful models can be built, but the results can go awry if not implemented correctly. As well, tracking schemes should be designed to evaluate the model's performance within a live campaign.

4. Implementation and tracking

The best way to demonstrate the significance of this phase is through an example. On the next page is a response rate model and its application within the validation sample during time of development and its application within a live marketing campaign. In this example (17-7), we are only looking at the top five deciles.

TABLE 17-7

% of list	Minimum score (validation sample)	Minimum score (current campaign)
0-10%	.080	.040
10%-20%	.070	.030
20%-30%	.060	.020
30%-40%	.050	.010
40%-50%	.040	.004

These results from the above table are a major warning flag to the analyst as the score ranges are different between the validation sample and the current campaign. Before implementing the model, investigation would have to occur in order to determine why we are seeing these drastically different score range results. As part of this process, the analyst would actually take a dump of 10 customer records along with their model scores. The analyst would then manually calculate the scores for each customer record to ensure that the modelling algorithm has been properly applied to the customer base. The next question would be whether this model is being currently applied to a different base of customers than the base that was used in model development. For instance, a model that has been developed across Canada but is only applied in Quebec would produce drastically different score range results. Another question to be asked is whether one of the model variables has changed between time of development and the current campaign. As customer databases evolve, some variables are either eliminated or are modified to reflect the new meaning of the variable. If all these questions are pursued by the analyst, then resolution will occur as to why these score range results are different. There may not be anything the analyst can do to change the model. However, expected results can be modified if we understand the reason for this gap in score range results.

In tracking the model within a live campaign, cell codes can be established, which evaluate the model's performance. As we stated before, the model's deliverable is performance lift and not actual response rates. As a result, we expect the model to rank names effectively in order to achieve a given expected lift. By placing cell codes at different intervals of a scored file, we can then see how well the model rank orders names and achieves its expected lift. In the response rate case, we might want to attach 10 cell codes at each decile of the list in order to obtain results. We could then compare the results of the live campaign versus the results experienced on the validation sample.

▶ Conclusion

Predictive modelling has become an extremely vital component of direct marketing programs. By targeting the appropriate customers, the overall customer relationship is further enhanced.

Technological advances now provide access to these tools by most organisations. However, the real challenge is identifying the appropriate persons to build the models. Developing predictive models involves much more than an advanced knowledge of statistics. In fact, an advanced knowledge of statistics, although desirable, is not a prerequisite for developing models. Certainly, analysts should have a strong quantitative background. They must also have strong business and programming skills. If organisations hire personnel with a good complement of business, technical, and quantitative skills, they will be more successful in their predictive modelling.

WHY SATISFIED CUSTOMERS DEFECT

18

The gulf between satisfied customers and completely satisfied customers can swallow a business.

Why Satisfied Customers Defect

by Thomas O. Jones and W. Earl Sasser, Jr.

The scene is familiar: the monthly management meeting attended by a company's senior officers and the general managers of its operating divisions. The company's eight divisions operate in diverse markets, including light manufacturing, wholesale distribution, and consumer services. All are feeling pressure from strong competitors, and the corporation has created a customer-satisfaction survey as one method of measuring the impact of its quality-improvement process.

After dispensing with several items on the agenda, the group turns to the third-quarter customer-satisfaction indices, and a transparency is placed on the overhead projector. (See the graph "Third Quarter Satisfaction Index.") The CEO proudly points out that 82% of the customers surveyed responded with an overall satisfaction rating of either 4 (satisfied) or 5 (completely satisfied). Everyone in the meeting agrees that the company must be doing pretty well because only 18% of its customers were less than satisfied.

There are three divisions with average ratings of 4.5 or higher. There is general consensus that they have reached the point of diminishing returns and that further investing to increase customer satisfaction will not make good financial sense.

The group next examines the results of the division with the lowest average rating, a 2.7. This busi-ness unit manufactures bulk lubricants and sells to companies that repackage the product for sale to the retail channel. It is a highly competitive, commodity-type business and operates with very tight margins. The group concludes that the lubricant division's market is difficult and that its price-sensitive customers will never be satisfied. Moreover, the division's rating is equal to or above those of most competitors. There is a general consensus that its customers are a lost cause and that it does not pay to make additional investments to try to satisfy them.

Finally, the discussion turns to four business units whose customers generally are neutral or pleased but certainly not delighted. Two divisions manufacture large industrial machinery. Two other divisions provide after-market service for the products of both the company and its competitors. Each division has an average rating between 3.5 and 4.5, meaning that, although the majority of their customers are not dissatisfied or neutral, a significant number are. "Our battle plan is to find out what's making the least-satisfied customers mad and fix it!" the head of one industrial-machinery division says. The others nod in agreement.

Implicit in this discussion are a number of beliefs widely held by managers of the dozens of manufacturing and service companies we have studied.

First, it is sufficient merely to satisfy a customer; as long as a customer responds with at least a satisfied rating (a 4), the company-customer relationship is strong. In other words, a level of satisfaction below complete or total satisfaction is acceptable. After all, this is the real world, where products and services are rarely perfect and people are hard to please. Second, the investment required to change customers from satisfied to completely satisfied will not provide an attractive financial return and therefore probably is not a wise use of resources. Indeed, there may even be instances – most notably, when competing in a cutthroat commodity market – where it doesn't pay to try to satisfy any customers. Finally, each division with a relatively high average rating (3.5 to 4.5) should focus on the customers in its lowest-satisfaction categories (1 to 2). Striving to understand the causes of their dissatisfaction and concentrating efforts on addressing them is the best use of resources.

The extensive research that we conducted on the relationship between customer satisfaction and customer loyalty, however, shows that these assumptions are deeply flawed. They either ignore or do not accord enough importance to the following aspects of the relationship:

□ *Except in a few rare instances, complete customer satisfaction is the key to securing customer loyalty and generating superior long-term financial performance.* Most managers realize that the more competitive the market, the more important the level of customer satisfaction. What most do not realize, however, is just how important the level of customer satisfaction is in markets where competition is intense, such as hard and soft durables, business equipment, financial services, and retailing. In markets like these, there is a tremendous difference between the loyalty of merely satisfied and completely satisfied customers. (See the graph "How the Competitive Environment Affects the Satisfaction-Loyalty Relationship.") As the steep curve for the automobile industry shows, completely satisfied customers are – to a surprising degree – much more loyal than satisfied customers. To put it another way, any drop from total satisfaction results in a major drop in loyalty. The same applies to commodity businesses with thin profit margins; the potential returns on initiatives to increase

Thomas O. Jones is president of Elm Square Technologies, a company in Andover, Massachusetts, that is developing advanced customer-service software. He formerly was a senior lecturer in the Harvard Business School's service management interest group. W. Earl Sasser, Jr., is the UPS Professor of Service Management and senior associate dean responsible for executive education at the Harvard Business School in Boston, Massachusetts.

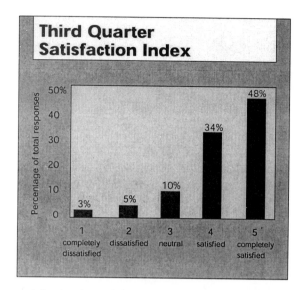

Third Quarter Satisfaction Index

Percentage of total responses

1 completely dissatisfied	3%
2 dissatisfied	5%
3 neutral	10%
4 satisfied	34%
5 completely satisfied	48%

satisfaction in such businesses can be as high as the return on initiatives in more profitable businesses. In fact, attempts to create complete customer satisfaction in commodity industries will often raise the product or service out of the commodity category. In most instances, totally satisfying the members of the targeted customer group should be a top priority.

□ *Even in markets with relatively little competition, providing customers with outstanding value may be the only reliable way to achieve sustained customer satisfaction and loyalty.* There are two types of loyalty: true long-term loyalty and what we call false loyalty. A variety of factors can generate false loyalty or make customers seem deeply loyal when they are not. They include: government regulations that limit competition; high switching costs such as the cost of changing hospitals in the middle of treatment; proprietary technology that limits alternatives; and strong loyalty-promotion programs such as frequent-flier plans. But we made a startling discovery about customers in such markets. Whenever these customers have choices and feel free to make a choice, they act like customers in markets with intense competition: They will only remain rock-solid loyal if they are completely satisfied. That is why seemingly loyal customers defect when they exhaust their frequent-flier miles, when they complete a course of treatment at a hospital, when a regulated market is deregulated, and when alternative technologies are offered. In such markets, it is the companies, rather than their customers, who ultimately have no choice. They must strive to provide their prized customers – those they can serve most profitably – with outstanding value. The message is clear: It is absolutely critical for a company to excel in both defining its target customers and delivering a product or service that completely meets their needs.

□ *Very poor service or products are not the only cause – and may not even be the main cause – of high dissatisfaction. Often the company has attracted the wrong customers or has an inadequate process for turning around the right customers when they have a bad experience.* Customers typically fall into one of two categories: the right customers, or target group, whom the company should be able to serve well and profitably, and the wrong customers, whose needs it cannot profitably serve. Having the wrong customers is the result of a flawed process for attracting or obtaining customers. The company that retains difficult-to-serve, chronically unhappy customers is making an expensive long-term mistake. Such customers will continually utilize a disproportionate amount of the company's resources, will hurt the morale of frontline employees, and will disparage the company to other potential customers. Managers should actively discourage such people or organizations from remaining customers and should do their best not to attract others like them. On the other hand, managers of companies that are generally delivering high-quality services or products obviously want to keep their targeted customers and should strive to make amends when, inevitably, something goes wrong. Marked unhappiness among targeted customers often means a problem was not resolved to their satisfaction.

□ *Different satisfaction levels reflect different issues and, therefore, require different actions.* The levels of satisfaction among targeted customers are a good indicator of the level of quality of the products or services that they are receiving. But the way to raise the level of customer satisfaction from neutral to satisfied or from satisfied to completely satisfied is not just a matter of doing a better job of delivering the same value or experience that the company is currently delivering. There are four elements that affect customer satisfaction: the basic elements of the product or service that customers expect all competitors to deliver; basic support services such as customer assistance or order tracking that make the product or service incrementally more effective and easier to use; a recovery process for counteracting bad experiences; and extraordinary services that so excel in meeting customers' personal preferences, in appealing to their values, or in solving their particular problems that they make the product or service seem customized. As we will discuss later, the satisfaction or dissatisfaction level of the majority of a company's customers helps determine which of these elements the company should focus on delivering.

□ *Even though the results of customer-satisfaction surveys are an important indicator of the health of the business, relying solely on them can be fatal.* Customer-satisfaction surveys can generate valuable information that enables a company to compare the performance of one business unit or several business units in different time periods and locations. They can provide leading indicators of market shifts and can provide a clear sense of the product or service attributes that individual customers most desire. However, customer-satisfaction surveys cannot supply the breadth and depth of information about customers needed to guide the company's strategy and product-innovation process. Satisfaction surveys alone will not enable a company to fend off new competitors or to keep products and services attuned to customers' changing needs. For this reason, companies must also utilize a variety of other methods to listen to existing, potential, and former customers. (See the insert "How to Listen to Customers.")

The Satisfaction-Loyalty Link

Executives at Xerox Corporation, which had conducted in-depth satisfaction studies of its office-products customers, played a major role in helping us define our research project. Xerox's intense interest in measuring customer satisfaction sprang from a set of beliefs that we share. High-quality products and associated services designed to meet customer needs will create high levels of customer satisfaction. This high level of satisfaction will lead to greatly increased customer loyalty. And increased customer loyalty is the single most important driver of long-term financial performance. Separate research has validated these beliefs. (See "Zero Defections: Quality Comes to Services," by Frederick F. Reichheld and W. Earl Sasser, Jr., HBR September-October 1990.)

Although these assumptions might seem relatively simple, one discovery by Xerox shattered conventional wisdom: Its totally satisfied customers were six times more likely to repurchase Xerox products over the next 18 months than its satisfied customers. The implications were profound: Merely satisfying customers who have the freedom to make choices is not enough to keep them loyal. The only truly loyal customers are totally satisfied customers.

The Research. Xerox's discovery intrigued us. Was this relationship between satisfaction and loyalty unique to Xerox? To investigate, we scrutinized more than 30 individual companies and analyzed data from five markets with different competitive environments and different types of customer relationships. The five markets were automobiles, personal computers purchased by businesses, hospitals, airlines, and local telephone services. To measure customer loyalty, we decided to rely mostly on customers' stated intent to repurchase products or services. (See the insert "Measures of Loyalty.") We selected the five markets for particular reasons.

□*Automobiles.* We chose automobiles to test whether Xerox's discovery–that its completely satisfied customers were significantly more likely to repurchase its products than its simply satisfied customers – was a fluke or the norm in highly competitive markets. By highly competitive markets we mean those in which there are many alternative products or services offered, the cost of switching is low, or the product is not important to the buyer (that is, where a valid substitute is no purchase at all). Our data on the buyers of 32 automobile models were provided by Robert Lunn of J.D. Power and Associates, the market-research company based in Agoura Hills, California. J.D. Power surveyed these individuals one year after they had purchased their vehicles.

How the Competitive Environment Affects the Satisfaction-Loyalty Relationship

Noncompetitive Zone
Regulated monopoly or few substitutes
Dominant brand equity
High cost of switching
Powerful loyalty program
Proprietary technology

Highly Competitive Zone
Commoditization or low differentiation
Consumer indifference
Many substitutes
Low cost of switching

local telephone
airlines
personal computers
hospitals
automobiles

Loyalty — high / low
Satisfaction — 1 completely dissatisfied ... 5 completely satisfied

The 32 nameplates included both foreign and domestic models with high, medium, and low prices.
□ *Personal Computers for Businesses.* We studied this industry to explore the satisfaction-loyalty relationship in a market where the user is not the actual purchaser. Although the personal-computer market is highly competitive, considerable barriers prevent individual business users from switching to another manufacturer's personal computer: for example, centralized purchasing and corporate standards. On the other hand, central purchasing departments do periodically reconsider their suppliers. And in the last ten years, corporate purchasing departments have placed a greater focus on pleasing their customers: the actual users of the equipment they buy. To test how satisfaction affected the loyalty of the end users, we analyzed data from J.D. Power's 1994 survey of more than 2,000 business users of personal computers.

□ *Hospitals.* We chose the hospital market because of two interesting characteristics: Although it is shifting from a market dominated by semi-monopolies to one characterized by intense competition, there still remain significant barriers that impede end users (patients) from switching. Several factors affect the choice of a particular hospital. The patient's physician, health maintenance organization, or insurer often determines where he or she goes for treatment; after beginning treatment in a hospital, a patient tends to complete treatment there; and finally, in many parts of the country, there is only one hospital within a convenient distance. Nonetheless, there are moments when the barriers drop and patients can and do switch. To test how these kinds of barriers affect the satisfaction-loyalty relationship, we relied on data taken from 10,000 surveys of patients treated at nearly 82 hospitals in a range of locations in the United States. David Furse, president of NCG Research – a company based in Nashville, Tennessee, that measures service quality and customer satisfaction in the health care industry – provided us with the data.

□ *Airlines.* This market interested us because it is one in which the varying level of competition on routes and strong loyalty-promotion programs affect purchasing decisions. Since airlines are relatively efficient in responding to competitors' price changes, most people flying on a particular route heavily base their purchasing decisions on two other factors: time of departure and frequent-flier programs. Although some routes are highly competitive, the fact of the matter is that people who have to go to a certain place at a certain time often have few if any alternatives: The route is a virtual monopoly. To explore the impact of all these factors on the satisfaction-loyalty relationship, we analyzed data from a survey that J.D. Power conducted in the first quarter of 1994. The survey questioned approximately 20,000 passengers who used the eight largest domestic airlines and flew on 72 routes.

□ *Local Telephone Services.* We analyzed data provided by a Bell operating company to explore the nature of the relationship in actual or virtual monopolies, in which satisfaction seems to have little impact on loyalty. More specifically, we wanted to understand better how the satisfaction-loyalty relationship might change if the competitive environment suddenly changed – a critical issue for monopolies facing deregulation, global competition, and technological change. By actual or virtual monopolies, we mean companies that operate in markets where, thanks to government regulations, proprietary technology, or very strong brand equity, there is little or no competition. Others in this category include: electrical utilities; cable television providers; transportation utilities with special rights of way; companies with brand identities that are so strong that the customers perceive there to be no other choice; and companies in competitive industries where the barriers that prevent customers from switching to another supplier are high (a restaurant at the top of a ski lift, for example).

The Indications. Of the five markets, local telephone service, with nearly complete control over customers, was the only one for which the relationship between satisfaction and loyalty turned out exactly as one would expect. Customers remained loyal no matter how dissatisfied they were. But our study of other actual or virtual monopolies did yield one vitally important discovery: When the source of a monopoly's hold on customers suddenly disappears – whether the cause is deregulation, the emergence of an alternative technology, or the arrival of new competitors – the curve can snap into the shape of a highly competitive market in an astonishingly short period of time.

According to conventional wisdom, the link between satisfaction and loyalty in markets where customers have choices is a simple, linear relationship: As satisfaction goes up, so does loyalty. But we discovered that the relationship was neither linear nor simple. To a much greater extent than most managers think, completely satisfied customers are more loyal than merely satisfied customers.

In markets where competition is intense, we found a tremendous difference between the loyalty of satisfied and completely satisfied customers. In the automobile industry, even a slight drop from complete satisfaction created an enormous drop in loyalty. This dramatic phenomenon is not limited

How to Listen to Customers

At the heart of any successful strategy to manage satisfaction is the ability to listen to the customer. There are five major categories of approaches that companies can use to listen to their customers. Most highly successful companies employ several, if not all. Many average or poor performers either use very few or, if they use many, do a poor job of incorporating the results into their strategies. The five categories are:

Customer-Satisfaction Indices. Surveying customers about their level of satisfaction and plotting the results can help managers understand just how satisfied or dissatisfied customers are with both their dealings with the company in general and with various elements of the company's product or service in particular. The fact that such indices are quantitative makes them a useful tool for comparing results from different time periods, locations, and business units.

Feedback. Customers' comments, complaints, and questions fall into this category. A company cannot implement a recovery strategy – a plan for making amends when something has gone wrong – if it does not know who has had a problem. Therefore, it is important to review the company's approach to soliciting feedback – especially complaints – on product and service quality.

Market Research. Although companies traditionally invest significantly in this area, they often overlook two critical listening points. Customers should be interviewed both at the time of arrival (when they become customers) and at the time of departure (when they defect) about the reasons for their behavior. New customers should not only be asked, "How did you hear about us?" but also, "What major experiences influenced your decision to try our product or service?" The answers to the first question will provide data about the effectiveness of the company's awareness advertising, and the answers to the second will supply information about specific factors that actually sparked the decision to try the product or service. It also is absolutely critical to understand why a customer defected. Gleaning that information requires a high degree of sensitivity and skill because most customers will blame the price or some other relatively basic product attribute in order to avoid discussing the real issue. Carefully questioning departing customers is important for two reasons: to isolate those attributes of the company's product or service that are causing customers to leave and to make a last-ditch attempt to keep the customer. One company we studied found that it recaptured a full 35% of its defectors just by contacting them and listening to them earnestly.

Frontline Personnel. Employees who have direct contact with the customer provide a superb means of listening. To take full advantage of frontline employees' interactions with customers, however, a company must train them to listen effectively and to make the first attempts at amends when customers have bad experiences. They also must have processes in place to capture the information and pass it along to the rest of the company. Many companies that excel in satisfying customers have institutionalized one other practice: All employees – not just those with frontline jobs – spend a significant amount of time interacting in depth with customers.

Strategic Activities. Some companies go to extremes to involve the customer in every level of their business. MTV, the cable music channel geared to 18- to 24-year-olds, insists that most of its employees must belong to the demographic target group. Southwest Airlines actually invites frequent fliers to its first round of group interviews with prospective flight attendants and considers these customers' opinions in decisions to invite certain candidates back for individual interviews. Intuit, the financial-software company, regularly brings in customers to participate in product-development sessions.

---

to markets for manufactured products: It also occurs in services. In his study of the loyalty of retail-banking depositors, John Larson, a vice president of Opinion Research Corporation in Princeton, New Jersey, found that completely satisfied customers were nearly 42% more likely to be loyal than merely satisfied customers.

How about the curves for hospitals, airlines, and personal computers sold to businesses – industries whose holds on customers fall somewhere between automobiles and local telephone services? They also held surprises. We discovered that customer satisfaction in those industries, too, can affect customer loyalty much more than managers generally assume. Equally if not more important, we discovered that at certain times or under certain circumstances, satisfaction has a much bigger impact on loyalty. In these cases, the curve can snap into the shape of a curve of a more competitive – even a highly competitive – market.

Of the three midrange markets, the steepest drop in the loyalty of end users relative to satisfaction was in the business-PC market. Why should manufacturers of personal computers care? Why should manufacturers care? Because, when the time comes for IT or purchasing departments to replace the cur-

Measures of Loyalty

Broadly speaking, customer loyalty is the feeling of attachment to or affection for a company's people, products, or services. These feelings manifest themselves in many forms of customer behavior. The ultimate measure of loyalty, of course, is share of purchases in the category. In the automobile business, it is share of garage. In the clothing industry, it is share of closet. And in the restaurant business, as Taco Bell president and CEO John Martin says, it is "share of stomach."

Unfortunately, such information is rarely available at the individual customer level. But there are alternative measurements, which we have grouped into three major categories.

Intent to Repurchase. At any time in the customer relationship, it is possible to ask customers about their future intentions to repurchase a given product or service. Although their responses are simply indications of future behavior and are not assurances, they have very important benefits. First, companies can capture this information when they measure satisfaction, making it relatively easy to link intentions and satisfaction for analytical purposes. The fact that intent to repurchase can be measured at any time in the customer relationship makes it especially valuable in industries with a long repurchase cycle. Finally, intent to repurchase actually is a very strong indicator of future behavior. Although this measure will generally overstate the probability of repurchase, the degree of exaggeration usually is fairly consistent, meaning that the future results can be predicted fairly accurately. For example, an average of 60% to 80% of automobile customers queried 90 days after buying a car say they intend to repurchase the same brand, and 35% to 40% actually do so three to four years later.

Primary Behavior. Depending on the industry, companies often have access to information on various transactions at the customer level and can measure five categories that show actual repurchasing behavior: recency, frequency, amount, retention, and longevity. Although they are important measures of actual behavior, they only provide a glimpse of overall share and are most useful as an indication of changes over time. Moreover, sometimes they can send the wrong message. For example, the credit-card industry traditionally measured the willingness of the consumer to pay the annual fee as its prime measure of retention. During the late 1980s and early 1990s, those same companies saw that willingness rise while actual "share of wallet" – the degree to which customers used their particular card for making purchases when they had the option of using a credit card – decreased. The consumer was willing to pay the fee to have the credit card available but often did not use it. Therefore, recency, frequency, and amount of purchase were significantly better measures of loyalty.

Secondary Behavior. Customer referrals, endorsements, and spreading the word are extremely important forms of consumer behavior for a company. In most product and service categories, word of mouth is one of the most important factors in acquiring new customers. Frequently, it is easier for a customer to respond honestly to a question about whether he or she would recommend the product or service to others than to a question about whether he or she intended to repurchase the product or service. Such indications of loyalty, obtained through customer surveys, are frequently ignored because they are *soft* measures of behavior that are difficult to link to eventual purchasing behavior. However, since secondary behavior significantly leverages the positive experiences of a single customer, it is very important to understand what types of experiences create such behavior.

rent generation of PCs, end-user satisfaction may suddenly have a big impact on customer loyalty. The curve snaps.

The next steepest drop in loyalty occurred in the hospital market – and it promises to become steeper as competition in the industry intensifies. Nonetheless, most hospitals are still operating as if they had little effective competition. They continue to place little emphasis on patient satisfaction. One can speculate about the reasons. Perhaps their managers think that the centralization of purchasing power makes health maintenance organizations and insurers, rather than individuals, the ones to please. Perhaps they think this centralization will only raise the barriers that block dissatisfied patients from switching. If so, they may be in for a shock. After all, many HMOs and insurers provide their subscribers with a menu of hospitals from which to choose. Moreover, individuals often can switch health plans if they don't like the hospitals on the menu – a fact not lost on HMOs. Although a patient may not be free to change hospitals at any time, there will be a time when the patient or HMO or insurer can. The curve snaps.

In mixed markets such as airlines, achieving a high level of customer satisfaction matters for several reasons. Although a combination of limited choice and artificial restraints such as frequent-flier programs often cause even completely dissatisfied airline customers to remain fairly loyal, the relationship between satisfaction and loyalty does resemble a competitive market on routes where several carriers offer flights at around the same time. This fact means that complete customer satisfaction is very important on both competitive routes and monopoly routes. Why is it important on monopoly routes? Because, as several larger airlines have learned, customers who have suffered years of mediocre or poor service on such routes can still take their revenge. When traveling on other routes where there is competition, they can choose another airline. And if a new, lower-priced competitor suddenly challenges the monopoly, even a frequent-flier program will not be enough to retain them.

Take heed. Although customers sometimes defect en masse, their departure may also occur in harder-to-spot dribs and drabs or spurts. Patients typically defect only after completing a course of treatment. An advertising agency client may defect only when it is time to undertake a new marketing campaign. A major corporate customer may defect from a bank only when an account executive with whom the customer had a personal relationship leaves. In these cases, the business is suddenly operating in a more competitive environment. The curve snaps. It is a time of maximum vulnerability for the company. And if it takes a while to lose such customers, it takes just as long to recapture them once they have moved to another supplier.

What is the overarching lesson? Customers are reasonable, but they want to be completely satisfied; if they are not and have a choice, they can be lured away easily. (See the table "They Suffered the Consequences.") In today's turbulent world, measuring customers' outward loyalty does not suffice. Nor does knowing whether the satisfaction-loyalty relationship a company enjoys with the majority of its customers is the norm for its market. It is essential to understand what portion of customers' seeming loyalty is true loyalty based on a company's delivery of superior value and what part is artificial. Measuring customer satisfaction is one of the safest ways to obtain this information. If there is a solid likelihood that the level of competition in a market is going to increase, it is obviously better to seek to increase customer satisfaction before the

They Suffered the Consequences

Industries or Companies That Experienced a Rapid Change in Customer Loyalty	Reason for Shift in Customer Loyalty
Telecommunications, airlines, electrical power, savings and loan associations	Deregulation
Xerox, Roche (Valium)	Loss of patent protection
Electronics, U.S. auto industry	Entrance of new competitors
American Express, IBM	Reduction in brand dominance
IBM, Digital Equipment Corporation	Advent of new technologies

curve snaps than after. The safest approach is to seek total customer satisfaction.

Consequently, most managers should be concerned rather than heartened if the majority of their customers fall into the satisfied category. Those customers have reasons for not being completely satisfied. Some element (or elements) of their experience with the company was not acceptable, and that shortfall in performance is sufficient for them to consider alternatives. Some might ask, Then why did these customers say they were satisfied in the first place? The answer is: Regardless of how they feel, customers of companies with reasonably good product or service quality tend to find it difficult to respond negatively to customer-satisfaction surveys. As a result, their satisfaction responses typically fall in the upper end of the scale – a 4 or 5 on a scale of 1 to 5. Rather than thinking of customers as loyal or disloyal, managers would be better off treating them as three separate groups. (See the table "Interpreting Levels of Satisfaction.")

Like the managers of the company described at the beginning of this article, most managers probably would be happy to learn that 82% of their customers fell into category 4 or 5. The more appropriate reaction would be, "We have a problem. Only 48% of our customers are completely satisfied, and 52% are up for grabs."

Using Customer-Satisfaction Information

Customer-satisfaction information can be a critical barometer of how well a company is serving its customers. This information also can show a company what it needs to do to increase its customer satisfaction level by level until the majority of its

Apostles and Terrorists:
A Company's Best Friends and Worst Enemies

Although it is important and valuable to track and understand the satisfaction and loyalty of customers as a group, it is equally critical to understand the attitudes and behavior of individual customers. Depending on their unique behavioral attributes (prior individual biases), intensity of satisfaction or dissatisfaction (attitude), and ability to act on their satisfaction or dissatisfaction (competitive market dynamics), customers behave in one of four basic ways: as loyalists, as defectors, as mercenaries, or as hostages. Turning as many customers as possible into the most valuable type of loyalist, the apostle, and eliminating the most dangerous type of defector or hostage, the terrorist, should be every company's ultimate objective. (See the table "Individual Customer Satisfaction, Loyalty, and Behavior.")

The Loyalist and the Apostle

In most cases, the loyalist is a customer who is completely satisfied and keeps returning to the company. The loyalist is a company's bedrock. This customer's needs and the company's product or service offerings fit exceptionally well, which, not surprisingly, is why loyalists often are the easiest customers to serve. Occasionally, the match is so good that even a 5 on a 1-to-5 satisfaction scale doesn't fully capture the strength of the relationship.

Within the loyalist camp are individuals who are so satisfied, whose experience so far exceeds their expectations, that they share their strong feelings with others. They are apostles.

One company that excels in creating apostles is Intuit, maker of Quicken, the phenomenally successful financial-management software. Although Intuit has fewer than ten sales employees, it has hundreds of thousands of salespeople: its highly satisfied customers, who found the company's product and its customer-service staff so responsive to their unique needs that they had to tell someone else. "When you treat a customer so well that he or she goes out and tells five

friends how great it is to own your product – that's when you're doing it right," says Scott Cook, Intuit's cofounder and chairman of the board.

Treating customers exceptionally well does not mean merely treating them well when everything basically is going right. It also means treating them exceptionally well when something goes terribly wrong. Highly dissatisfied customers typically include people who were highly satisfied until they purchased a single shoddy product or suffered a service failure or a sequence of unrelated failures. If a company excels in making amends – that is, in recovering – when such failures occur, customers' faith in the company is not just restored, it is deepened; and they become apostles, spreading the good word about the company to potential customers.

Of course, a company can only turn such customers into apostles if they come forward. For this reason alone, it more than pays to provide customers with numerous opportunities to express their dissatisfaction. Companies with world-class recovery organizations frequently ask customers if they are satisfied, provide toll-free customer comment numbers, fully involve frontline employees in the crusade to identify and help customers frustrated by service or product failures, and regularly review their approaches to dealing with customer problems.

The Defector and the Terrorist

Defectors' ranks include those who are more than dissatisfied, quite dissatisfied, and neutral. The merely satisfied – many more than most managers realize – defect, too. And as we've said, so do once highly satisfied customers who have encountered failures. Letting those customers defect is perhaps the biggest mistake managers can make. When a company has strong processes in place to understand such customers' needs better and to shower attention on them if isolated problems strike, most of them can be converted or turned once again into highly satisfied customers.

customers are totally satisfied. The key is understanding what customers are saying when they provide various responses.

The first step is to make the measurement of customer satisfaction and loyalty a priority and to ensure that the process is unbiased, consistent, broadly applied, and able to capture and store information on individual customers. The process should be unbiased because typically there are forces within the company that will attempt to dis-

tort it for their own purposes. It should be consistent so that period-to-period changes have meaning. It should be broadly applied so that products, locations, and business units can be compared in order to help managers decide how to use the company's limited resources most effectively. Last but not least, the measurement process should capture information on individual customers so that the company can tailor its satisfaction-improvement programs to its individual customers' situations.

Not all defectors should be retained, however. The unreasonable demands of unhappy customers whose needs do not fit with the company's capabilities can devour excessive resources and wreak havoc on employee morale. For just this reason, such outstanding service organizations as Nordstrom department stores, Sewell Village Cadillac Company in Dallas, and Southwest Airlines regularly "fire" customers they cannot properly serve. They recognize counterproductive efforts when they see them.

The most dangerous defectors are the terrorists. These are the customers who have had a bad experience and can't wait to tell others about their anger and frustration. They are the airline passengers who because of bad weather were stranded at an alternate airport and were not given appropriate assistance. They are the retail customers who found that the product they just bought did not work and encountered an inept or uncaring service employee when they tried to get help or compensation. They are the new car owners who had to return countless times to try to get the same problem fixed. With each telling, their stories grow in intensity and the actual facts become increasingly distorted.

Unfortunately, terrorists generally are far more committed and hence more effective at telling their stories than apostles. Like many apostles, they had bad experiences. But in their case, no one listened, no one responded, no one corrected the problem.

The Mercenary

Another customer who can make a company's life miserable is the mercenary. This individual defies the satisfaction-loyalty rule: He may be completely satisfied but exhibit almost no loyalty. These customers are often expensive to acquire and quick to depart. They chase low prices, buy on impulse, pursue fashion trends, or seek change for the sake of change. Although it often takes as much effort to please them as to please long-term loyal customers, they do not remain long enough for the relationship to turn a profit.

The Hostage

Hostages are stuck. These individuals experience the worst the company has to offer and must accept it. Many companies operating in a monopolistic environment see little reason to respond to the plight of hostages. After all, these customers can't go anywhere. So why bother to correct the problems?

There are two important reasons why companies should bother. First, if the competitive environment suddenly shifts, these companies will then pay the price. Their customers will defect quickly and many will become terrorists. Second, hostages are very difficult and expensive to serve. They may be trapped, but they still take every opportunity to complain and to ask for special service. Hostages can devastate company morale, and their negative impact on per unit costs is astounding.

Individual Customer Satisfaction, Loyalty, and Behavior

	Satisfaction	Loyalty	Behavior
Loyalist/Apostle	high	high	staying and supportive
Defector/Terrorist	low to medium	low to medium	leaving or having left and unhappy
Mercenary	high	low to medium	coming and going; low commitment
Hostage	low to medium	high	unable to switch; trapped

The second step is to create a curve by plotting individual customer responses. In addition to assessing how satisfied or dissatisfied customers are, managers should compare their company's curve with those shown in the industries we surveyed and consider the factors that shaped their own company's curve. Is the company retaining its customers through false-loyalty mechanisms, or is their loyalty the result of the value that the company provides through its product or services?

The third step is to determine the most appropriate strategies for raising customer satisfaction. (See the table "How to Decide What Actions to Take.")

A dissatisfied customer is probably having problems with the core value of the company's product or service – the basic elements that customers expect everyone in the industry to be able to provide. Although it may seem obvious that the basic product desired by customers often shifts as competitors improve, new competitors arrive, and new

Interpreting Levels of Satisfaction

Response	Description	Loyalty
5	completely satisfied	very loyal
3-4	satisfied	easily switched to a competitor
1-2	dissatisfied	very disloyal

technologies redefine the game, it is even more obvious from business history that keeping up with such shifts is one of management's most difficult challenges. The match between the basic product or service and the customers it is designed to serve must be reviewed continually to ensure that there is still a good fit.

A neutral customer is probably happy with the basic product or service but would like to be offered a consistent set of support services. And to ensure that neutral and satisfied customers do not slip back into the realm of the dissatisfied if bad luck happens to strike, companies also need highly responsive recovery processes. Well-designed support services – and they almost always are *services* – make the basic product or service easier to use or more effective. And recovery processes help the customer get back on track if problems occur.

The vast majority of companies that excel in satisfying customers rank the ability to react when something goes wrong as one of the most important factors in satisfying customers. That ability greatly influences whether customers heap scorn or praise on the company when talking to others. (See the insert "Apostles and Terrorists: A Company's Best Friends and Worst Enemies.") Strong recovery processes are especially vital in industries such as airlines, automobiles, production equipment, and mail-order retailing – businesses in which the product or service is complex or some delivery and servicing processes lie outside the company's control.

A completely satisfied customer typically believes that the company excels in understanding and addressing his or her personal preferences, values, needs, or problems. To figure out how to satisfy customers in this fashion, a company has to excel at listening to customers and interpreting what they are saying.[1]

Consider the experience of having a car repaired. A customer's basic goal is to have it fixed properly. To obtain a relatively neutral customer, a dealership or service station must repair the customer's vehicle competently. In the last decade, a large number of dealerships have expanded their services to include overnight and express drop-off, loaner vehicles, and free washing and waxing. Some also have instituted the practice of checking back with customers within 24 hours to make sure the problem was properly fixed, and a handful of really great dealerships check again after two weeks. If there is still a problem, fixing it becomes the top priority. These value-added support and recovery services are crucial for moving customers from neutral to satisfied. In recent years, dealerships that sell Japanese cars – most notably, Lexus dealerships – have reexamined the car-servicing experience from the customer's perspective. They found that what most customers want is to have their car repaired with minimum inconvenience and that *their* definition of the car-servicing experience includes taking the car to the dealership, arranging for transportation while it is in the shop, and picking it up once it is fixed. These dealers *completely satisfy* customers by picking up their cars at their homes or offices, leaving loaner vehicles, competently repairing, cleaning, and waxing the cars, returning them later in the day, picking up the loaners – and, of course, checking later to make sure that the cars were properly repaired.

An independent multiplex movie theater that we came across in the Southwest last year is another example of a business that excels in figuring out

How to Decide What Actions to Take

	Bulk of Responses	Strategic Response
Stage 1	2-3 (dissatisfied)	Deliver the basic product or service elements as expected of anyone in the industry
Stage 2	3-4 (neutral)	Provide an appropriate range of supporting services. Develop proactive service recovery to make amends when something goes wrong
Stage 3	4-5 (satisfied)	Understand and achieve results in customers' terms

what its customers really want and giving it to them. Its managers discovered that customers' actual movie-going experience started about two blocks from the theater, where the typical customer, especially one who is running a bit late, enters the traffic approaching the parking lot and starts to become anxious about parking and purchasing a ticket. To address such concerns, the theater's managers placed attendants two blocks from the theater to sell tickets and help people enter the parking lot. The managers discovered that customers also resented having to leave the viewing area and then stand in line in the lobby to buy food. In response, the theater began to serve food throughout the facility; it even served seated customers until the main features began. Finally, the managers learned that customers detested dirty bathrooms. In response, the theater began cleaning its bathrooms four times an hour. The end result: a large number of highly satisfied, highly loyal customers.

The three-phase approach to increasing customer satisfaction has important implications. First, different actions are required to raise the satisfaction of customers of a family of products or services whose level of satisfaction differs. Second, it is absolutely critical to accomplish the three stages in order. It is possible to make a quantum leap – to move customers from neutral to completely satisfied, for instance – by completely redesigning the product or service, by introducing new technology, or by reengineering the underlying delivery process. But we have found that not many companies succeed at that. Such leaps often fall short because the company overlooked the support services that had evolved informally over the years and did not redesign them, too.

In the final analysis, the company that will survive and flourish over the long term is the one that continually works to understand the relationship between satisfaction and loyalty for each of its customers, for each of its business units, and for each of the industries in which it competes. Horst Schulze, president and COO of the Ritz-Carlton Hotel Company, the 1992 winner of the Malcolm Baldridge National Quality Award, put it the best. "Unless you have 100% customer satisfaction–and I don't mean that they are just satisfied, I mean that they are excited about what you are doing – you have to improve," he said. "And if you have 100% customer satisfaction, you have to make sure that you listen just in case they change...so you can change with them."

1. Not all customers are saying the same thing. Opinion Research Corporation's John Larson has performed several studies comparing the satisfaction drivers for customers at different levels of satisfaction. In a study for a large information-services company, he found that dissatisfied customers were interested in core product attributes such as accuracy of data. Neutral customers were interested in account management issues such as the account manager's ability to relay account status quickly and accurately. And satisfied customers were interested in the degree to which the company's services supported the customer's strategic business objectives.

Reprint 95606

DIRECT MARKETING SUPPLIERS

19

DIRECT
MARKETING
SUPPLIERS

An integral part of
your delivery to
the consumer

This book has been devoted to the business of direct marketing and is meant to demonstrate the discipline necessary to apply your marketing knowledge to a new communication vehicle.

One of the key areas that distinguishes the direct marketing process, in particular direct mail, is that you must be familiar with all aspects of the process. This chapter is designed to introduce you to the important role printers and lettershops play in your up-front planning and your back-end results.

Although the idea that drives your creative product may not be influenced by your printing partner, it is a fact that the end product can be greatly affected. When searching for a print partner for direct mail, contact a printer that has experience in this area. Make sure your printer knows and understands direct mail with all its intricacies of personalisation, printing, and mailing. The slightest increase in outer envelope dimensions can dramatically increase your postage costs. Not knowing where personalisation will be inserted can result in an unacceptable direct mail package. Unfortunately, I have experienced more than once, a BRE that is too large for the outer envelope, or a brochure that will not accommodate machine inserting. A good, knowledgeable printer that specialises in direct mail can be your one-stop shop for all your direct mail needs. A printer's knowledge and service can be invaluable to the complicated process.

Lettershops carry out the personalising, labelling, bursting, collating, inserting, bagging, and delivery of your direct mail programs to Canada Post. They can also play an important role in order fulfillment, customer service, and the all-important billing of your customers with accounts receivable documentation and follow-up. A few of the lettershops offer full database services and do it extremely well. They are worth adding to your list when shopping for a database supplier.

The decision to use personalisation plays a large role in the selection of your lettershop. Personalisation can be handled by selected printers, by an outside computer service bureau, or by your lettershop. The overall dimensions of your mailing piece and its related quantities will also be factors in considering your lettershop selection. Be sure to include these considerations in your up-front planning.

The size and capability of your selected lettershop's inserting equipment may also affect the overall size of your package. There's nothing worse than having to approve a wonderful-looking package, only to find out that it is not machine insertable and must be inserted by hand. Hand insertion, of course, can put you over your budget and increase your break-even point. If you are using a separate printer and lettershop, be sure your package components are reviewed prior to printing with your chosen lettershop to establish optimum efficiencies for its automated and sophisticated equipment.

If your material is not compatible with today's complex lettershop machinery, the cost of hand-inserting thousands of packages will increase your costs and decrease your opportunity for success. Remember. Your success is based on your total program cost. The higher your costs to produce your campaign, the higher your needed response rate. Again, careful up-front planning is the key.

Your production department must cultivate relationships with a number of printers and lettershops, and therefore should know their specifications intimately. Here's a preliminary list that I hope will be of help:

Full service house

- From the beginning to the end of a project, the services vary — pre-press production, finishing, data management, personalisation, and lettershop.

Data houses or computer service bureau

- They specialise in managing and manipulating data. Some data houses also offer laser personalisation and lettershop services.

Printing

- **Pre-press** offers front-end services, such as film preparation and proofing. Some film houses also offer pre-press services.

Types of printers

- **Web printers** are primarily geared toward long-run, high-volume production. Most web printers have in-line finishing technology capable of producing sophisticated self-mailers.

- **Sheet fed printers** handle a variety of short and medium size production projects. Most sheet fed printers also have in-line finishing capability.

- **Silk screen** printers are generally used for point-of-sale material, display, and in-store promotion material.

I strongly recommend that you personally take a tour of your chosen direct marketing supplier's facility for a better understanding of its capabilities and how it fits in with your marketing requirements. Suppliers that specialise in direct mail are constantly exploring new technologies. The real learning process comes from listening to their ideas and seeing their equipment at work. Make sure you take them up on their offer to tour their facilities. You'll learn something new every time. I know, I do.

If your material is not compatible with today's complex lettershop machinery, the cost of hand-inserting thousands of packages will increase your costs and decrease your opportunity for success.

CAREERS

20

CAREERS

Set personal goals.
Conduct research on
potential employers.

W hen I began my direct marketing career in 1966, it was not really by choice, it was by chance. There were a limited number of companies in the field and even fewer people to learn from. I was one of the lucky ones. I learned from the best … and from the worst. I learned very quickly what worked and what didn't. Somewhere in between, there was a happy medium of training.

Today, with the corporate focus moving toward building customer relationships, the scope of opportunity is coming from call centres, cataloguers, computer services, database management groups, direct marketing agencies, financial institutions, fulfillment operations, fundraisers, list management and broker groups, pharmaceutical companies, printers, retailers, and any company interested in knowing its customer and building customer loyalty. Expenditures on direct marketing have increased, as illustrated by the dramatic double-digit growth year after year. The need for trained professionals has never been so great, nor has the opportunity for an exciting long-term career.

▶ Education

Our education profile in Canada is lower than in the United States with existing penetration into only a few colleges and universities. But this is changing as I write. As part of CDMA's new education initiatives, a benchmark survey of Canadian post-secondary direct marketing education was conducted. This survey reveals the need for new programs and the necessity for this exciting marketing specialty to be included in marketing program curriculum. We can look for changes in this area in the near future Although there is a call for expansion, there are programs available today that will introduce you to the exciting world of direct marketing: the CDMA Certificate Program, CDMA seminars and conventions, Simon Fraser University in British Columbia, Humber College, Centennial College, Seneca College, York University and the University of Toronto in Ontario, and Dalhousie University in the east to name but a few. Check with your local college or university for available courses. CDMA also offers students insight into the world of direct marketing at its Annual Student Day.

A CDMA study conducted in 1997 of entry-level recruiting and training practices in Canada delivers good news for recent graduates. The majority of companies indicated they would be recruiting entry-level employees for their firms within the next 12 to 18 months. Over 85 percent of the respondents said they would provide both on-the-job training and give new recruits the opportunity to attend outside seminars for additional training.

Before you embark on your search for the perfect entry-level position, re-read some of the chapters in this book to learn how to market yourself (no better way to get attention than to use direct marketing techniques in all your contacts), consider enrolling in CDMA's Certificate Program, attend seminars, and read direct marketing trade publications.

▶ The opportunity

Two of the highest priorities companies factored into hiring for entry-level positions in the CDMA study for job opportunities were:

1) Values and ethics
2) Interpersonal and communication skills

As you begin to prepare your résumé outline, be sure you keep these factors in mind. Your résumé is the beginning of the relationship between you and a company and should demonstrate these important factors to secure an interview. Getting an entry position is tough work today. You must stand out from the crowd. You must make a commitment to the company to do the best job you can do. And the company must make a commitment to you for training and your personal growth. Direct marketing is hard work, coupled with long hours full of deadlines that bring a unique kind of pressure and enjoyment to your career. If you are committed, no other position will give you as many rewards — rewards that can only come from working in a measurable and accountable marketing environment.

▶ Preparing your résumé

If you have decided that direct marketing is for you, make sure you start off on the right foot. Your résumé should send a clear message about your personal goals and accomplishments and demonstrate that you have done your homework on your prospective employer. Before preparing your résumé, be sure to:

Do your research

Learn something about your prospective employer. Keep up-to-date on business news. Request a copy of the company's annual report. Contact friends who may know the company, its products, and corporate values. Become a customer.

Identify your targets

Prioritise the companies by linking your skills, hobbies, or involvement as a customer. Do not do mass mailings. Be selective. Target your prospects.

Prepare your résumé with your target audience in mind

Try to personalise your résumé and covering letter to your potential employer's needs or its type of business. Position yourself as the product. Use action words. Measure your growth back against your achievements.

> Try to personalise your résumé and covering letter to your potential employer's needs or its type of business.

Use some direct response techniques in your covering letter

Always include a covering letter with your résumé. Remember. Just like in a direct mail package, the letter begins or cements the relationship. Re-read the chapter on Direct Mail and Creative to incorporate some helpful hints into format and personalised language. It's important to remember to highlight the benefits of hiring a person such as yourself. And don't forget to ask for the job.

Telemarketing

As illustrated in the Telemarketing chapter of this book, a follow-up phone call can help increase your response. When you look for an entry-level position, your efficient use of the phone demonstrates to your prospective employer that you know how to get things done efficiently and effectively.

Of course, these techniques may get you in the door, but will not guarantee you a position. Even if you don't get the first position you go after, be sure to inquire as to why you were not suitable for the position. Learn as you go along. Test, test, test, and improve your approach.

Prior to sending out your résumé, you should familiarise yourself with some of the job descriptions that exist in the direct marketing field. Although the specific responsibilities of a given position may differ from company to company, the following list can serve as a good guide.

What are my career options?

The entire industry can be divided into three tracks: agency, client, and supplier. To serve? Or to be served? That is the question. There are pluses and minuses to both: the decision must rest with each individual. Identify your own strengths, weaknesses, and personal interests, then match them up to your prospective employer's available position. If your satisfaction comes from helping others achieve their goals, you may want to consider the agency or service track. No matter which track you choose, make sure you have a personal long-term plan before accepting any position.

For clarification, I have chosen to expand on the job descriptions in a direct marketing agency — filtered throughout these job descriptions are client and supplier tracks.

▶ Job descriptions

Most agencies are structured into: account services, creative services, media, production, traffic, research, database management, and analytics.

Account services

Account services can be subdivided into various levels of experience. Account director, account supervisor, account executive, and associate account executive. The associate is the entry-level position. This is where your entry ladder of opportunity begins.

The associate

All account services are centred around your client. You are the liaison between the client and the other service groups within your organisation. You get involved in all stages, from the marketing strategy right up to and including the execution of agreed-upon strategies. Your training will come from account executives, supervisors, and directors. A background in marketing, business, or communications would be a solid base from which to build your career in this position.

Creative services

The creative department of an agency is usually divided into creative director, senior writer, junior writer, senior art director, and junior art director. The two entry-level positions are junior writer and junior art director. A background in journalism or art school will give you good entry credentials for these positions. Make your résumé or letter stand out. Get noticed. Be creative.

Junior writer

Applicants for the position, though they cannot be expected to have direct response copy experience, are expected to have a love for words, and the ability to write long copy in a conversational tone to a specific strategy. Also, a background in sales promotion or retail writing is helpful. But the rest must come from carefully learning the craft. Direct response writers are made, not born.

Junior art director

Again, a background in sales promotion or retail is certainly helpful. But the key to success is to know how to sell, visually. Knowing and understanding how to design the components of a direct mail package, print ad, or statement stuffer, will only come with long years of training. For a company to invest in your training, it must be able to see your potential — your ability to "make the cash register ring."

Media

Media departments are very often structured around a media director, media supervisors, and media associates. Responsibilities span broadcast, Internet, magazine, and newspapers. There is very little business training that

The production department is responsible for producing the final product — whether it is a direct mail package, an insert, or an on-page ad.

can equip you for an entry-level position in media. But if you are great at math and love spreadsheets, this may be for you. An analytical mind and good negotiation, communication, and interpersonal skills are vital to your success and happiness with this position.

Production

A production department can be divided into production manager, production supervisor, and production co-ordinators. The entry-level position is production co-ordinator.

Production co-ordinator

The production department is responsible for producing the final product — whether it is a direct mail package, an insert, or an on-page ad. It is responsible for all activities involving typesetting, film, data work, printing, and lettershop, to name a few. Production co-ordination is a detailed and exacting job; for those who do not have related experience, a print course and love of numbers is recommended, and almost mandatory. But for those who love detail work, deadlines, and get joy out of being the one who produces the final product, this may be the job for you.

Traffic

Traffic is responsible for the co-ordination of all activities — ensuring that each component is kept to the company's standards and on schedule. Traffic reports to either the creative director or the production manager. Any position in the traffic department plays a vital role in the success of each program and can be a stepping stone to other areas within the company.

Research

More and more today, companies have their own research department and it plays a vital role in better understanding what the customer wants. Its function is to research the executions of specific strategies and produce an actionable document of the findings. This research may take the form of focus groups, in-the-mail research, such as questionnaires to existing customers, or phone research to customers based on database information. The structure of a research department varies, but a research director and an assistant seem to be standard. If you have been involved in research of any type, and have a good understanding of research techniques, you should consider this entry position.

Database

Database is the backbone of direct marketing today. There are various levels within a database group. Generally, senior-level positions cover the design and management of the system, profiling and segmenting customers.

But there are entry-level opportunities at the data analysis level. If you have related experience or have an economic or computer science background, you may qualify for a position in this exploding area.

▶ Other opportunities

If you re-read the chapters on The Role of the Agency, Lists, Telemarketing, Direct Marketing Suppliers, you may find many additional opportunities, not unlike those listed here but more closely aligned to your skills and interests.

▶ Where to go for help

There are a few recruiters who specialise in placing people in direct marketing. You can find them in trade publications and the career section of your newspaper. There is also a strong network of direct marketers in Canada, all willing to assist you in your search. Don't be afraid to make a few phone calls to ask for help. Many of the available positions are filled through the network and may never be advertised. CDMA offers interested parties an opportunity to advertise in the career section of its newsletter, *Communicator*. You can locate CDMA on the web at http://www.cdma.org, where you'll find lots of information helpful in your search.

As you embark on your career in direct marketing, you will learn that salaries, the commitment to training, and your responsibilities will differ from company to company. Be sure you make a wise choice. Do your research.

▶ Summary

Today, there is a wealth of companies doing business by incorporating direct marketing techniques into their marketing mix. Your choice of specialty can range from consumer products and services, to business products and services, to products marketed by catalogue. The opportunities are there — at record clubs, such as Columbia House, at financial institutions, including all Canadian banks, trust companies, mutual funds and insurance, at Canada Post Corporation, at other Fortune 500s, and at the firm of the entrepreneur around the corner. Never before have there been so many choices. Make sure you choose wisely. Good luck.

> Today, there is a wealth of companies doing business by incorporating direct marketing techniques into their marketing mix.

APPENDIX

Advertising by Mail

Industry

Business to Business

Client

Kodak

Agency

Relationship Marketing
Resources, Toronto

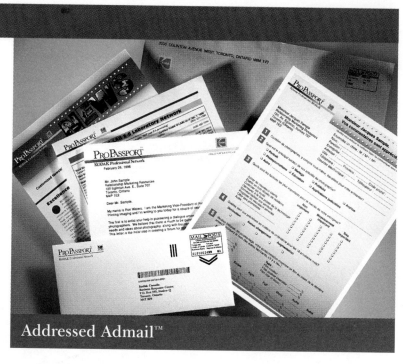

Addressed Admail™

Background

Kodak had employed a variety of communication tools to reach the professional photographer – a very demanding customer base. Kodak determined that they needed to be more efficient and effective with their sales and marketing efforts in order to penetrate the market, gather vital customer feedback, and generate qualified leads for the sales force.

Objectives

Develop an interactive customer relationship marketing program
- Position Kodak as the answer to expressed needs and wants
- Effectively build customer loyalty
- Help field sales make productive calls
- Solicit basic customer information

Strategy

- Using admail, distribute a newsletter with a questionnaire
- Build a proprietary database of professional photographers, qualified through their responses on the basis of potential value and buying motivations
- Create an added-value communications tool — a newsletter customized for each respondent, based on their expressed needs
- Maintain responses online for access and follow-up by field sales

Program In Action

1. The initial newsletter mailing to professional photographers and studios included a personalized letter from Kodak Professional's VP of Marketing, asking for help in starting a dialogue. The stated aim was to share ideas about photography and effective business management practices.
2. A questionnaire solicited photographers' business-related statistics, plus their purchase motivation factors, and asked how Kodak can assist with their business needs. Responses were grouped into similar data buckets, and stored online for access by field sales.
3. Using the data, a personalized newsletter, "ProPassport," was developed. It responded to the specific needs of the participants, to ensure relevance and interest. The newsletter also functions as an industry forum highlighting upcoming events and frequently-asked questions.

Results

- 40% industry response
- Excellent feedback from customers
- Significantly reduced growth marketing/ sales costs
- Online database of responses

Keys To Success

A Value-Added Relationship

Kodak achieves market leadership growth by successfully leveraging admail to obtain customers' feedback, and then selling the Kodak products and services that are most relevant to the customers' self expressed needs.

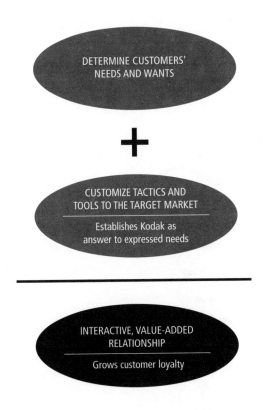

Please contact your Canada Post Corporation representative to receive copies of other case studies in this series.

Advertising by Mail

Industry

Packaged Goods

Clients

Lever / Ponds, Johnson & Johnson, General Mills, McNeil, Ralston Purina, Warner-Lambert, and many others

Supplier

ICOM • Target Dimensions, Toronto

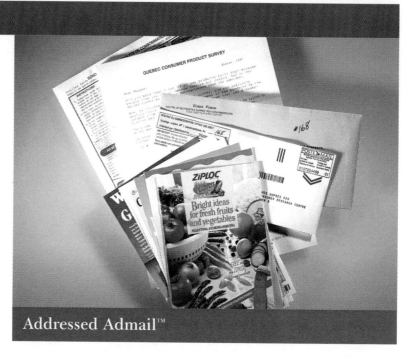

Addressed Admail™

Case Study

Background

Branded packaged goods managers have long recognized that traditional mass marketing techniques can fall short of their target due to three types of costly waste: reach waste – addressing people to whom your product is irrelevant; opportunity waste – saying or sending the wrong thing; and subsidization waste – giving people more than they need or merit. The challenge to the marketer is to cost-effectively apply direct marketing disciplines to fast-moving, low margin goods. ICOM • Target Dimensions has invented unique ways to create the economies of scale associated with mass marketing while achieving the persuasiveness of one-to-one selling.

Objectives

- Segment the market based on actual usage
- Isolate individual target consumers according to their specific purchase behaviors
- Design creative targeted to the unique habits and usage of each consumer
- Target creative and incentives flexibly to different consumers
- Create a cost-effective delivery vehicle

Strategy

- Tap into TargetSource™, Canada's largest up-to-date behavioral consumer database, with purchase and usage profiles on 2.2 million individual households
- Use the database to identify and isolate selected target groups, based on desired criteria (e.g., category usage, brand usage, frequency of purchase, etc.)
- Develop specific creative for each consumer group, ranging from customized ads to samples and promotion incentives
- Use the TargetMail™ co-op to cost-effectively distribute the appropriate creative to each chosen target
- Measure the results for each segment to evaluate return on investment

Program In Action

ICOM•Target Dimension's targeting expertise enables clients to acquire and apply recent consumer data to improve their marketing effectiveness. Millions of consumer survey profiles are run against a flowchart designed to determine which consumers should receive which mailings, for minimum waste and maximum return on investment. (Refer to chart below)

Results

- This successful marketing approach has a solid track record of results
- Typical redemption rates are in the double digits
- Payout typically occurs within 12 months

Keys To Success

- Recent, actual behavioral data gathered from millions of representative households are used to create an accurate and actionable segmentation
- Proprietary selective insertion technology allows packaged goods brands to share mailing costs, without compromising the ability to target down to the household level
- Waste is minimized by applying consumer data against marketing program flowchart

Program In Action

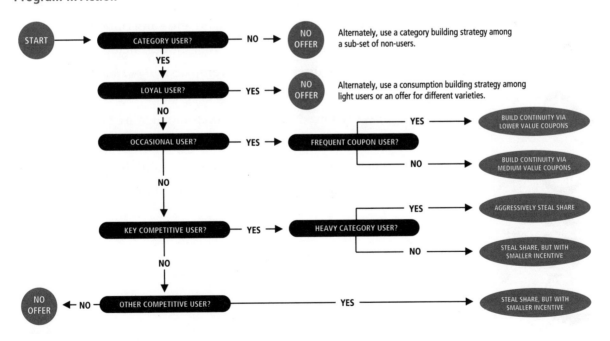

Please contact your Canada Post Corporation representative to receive copies of other case studies in this series.

Advertising by Mail

Industry

Communications – Newspaper

Client

The Financial Post

Agency

Wunderman Cato Johnson,
Toronto

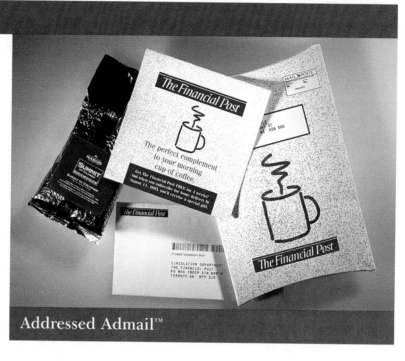

Addressed Admail™

Background

The Financial Post is Canada's premier daily financial newspaper. The paper is published Tuesday through Saturday and is sold through both newsstand and subscription. Subscribers are acquired through integrated general advertising and direct response campaigns. *The Financial Post*'s key challenge was to create a direct mail package that would meet required acquisition levels in a mature and highly competitive marketing environment. The creative had to be impactful, break through the clutter and distinguish itself to appeal to an up-scale, discriminating target market.

Objectives

- Develop an effective campaign to acquire new subscribers
- Measure the relative performance of alternative approaches

Strategy

- Develop a direct mail package that positions *The Financial Post* as an essential component of the morning ritual
- Partner with Kraft General Foods to include an appropriate, high value premium: Nabob coffee
- Extend the creative theme with freefall insert in *The Financial Post* newsstand editions

Program In Action

A mailing list was compiled from a selection of over 100 broad-ranging business, investment and consumer lists targeted to residential prospects.

The control version of the direct mail package offered four weeks of *The Financial Post* free, a subsequent cost of $3.95 per week, plus a personal sound system premium. The test campaign, which ran nationally with a total quantity of 40,000, did not include the premium. The freefall was inserted in newsstand copies of *The Financial Post*.

By including a packet of Nabob coffee in its direct mail pieces, *The Financial Post* created a dimensional, high-impact mailing. The theme – "The perfect complement to your morning cup of coffee" – leveraged one of *The Financial Post*'s key attri-butes: daily home delivery before 6 a.m.

The creative carried out the theme through the use of a granular background, visuals of steaming mugs and copy references such as "100% pure profitable information." Because of its upscale image, Nabob coffee was likely to be considered a high value premium by the desired target market. The freefall insert synergized with the mail package, leveraging the coffee theme and reinforcing the message of early morning delivery. Prospects were invited to subscribe by mail, fax or 1-800 number.

Results

- The direct mail piece achieved outstanding results, exceeding plan by 50%
- Winner of 1995 Canadian Direct Marketing Association RSVP Award
- Program was extended further to a neighbour sampling program

Keys To Success

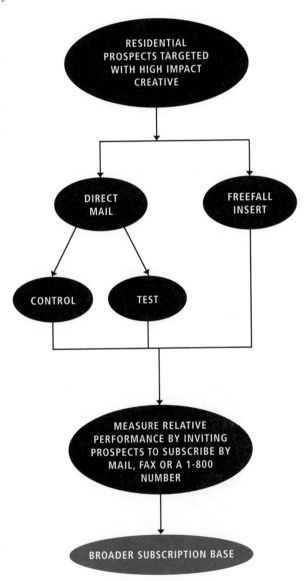

Please contact your Canada Post Corporation representative to receive copies of other case studies in this series.

Advertising by Mail

Industry
Collector Coins

Client
Royal Canadian Mint

Agency
FCB Direct Montréal

Addressed Admail™

Case Study

Background

The Royal Canadian Mint traditionally introduces most of its new products in the winter period (January to March). This is when customers acquire most of their collectibles for the year and spend the greater part of their coin collection budget. In 1996, for the first time, an additional mailing (for the numismatic $2 product line) preceded the Winter Campaign. The challenge: generate traditional revenues from the Winter Campaign despite the additional mailing, just four weeks prior.

Objectives

- Create excitement about the new products and position the new themes, materials and finishes as desirable characteristics of Royal Canadian Mint products
- Maintain a 30% response rate among active buyers (those who made a purchase in the past two years)
- Test new offers in order to increase performance and beat the control offer
- Maintain high creative standards without increasing costs

Strategy

- Roll out the control offer – a coin catalogue with an incentive based on a minimum order
- Test the control offer with a higher minimum purchase threshold to seek ways of increasing revenues
- Personalize the communication based on the individual history of the customer segments
- Maintain high production values to increase the coins' perceived value

Program In Action

1. The aim of the campaign was to create excitement and make the customers feel as though they were actually entering the building to attend the Premiere of the 1996 Collection.
2. The catalogue continued the "unveiling" theme. The direct mail campaign established interest and anticipation with its envelope design: it showed the Royal Canadian Mint building, with its doors opening for a big event.
3. A personalized letter, order form and return envelope completed the package. The visuals leveraged the success of the Winter 1995 creative approach, which displayed the coins bigger than life and featured them as works of art. High production standards were maintained to convey the idea of coin collecting as a sophisticated and prestigious hobby.

Results

- Response rate: 37.3% for the entire active buyer group (24.3% above projections)
- Revenues: 30% above projections
- Generated the same revenue per order as the previous year, even with the $2 mailing just four weeks prior
- Winner of the 1996 Canadian Direct Marketing Association RSVP Award

Keys To Success

Skillful Direct Marketing

This successful campaign illustrates that skillful direct marketing can achieve the gentle balance between compelling creative, selective personalization, and tested offer structures to a precise target.

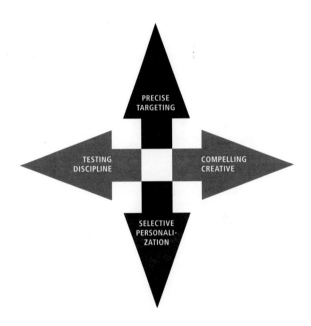

Please contact your Canada Post Corporation representative to receive copies of other case studies in this series.

Advertising by Mail

Industry

Communications

Client

Groupe Vidéotron (Cable TV)

Agency

Sprint Communication Marketing Inc.,
Montreal

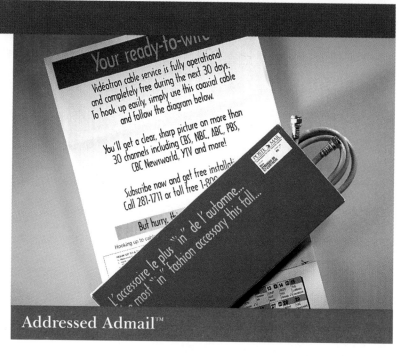

Addressed Admail™

Background

Cable TV company Groupe Vidéotron identified a significant opportunity to expand their market reach. The target consumer group? Residents of apartments which were built pre-wired for cable. Unfortunately, historical efforts to attract these non-subscribers had proven to be both challenging and expensive. Conventional media was inefficient. Groupe Vidéotron chose to communicate its compelling message through Addressed Admail.

Objectives

- Build the subscriber base among apartment dwellers in Montreal, Quebec City and Sherbrooke
- Obtain a 2.5% response rate by emphasizing the ease of plugging into the cable network

Strategy

- Use personalized Admail
- Offer a free month of cable service, plus no installation fee

Program In Action

To create a sense of urgency and special value, the campaign was restricted to a ten-day period. Non-subscribing households on the Vidéotron database received a personalized Admail package which included:

1. A three-dimensional teaser box.
2. A pamphlet describing the offer, including a channel listing.
3. A co-axial cable – consumers could simply plug it into the TV set, and Vidéotron would unscramble the signal by computer.
4. An exciting programming schedule.

Results

- Response rate: 11% (over four times the expected rate)
- Research showed favourable consumer feedback
- Solid return on investment
- Winner of the 1996 Canadian Direct Marketing Association RSVP Award

Keys To Success

Message in Admail

Starting with an up-to-date database of current and potential prospects, Groupe Vidéotron built on the strengths of Admail in a successful campaign. Features included:

PERSONALIZED

CREATIVE, THREE-DIMENSIONAL PACKAGE

VALUABLE OFFER TO CONSUMERS

STRONG CALL TO ACTION

Please contact your Canada Post Corporation representative to receive copies of other case studies in this series.

Advertising by Mail

Industry
Financial Services

Product
Mutual Funds

Client
Scudder Funds of Canada

Agency
Taylor – Tarpay, Toronto

Addressed Admail™

Case Study

Background

Scudder Funds of Canada launched in the fall of 1995. Although Scudder had administered Canadian institutional accounts since the 1960s, primary research revealed no awareness in the Canadian public to either the name "Scudder" or the types of funds the company offered.

The Canadian mutual fund market is extremely cluttered with well over 1,400 different mutual funds available to Canadian investors. Each fund and fund company is aggressively trying to create a unique brand identity and capture marketshare. The 1997 Ascot study reported a record total print advertising spend of $5.8 million in the Toronto market alone by the top mutual fund companies during the months of Jan. '97 through Feb. '97. Adding further to the clutter, Scudder noted that the traditional RRSP season was beginning earlier than ever before (October) and intensifying all the way through February.

Scudder is different from the majority of mutual fund companies. They sell directly to the consumer without the aid of a sales force of brokers/planners. This created a unique challenge for the company with a formidable US heritage but no track record in Canada – will Canadians buy from an unknown financial company without a Canadian track record, or the track record of a flamboyant fund manager? Will they buy through the mail?

At the beginning of the 1996/97 Scudder had $23 million in funds under management.

Objectives

Significantly increase assets under management by:

- increasing response rates versus benchmark controls by 100% via careful targeting
- reducing cost of out bound mail by 20% by efficient targeting using Addressed Admail

Strategy

- Utilize an integrated direct marketing program to reach an affluent, financial savvy audience

Program In Action

Direct Mail

2 mailings were used:

Timing	000	Lists*
Fall '96	140	21
Winter '97	360	31

*Unduplicated prospect names were compiled from:
'A' Lists: investing and related publications or newsletters
'B' Lists: business publications and newspapers
'C' Lists: compiled lists with investing criteria
'D' Lists: lifestyle selection lists, compiled and publications

Offer

The unique offer featured a Free Scudder Guide to Global Investing

Creative Strategy

1. A reverse format, 2 colour, #10 outer envelope was designed to increase the chances of having the package opened. The design instilled a sense of curiosity in the target audience. The front of envelope offered "Yours free: the Scudder Guide to Global Investing", while the back of the envelope showed a world map with the headline "Are your investments all over the map?"

2. Inside: Personalized, long format (4 pages) letter with strong "sales" message stressing the benefits of global investing and superiority of Scudder as a global investor.

3. Brochure: 4 colour, simple roll brochure that summarized the benefits of global investing and superiority of Scudder as a global investor.

4. Business Reply Card: Personalized, return postage paid.

Financial Press

The Globe & Mail and *The Financial Post* formed the cornerstone of the print campaign for Scudder. Keeping in mind the business objectives of this campaign (to maximize exposure while reducing costs), Scudder pioneered different ad formats, including stock-islands on the mutual fund pages, banner ads and bookend ads (banners at top and bottom of the page). This gave Scudder extensive exposure, while limiting the expense. In the *Mutual Funds Advertising Performance Report* published by Ascot Marketing, Scudder was found to have the most compelling and motivating ("This ad makes you want to find out more about, and/or buy, the mutual funds advertised"[1]) print advertising of all mutual fund companies advertising during the 1996-97 season.

1. Source: Scudder Performance Research Report.

Results

All objectives met and surpassed

- 3.13% response rate to the Fall 1996 mailing
- 3.25% response rate to the January 1997 mailing
- Incremental increase of more than 225% over last year
  – 125% over target
- Over $12 million in new assets under management were directly attributable to the direct mail portion of the campaign – 300% increase over 1996 levels
- A 30% decrease in the cost of outbound mailing – 10% better than target
- A 462% improvement in the cost per response
- 82% of all responses, from all media, were to the Scudder Guide to Global Investing offer
- 1996 RSVP Award certificate

Keys to Success

Discipline	Goal	Result	Outcomes
Market Research	▶ In-depth Customer Knowledge	▶ Careful Targeting	▶ Improved Cost-Efficiency
Advertising	▶ Innovative Creative and Media Selection ▶ Unique Offer	▶ Consumer Appeal and Relevance	▶ Memorability ▶ Increased Response Rates ▶ Sustained Competitive Advantage ▶ Branding
Fulfillment	▶ Measurement vs Benchmarks	▶ Spending Leverage	▶ Innovation ▶ Improved ROI vs Industry norms

Please contact your Canada Post Corporation representative to receive copies of other case studies in this series.

Incentive Lettermail™

Case Study

Industry

Financial Services – Insurance

Client

London Life

Agency

Relationship Marketing
Resources, Toronto

Background

London Life acquired the Canadian operations of Prudential Insurance Company and understood that a key asset was the 600,000-plus customer database. London Life's business imperative was to develop an understanding of the needs and expectations of this new customer base, in order to tailor their marketing plans.

Objectives

- Leverage the mandatory London Life Certificate of Assumption mailing to Prudential policy holders, to learn more about their needs and expectations
- Provide an effective means of segmenting the new customer base into customer stages and selling strategies

Strategy

- Turn a legally required Lettermail mailing, and the associated cost, into a strategic asset
- Build on the initial Lettermail customer contact to create a proactive relationship marketing process

The Lettermail selling process is similar to personal selling.

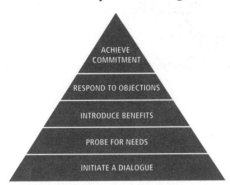

ACHIEVE COMMITMENT

RESPOND TO OBJECTIONS

INTRODUCE BENEFITS

PROBE FOR NEEDS

INITIATE A DIALOGUE

Program In Action

1. With each mailing, London Life included a personalized letter introducing the company.
2. An enclosed questionnaire invited customers to share their attitudes and perspectives on key issues such as products offered or wanted, evaluation of service levels, and desire for more information. The questions enabled a quantitative understanding of the customer's lifetime value. Customized software used the feedback to formulate a selling strategy for each respondent. Detailed lead sheets and call priority reports were generated for the London Life sales force, identifying opportunities and challenges. The relationship database permits desktop querying across markets.

Visit our web site at:
www.mailposte.ca

Printed in Canada
AD-LM1006-01 (03-98)

Results

- Excellent customer retention and enthusiastic support from London Life sales management
- Double-digit response rate to survey
- 83% of respondents stated that their preferred method of staying in touch was via personalized Lettermail

Keys To Success

Soliciting customer feedback through Lettermail can be a key building block in an effective relationship marketing program. While Lettermail was the primary method, it points the way to viewing all customer contact opportunities as a means of building the relationship. The results of an interactive process and ongoing dialogue can result in more effective sales leads and agent support, new product development, and sophisticated predictive models.

Integrated Relationship Marketing Process

Corporate Objectives

Customer Contact Opportunities

PERSONAL SALES CALLS

DIRECT MARKETING

SALES PROMOTION

GENERAL ADVERTISING

BILLING STATEMENTS

Customer Relationship Marketing Systems

SALES LEADS / SUPPORT

LEGAL MAILINGS e.g., annual report

NEW PRODUCT DEVELOPMENT

PREDICTIVE MODELING

LIFETIME VALUE ENHANCERS

Please contact your Canada Post Corporation representative to receive copies of other case studies in this series.

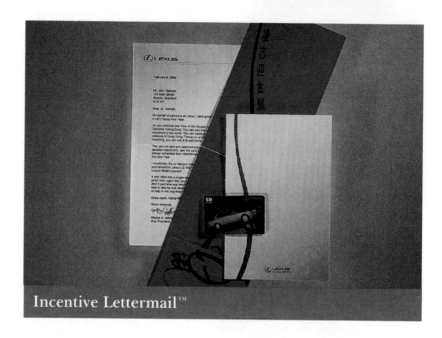

Incentive Lettermail™

Industry

Automotive

Client

Lexus

Agency

SMW Advertising Toronto

Background

The standard of luxury cars continues to be pushed upwards. European companies keep churning out new and exciting models...the Japanese entries are being built better than ever...the domestic cars continue to show promise. In this competitive context, the retention of current customers becomes paramount to ongoing success.

Objectives

- Build a strong customer bond with current Lexus owners

Increasing Loyalty

Advocacy

Community

Relationship

Identity

Awareness

Strategy

- Focus on all existing Lexus owners who are of Chinese origin
- Recognizing the high level of language retention and the strong ties with their homelands, communicate with these owners in their own language
- Use lettermail to demonstrate that Lexus goes the extra mile, recognizing cultural diversity and values

Program In Action

Due to the lifestyle and congregation pattern of the Chinese ethnic market, "word of mouth" advertising plays a key role in the purchase decision. Lexus firmly believes a happy customer is the best Lexus spokesperson. Lettermail provided the quality context for delivering the message.

A high quality mailing was created to wish all Chinese Lexus owners "A Prosperous Year of the Mouse" in the celebration of the Chinese New Year. The components included: customized, Chinese-language New Year's greeting card, and a red packet – considered a lucky charm in the Chinese culture. Inside the red packet was a prepaid Lexus long distance calling card. A bilingual (Chinese and English) covering letter was included as a safety device, in case the recipient did not read Chinese.

Results

- Very positive feedback from the dealer network
- Units sold to Chinese customers increased 160% compared to the month prior to the mailing

Keys To Success

This lettermail project is outstanding for the following reasons:

- It is a unique example of target segmentation and effective customer communication. The customer base is not homogeneous. The creative approach showed that Lexus recognized that owners deserve customized treatment. Lettermail was judged to be the best medium to deliver this message.
- The "Year of the Mouse" mailing demonstrated Lexus's commitment to developing the Chinese market. Not only did the quality mailing recognize the Chinese New Year as the biggest festival of the year for these customers, it also communicated Lexus's thoughtfulness in providing a free calling card on an occasion when many would be calling family and friends to wish them Happy New Year.

POSITIVE DEALER FEEDBACK

INCREASED CUSTOMER BASE

Visit our web site at:
www.mailposte.ca

 Printed in Canada
AD-LM1007-01 (03-98)

Please contact your Canada Post Corporation representative to receive copies of other case studies in this series.

CANADA POST | POSTES CANADA

Industry
Chemicals Fibres

Client
DuPont

Agency
FCB Direct, Toronto

Case Study

Incentive Lettermail™

Background

TYVEK®, a synthetic paper stock manufactured by DuPont Canada Inc., is used primarily as a durable paper for tags and signs. DuPont needed to capture growth opportunities in the banners/signs market, and to promote the product for broader applications. They recognized the importance of establishing a customer database and building loyalty in the graphic designer market and the printing industry. The major challenge: many designers and printers had a limited understanding of the product or believed it to be difficult to print. FCB Direct was asked to develop a direct mail campaign to promote new uses of TYVEK® and increase the target groups' comfort level for specifying or printing with TYVEK®.

®Registered trademark of E.I. du Pont de Nemours and Company

Objectives

- Immediately strengthen top-of-mind awareness of TYVEK® and its exclusive Canadian distributors
- Increase knowledge and comfort level of printing and designing with TYVEK®
- Generate a 5% response rate from each of two customized surveys
- Encourage incremental sales in the graphic industry, indicating trial or repeat usage, during a three-month promotion period

Strategy

- Position TYVEK® as the tough, durable substrate of choice for dynamic promotional mailings
- Encourage replies with a database-building offer
- Motivate trial and re-usage with an additional incentive

Program In Action

A graphically exciting, three-dimensional promotion was distributed by lettermail. The customized mailings, printed on TYVEK®, were created to appeal to a designer's sense of flair and flexibility and to a printers' sense of printing capability.

A recipient list was culled from DuPont business records, magazine lists and TYVEK® distributor lists. To improve customer knowledge and collect marketing data, a short survey was included. To encourage response and trial or re-usage, incentives were offered.

For Designers:
Responding designers qualified for a prize – a trip to the prestigious HOW Design Conference. With specification of TYVEK®, designers earned a free annual subscription to HOW magazine.

For Printers:
Responding printers qualified for a trip to the print show DRUPA in Dusseldorf, Germany. Printers were also offered additional information or a visit from a sales representative.

®Registered trademark of E.I. du Pont de Nemours and Company

Results

- Survey responses: 77%
- Aggressive 1994 sales objectives were met
- Winner of the 1996 Canadian Direct Marketing Association RSVP Award

Keys To Success

A Value-Added Relationship

Creative Lettermail Hits the Target

The fact that DuPont was able to reach 1994 annual sales objectives – which appeared out of reach only four months earlier – was directly attributed to the success of the mailings, according to DuPont senior management. This lettermail campaign represented the only marketing/sales activity in the second half of 1994.

CREATIVE AND
COMPELLING PROMO
....
Product Info
Distribution Info
Strong Offers

+

WELL-DEFINED
TARGET
....
Graphic Designers
Printers

Please contact your Canada Post Corporation representative to receive copies of other case studies in this series.

Advertising by Mail

Industry

Retail

Client

Eaton Centre,
Downtown Edmonton

Data Centre

HKA Data, Toronto

Addressed Admail™

Case Study

Background

The Eaton Centre in Edmonton faced tough, escalating competition from large suburban malls. Merchant sales were sluggish and customers were dwindling. How could the Eaton Centre win back customers without resorting to deep discounting tactics? The challenge was to develop a comprehensive marketing strategy that would position the Eaton Centre as the best value provider, engage the customer in a long-term relationship, and create sustainable, competitive advantages for the mall.

Objectives

- Increase revenue from existing customers
- Reach new customers
- Increase shopper loyalty and frequency
- Enhance the value equation

Strategy

- Utilize direct marketing to build a customer database
- Create a personalized, electronic, card-based preferred shopper program
- Track and measure customer shopping activity (frequency, retail location, purchase amounts)
- Customize offers to match spending habits

Program In Action

A unique and proprietary frequent-shopper program was developed that could be easily implemented for any mall retailer.

Mall outlets throughout the Eaton Centre participated in the new electronic point system. A direct mail package invited area householders to enroll at no cost.

Members present a personalized, magnetic-striped card each time they make a purchase. The purchase data are automatically entered into the program, which facilitates tracking of shopping habits.

Members receive a quarterly point-summary statement, plus a newsletter communicating the latest retail offers and shopping centre promotions. Mailings are targeted by postal code, personalized mailings are sent out quarterly, and customer-specific offers are made periodically based on the shopper's activity profile.

Results

Total Sales	+20.3% vs. year ago
Transaction Amount	+18% vs. year ago
Member Enrollment	+27.8% vs. target
Retail Sales Per Sq. Ft.	+44% vs. year ago

Winner of Marketing's 1993 Gold Promo Award in the retail category.

Keys To Success

ELECTRONIC CARD FOR
POINTS-BASED SHOPPING

IN-DEPTH CUSTOMER
SHOPPING DATA COLLECTED

DATABASE SUPPORTS ACTIVE,
TARGETED MARKETING

DIALOGUE WITH CUSTOMERS
ENHANCES RELATIONSHIPS

Please contact your Canada Post Corporation representative to receive copies of other case studies in this series.

Canadian Direct Marketing Association
Code of Ethics and Standards of Practice

A. Introduction

A1. Purpose of Code of Ethics and Standards of Practice

Preamble: Direct marketers acknowledge that the establishment and maintenance of high standards of practice are a fundamental responsibility to the public, essential to winning and holding public confidence, and the foundation of a successful and independent direct marketing industry in Canada.

Canadian Direct Marketing Association members include Canada's major financial institutions, retailers, publishers, cataloguers, and charities, as well as a wide range of suppliers of goods and services to direct marketers.

A2. Application and Governing Legislation

A2.1 This code of ethics is designed to set and maintain standards for the conduct of direct response marketing in Canada.

A2.2 Members of the Canadian Direct Marketing Association recognize an obligation — to the public, to the integrity of the discipline in which they operate and to each other — to practice to the highest standards of honesty, truth, accuracy, and fairness.

A2.3 All persons involved in the direct response marketing industry in Canada shall be cognizant of and conduct themselves according to the laws of Canada.

A2.4 No direct marketer shall participate in any campaign involving the disparagement of any person or group on the grounds of race, colour, religion, national origin, gender, sexual orientation, marital status.

A2.5 Unless obliged by law, no direct marketer shall participate in the distribution of unsolicited material which is derogatory, vulgar, or indecent in nature, including that which portrays, describes, or includes explicit: sexual conduct, mutilation, or torture.

A2.6 No person involved in any aspect of any direct marketing program shall knowingly participate in any direct marketing programs that contravene Directives A2.4, A2.5 or Section G respecting marketing to children. Further, suppliers should actively encourage their non-member clients to adhere to other provisions of this Code of Ethics and Standards of Practice.

B. Accuracy of Representation

B1 Accuracy: Offers must be clear and truthful and shall not misrepresent a product, service, solicitation, or program and shall not mislead by statement, or technique of demonstration or comparison.

B2 Timeliness: Descriptions and promises shall reflect actual conditions, situations, and circumstances existing at the time of the promotion.

B3 Evidence: Test or survey data referred to shall be competent, reliable, and must support the specific claim for which it is cited. Direct marketers shall be able to substantiate the basis for any claim or comparison. No claim shall imply — by statement, illustration, or presentation — a scientific, factual or statistical basis where none exists. (See also B8, Testimonials).

B4 Identity: Every offer and shipment shall identify the direct marketer and provide the consumer with sufficient information to be able to contact the direct marketer.

B5 Disguise: No person shall make offers or solicitations in the guise of research or a survey when the real intent is to sell products, services, or to raise funds.

B6 Disparagement: No offer shall attack or discredit, or disparage products, services, advertisements or companies using inaccurate information.

B7 Representation: Photography, artwork, or audio-visual representation must accurately and fairly illustrate the product offered.

B8 Testimonials: Testimonials and endorsements must be:
- Authorized by the person quoted;
- Genuine and related to the experience of the person quoted; and,
- Not taken out of context so as to distort the opinion or experience of the person quoted.
(See also B3 Evidence)

C. **Constituent Elements and Characteristics of the Offer**

C1 Disclosure: The offer shall contain clear and conspicuous disclosure of the following terms:
- The exact nature of what is offered;
- The price;
- The terms of payment, including any additional charges, such as shipping and handling; and,
- The consumer's commitment and any ongoing obligation in placing an order.

The following additional disclosures are to be made with the offer (or, provided the consumer can return goods or refuse services, with the shipment):
- Credit, late payment penalties;
- Returns/cancellations policies and procedures;
- Substitution policy (where applicable);
- Shipping terms and delivery times, FOB point, substitution policy (See also D1 Shipment);
- How to update a customer record;
- How to contact the seller; and,
- Method of transferring title (if applicable).

In addition:

Full and fair disclosure of the terms of the offer shall include not just wording, but the manner of presentation of the price, terms and conditions, and customer commitments and obligations: printed information which, by the use of type size, placement, color, contrast, or other means materially affects the legibility of the offer or exceptions to it shall not be used.

C2 Comparisons: Comparisons included in offers must be factual, verifiable, and not misleading.

In addition:

No offer shall include a deceptive price claim or deceptive suggestion of a discount, or exaggerated claim as to worth or value;

Terms such as "Regular price", "Suggested retail value", "Manufacturer's list price", and "Fair market value", must represent prices at which a reasonable quantity of the item has been sold in the relevant marketplace as defined in the competition laws of Canada.

Where qualified price discounts are offered, statements such as "up to", and "xx off" must be presented in easily readable type, and in proximity to the prices quoted.

C3 "Free": Products or services offered without cost or obligation on the part of the consumer or as a premium incentive to purchase goods or services, may be described as "Free". Where any cost or obligation is incurred by the consumer, it shall be so identified or the offer shall use another term, such as "A bonus". (See also C1 Disclosure.)

C4 Unordered Goods and Services: Consumers are not responsible to pay for unordered goods or services.

C5 Automatically Billed Goods and Services: Automatically billed goods and services — in which the consumer agrees to receive goods or services on a continuing basis and be billed — is permitted.

The marketer shall clearly inform the customer of all material terms and obligations in the original offer including whether there is a right to cancel.

Any material change in the goods or services offered to a customer who has previously consented to be automatically billed for those goods or services shall require the marketer to obtain new consent. Such new consent may be inferred from the customer's acceptance or use of the goods or services, provided that the customer has a meaningful opportunity to decline the services without incurring cost or further obligation.

C6 Negative Option Prenotification Membership Plans: A negative option prenotification subscription membership plan is a contractual plan offered by direct marketers. Under these plans, the seller prenotifies the member of a selection that will be sent to the member and billed for unless the member instructs the seller, in a method provided by the seller, not to provide the selection.

Advertising and promotional material for a negative option membership must clearly and conspicuously disclose material terms and a consumer must give prior expressed request or consent to join. Material terms include: number of selections in a 12-month period; number of days to instruct the seller not to ship; and any minimum purchase or membership term.

C7 Contests, Sweepstakes: The use of contests, sweepstakes, or prizes in the promotion of goods or services shall conform to the laws of Canada.

The rules of any contest, sweepstake, or prize give away shall be clearly stated or easily obtainable. (See B1 Accuracy, and C1 Disclosure.)

C8 Pricing: Prices quoted in Canada shall be in Canadian dollars, unless otherwise identified.

C9 Other: Offers that appear to be bills or invoices may not be used.

C10 Guarantees and Warranties: Where an offer includes a guarantee or warranty, the terms and conditions shall be set forth in full with the offer, or made available to the consumer upon request.

D. Fulfillment Practices

D1 Shipment: Goods offered shall be shipped within 30 days of the receipt of a properly completed order, or within the time limit stated in the original offer.

D2 Delay: The customer shall be advised within 30 days of the receipt of the order, or within the time limit stated in the original offer, if delivery will be late.

D3 Order Cancellation: The customer has the right to cancel an order for goods that cannot be delivered within 30 days, or the time stated (or which are described as "back ordered"), without cost or obligation to the customer.

D4 Substitution: Any substitution of goods to those originally offered and ordered shall be disclosed to the consumer and shall be of the same or better quality, or be approved by the customer before shipment. The customer shall be informed that he or she has the right to accept or reject goods substituted, without additional obligation or cost, including return shipping cost.

D5 Guarantees and Warranties: Any guarantee provided in conjunction with the provision of goods or services shall clearly identify the name and address of the guarantor and the duration of such guarantee.

D6 Prompt Response: Any request under the terms of a guarantee for repair, replacement, refund, or other remedy shall be honoured promptly.

E. Media-Specific Standards of Practice

Introduction: Beyond the standards of practice that govern direct marketing in Canada generally, and which are described in the preceding paragraphs, certain additional standards of practice are mandated according to the medium in which direct marketing is conducted:

E1. Broadcast

E1.1 Application: These standards of practice apply to all direct response broadcast commercial solicitations or requests for charitable contributions delivered to private residences by any electronic means.

E1.2 Misrepresentation: Direct response marketers shall not employ presentations likely to mislead reasonable consumers that the presentation is news, information, public service or entertainment programming.

CDMA Code of Ethics

E1.3 Endorsement: Except where the endorser is identified as an expert or is a generally recognized celebrity (whose sole connection with the marketer is the payment of a fee for the endorsement), any material connection between the endorser and the marketer shall be disclosed; and,

The results, experiences, or findings of the endorser shall be generally representative of the results to be expected by the average consumer. In the alternative, the marketer shall clearly and conspicuously disclaim that such results, experiences, or findings are or will be typical of the experiences of the average consumer.

E1.4 Sponsorship: Each video presentation (infomercial) shall be preceded and followed by a clear or prominent video and oral announcement that the presentation is a paid commercial message, and which identifies the product or service on offer, and the soliciting party. The video announcement shall also be presented prior to each ordering opportunity.

E2. Printed Media

E2.1 Application: These standards of practice apply to all forms of commercial solicitation or requests for charitable donations employing printed media, including (but not limited to) direct mail, catalogues, and periodical advertising.

E2.2 Description: All printed materials shall accurately and fairly describe the product or service offered. Type size, colour, contrast, style, placement, or other treatment shall not be used to reduce the legibility or clarity of the offer, exceptions to the offer, or terms and conditions.

E3. Telephone

E3.1 Application: These standards of practice apply to all forms of commercial solicitation or requests for charitable donation conveyed by telephone (also known as telemarketing), including the presentation of offers for goods or services or requests for charitable donations by means of telephone facsimile (also known as fax).

E3.2 Identification: Marketers shall identify themselves and the business or organization represented promptly at the beginning of each outbound telemarketing call.

E3.3 Privacy: No marketer shall knowingly call any person who has an unlisted or unpublished telephone number, except where the telephone number was furnished by the customer to that marketer. In addition:

Marketers will promptly remove from their lists the telephone numbers of consumers who request them to do so, or non-customers who have registered with the CDMA's Do Not Call Service; and, Marketers who contact consumers by telephone shall employ lists which contain at least the surname and telephone number of the household called.

E3.4 Calling Hours: Marketers will respect consumers by limiting the hours of outbound telemarketing to: 9:00 am to 9:30 p.m. weekdays, 10:00 a.m. to 6:00 p.m. Saturdays and Sundays. Calling shall not be undertaken on statutory holidays.

Outbound telemarketing by facsimile is excluded from the restrictions on calling hours as described in this section.

E3.5 Frequency: Marketers (that is, the same organization or business) shall not knowingly contact a consumer who is not already a current customer more frequently than once per month for the same product or service. A current customer is defined as any consumer who has made a purchase from the direct marketer within the last six months or during a normal buying cycle.

E3.6 Observation: Call monitoring or observation shall be undertaken only according to federal and/or provincial regulations.

E4. Other Electronic Media

E4.1 Application: The general provisions of these standards of practice apply to all other forms of electronic media. In addition, the following media specific standards of practice apply to electronic media, including (but not limited to) the Internet, electronic mail, interactive kiosks, databases, and computer-based information services.

E4.2 Consent: Marketers shall not transmit marketing e-mail without the consent of the recipient or unless the marketer has an existing relationship with the recipient.

E4.3 Reply: Every e-mail message shall clearly identify the marketer and provide the recipient with a simple and easy to use e-mail means to reply to the marketer.

Marketers shall not send e-mail to recipients who have indicated they wish not to receive further communications from that marketer.

E4.4 Protection of the virtual environment: Direct response marketers acknowledge that their continuing responsibility to manage their businesses to reduce unwanted marketing offers applies also to the maintenance of the electronic distribution environment, including e-mail and the Internet.

E4.5 Disclosure: When gathering data from individual consumers that could identify the consumer, and which will be linked with 'clickstream'[1] data, direct marketers shall advise consumers: a) what information is being collected; and, b) how the information will be used. The marketer shall provide access to this advisory before consumers submit data that could identify them.

Marketers shall also provide a meaningful opportunity for consumers to decline to have information that identifies them collected, or transferred, for marketing purposes. In addition, access to this advisory shall be provided in every location, site, or page from which the marketer is collecting such data.

F. Product Safety

F1 Introduction: Products offered by direct marketers shall be safe in normal use and, where applicable, shall conform to product safety regulations established by Health and Welfare Canada and by the Canadian Standards Association and/or other recognized Canadian authorities.

F2 Information: Information provided with the product shall include full directions for assembly (if applicable), directions for proper use of the product and full and fair disclosure of known hazards of improper use, handling, storage, or disposal.

G. Special Considerations in Marketing to Children

G1 Responsibility: Promotions to children impose a special responsibility on direct marketers.

G2 Credulity: Advertisements shall not exploit children's credulity, lack of experience, or sense of loyalty.

G3 Safety: Products whose use may result in physical harm shall not be promoted to children.

G4 Authorization: No direct marketer shall knowingly accept an order from a minor unless a parent or guardian's authorization is provided.

H. Protection of the Environment

H1 Environmental Responsibility: Direct marketers recognize and acknowledge a continuing responsibility to manage their businesses to minimize environmental impact.

This responsibility shall include: use of targeted marketing techniques to improve mail efficiency; the use of recycled papers and environmentally benign inks and other materials; use of materials recycling programs; and, the active encouragement of environmental responsibility among members of the business community.

In addition, direct marketers shall use the CDMA's Do Not Mail program to reduce unwanted mailings, and thereby reduce wasted materials.

H2 Three Rs: Direct marketers shall incorporate the "Three Rs" of environmental responsibility in the operation of their businesses.
More specifically, to:
- Reduce material use
- Reuse materials and
- Recycle materials

I. Protection of Personal Privacy

I1 Privacy: All direct marketers shall recognize and abide by the seven principles of personal privacy adopted by the Canadian Direct Marketing Association:

Principle #1: Giving Consumers Control of How Information About Them is Used

1.1 Consumers must be provided with a meaningful opportunity to decline to have their name or other information used for any further marketing purposes by a third party.

1.2 This opportunity must be provided to the consumer before any information is transferred and must be repeated once every three years, at a minimum.

1.3 Third parties are defined as: a) unrelated companies; and b) companies associated with or forming part of the same group where such a relationship is either not obvious or would not generally be known to the consumer.

1.4 In addition to the above, the marketer must remove the consumer's name from all internal marketing lists or lists for rental to a third party at the request of the consumer at any time, e.g., all member companies of CDMA must maintain internal suppression lists for all media employed by the marketer.

1.5 CDMA member companies are strongly encouraged to adopt a list rental policy, which restricts rental of information to companies that agree to comply with this policy.

Principle #2: Providing Consumers with the Right of Access to Information

2.1 The industry endorses the right of the consumer to know the source of his or her name used in any direct marketing program. Marketers must make all reasonable efforts to provide this information to the consumer on request.

2.2 Additionally, consumers have the right to know what information is held in their customer files and the right to question and request correction of any erroneous information. Marketers must make all reasonable efforts to provide this information to the consumer on request. In the case of disputes between consumers and marketers, CDMA will act as mediator and may require that marketers adjust data or annotate customer files.

Principle #3: Enabling Consumers to Reduce the Amount of Mail They Receive

All CDMA members must use the Do Not Mail/Do Not Call services of the Association when conducting a direct marketing campaign in order to delete the name of any consumer, other than a current customer, who has requested that he or she be removed from mail and telemarketing lists. A "current customer" is defined as any consumer who has made a purchase from the direct marketer within the last six months or during a normal buying cycle.

Principle #4: Controlling the Use of Information by Third Parties

The purposes for which information is collected shall be identified by the organization at or before the time the information is collected.

The collection of personal information shall be limited to that which is necessary for the purposes identified by the organization.

All those involved in the transfer, rental, sale, or exchange of mailing lists must establish and agree upon the exact nature of the list's intended usage prior to permission being given to use the list or to transfer the information.

Principle #5: Safely Storing Information About Consumers

All those involved in the transfer, rental, sale, or exchange of mailing lists must be responsible for the protection of list data and should take appropriate measures to ensure against unauthorized access, alteration, or dissemination of list data. Those who have access to such data should agree in advance to use data only in an authorized manner.

Principle #6: Respecting Confidential and Sensitive Information

All list owners and users must be protective of the consumer's right to privacy and sensitive to the information collected on lists and subsequently considered for use, transfer, rental, or sale.

Where a use of personal information that a reasonable person would consider to be sensitive and confidential has not been identified to the individual at the time of collection, then positive consent must be obtained prior to such further use of the personal information.

The industry recognizes that private personal data, such as medical, financial, and credit data must be protected by sectoral regulatory codes.

CDMA Code of Ethics

Principle #7: Enforcement

7.1 The Privacy Code is an integral part of the Association's "Code of Ethics and Standards of Practice" and will therefore be enforced in the same manner as the existing Code. Specifically, any complaints of violation by members — e.g., from consumers or government bodies —will initiate a process of review and hearings by CDMA. Members found to be in violation of the Code will have the opportunity to correct their practices; if further complaints are proven justified, members will be expelled from the Association.

7.2 All CDMA members must designate a staff manager to be responsible for adherence to the Principles of the Privacy Code.

The privacy provisions of the Code were developed in accordance with the privacy principles of the Organization for Economic Co-operation and Development (OECD).

J.   Enforcement Procedures for the Standards of Practice

1. Upon receipt of information that would indicate a violation of the criminal laws of Canada the Association will promptly forward such information to the appropriate authorities and the organization concerned.

2. Upon receipt of a customer complaint regarding violation of this Code, whether regarding a member or a non-member, the Association will contact the company and use its mediation procedures to attempt to resolve the consumer complaint.

3. If no response is received within 30 days to the Association's inquiry, or the company fails to satisfy the consumer complaint within 90 days, the President will write to the company and ask for its compliance with the Code of Ethics and Standards of Practice if he is satisfied that a violation has occurred.

4. If the President is not satisfied that the company has made best efforts to comply with the Code of Ethics and Standards of Practice or is satisfied that there is a pattern of non-compliance, he shall:

a.   Strike a committee of members and a representative of a consumer group to investigate the conduct of the company; or

b. File a report with the Board of Directors, with or without the committee's report, with a recommendation for further action and an explanation of why no committee was formed pursuant to 4 a.

5.1 Upon receipt of the President's report, in the case of a member company the Board of Directors shall:

a. Order further investigation; or

b. Hold a special meeting with the attendance of the member complained about and subsequently:
   · Expel the member and make a broad public announcement that it has done so; or
   · Determine that no further action is appropriate.

5.2 Upon receipt of the President's report, in the case of a non-member company the Board of Directors may, after a fair hearing, make a broad public announcement of the facts found by the President's or the Committee's investigation.

6. Where the Board of Directors, after a fair hearing, is satisfied that there has been a pattern of willful non-compliance with the Code of Ethics and Standards of Practice of the Association, the Board shall expel the company from membership in the Association and make a broad public announcement that it has done so.

7. In cases that are urgent or otherwise constitute flagrant or egregious violation of the Code by a member or non-member, after communication with the offending organization the President may report directly to the Board with a recommendation for action. The Board shall take such action as it deems appropriate after providing an opportunity for the offending company to respond.

K. CDMA Mission Statement

Our Mission: To create an environment which fosters the responsible growth of direct marketing in Canada.

Objectives of CDMA:

1) To represent the interests of the industry on key issues;

2) (a) To take a leadership role in identifying, planning for, and reacting to issues affecting the direct marketing industry and,

    (b) To influence and shape policy initiatives which impact the industry, through education of government, media, and the public;

3) To establish and promote standards of practice for the industry and to take an active role in ensuring compliance (e.g., CDMA will enforce its Code of Ethics and CDMA will act as a conduit of information to regulatory bodies);

4) To promote integrity and high standards of business conduct among our members in the interests of consumers (e.g., Do Not Mail/Do Not Call and consumer satisfaction programs);

5) To be a major source of education and skills development (e.g., gathering and maintenance of statistics, resource centre for industry, seminars, and conventions); and,

6) To provide opportunities for members to meet, network, exchange information, and do business together.

Printed October 1997
1997 © Canadian Direct Marketing Association

CDMA Code of Ethics

CDMA Special Interest Councils

Business-to-Business Council

The Business-to-Business Council is a forum for direct marketers whose campaigns are directed to business buyers rather than consumers to examine the unique issues and approaches they require. The council holds two annual full day events, one focused on the Small Office/Home Office market and the other on more general business-to-business topics.

Call Centre Council

The Call Centre Council is the voice of the Canadian telemarketing industry. The council provides a forum for the discussion of common problems and concerns, and closely monitors and intervenes on regulatory issues affecting telemarketers. The council also holds regular breakfast meetings and an annual Call Centre Day to keep its members informed about new regulations, services, and technology.

Catalogue & Direct Merchants Council

The Catalogue & Direct Merchants Council is driven by issues identified by its members, and encourages excellence in catalogue operations as well as promoting regulation affecting cataloguers, and has worked on issues, such as cross-border shopping, the postal and courier remission orders, and removing the tax-included pricing requirement of HST legislation. The council is planning a variety of educational forums to explore the issues of greatest concern to the catalogue industry.

Database & List Council

The Database & List Council serves as a forum for discussion, networking, and problem solving among list brokers, owners, users, and processors. Some of the issues it tackles are list ethics, privacy, list standards, use of new technology, postal requirements, and taxation. The council holds regular luncheons meetings, an annual Database & List Conference, and seminars to educate its members about new developments.

DRTV/Teleshopping Council

The council's main activities are to monitor regulatory issues related to direct response television advertising and to uncover opportunities to air more direct response television messages.

Financial Services Council

The Financial Services Council provides a collective voice on industry issues and problems for companies involved in the direct marketing of financial products and services. A forum for education, communication, and networking, this council is committed to the growth of direct marketing of financial services in Canada. The council plans four breakfast programs for the year with speakers on topics of interest to its members.

Fundraisers Council

The Fundraisers Council was established to benefit not-for-profit direct marketers. Activities include regular luncheon meetings with speakers and roundtable sessions focusing on issues of common concern to this unique group. This group is also involved in outreach to other fundraisers who are interested in including a direct marketing component in their programs, and actively monitoring fundraising, postal, and legislative issues.

Interactive/Online Council

Monitoring regulatory issues pertaining to marketing through electronic media and keeping its members up to date on the use of emerging media for direct response are among the key initiatives of the Interactive/Online Council.

Mailing Services Council
The Mailing Services Council's members are experienced mail professionals who work together to monitor postal issues affecting mail service suppliers. The council holds regular dinner meetings to discuss issues of concern to the industry and hear speakers on topics of interest to its members.

Publishing Council
The Publishing Council focuses on issues of importance to magazine and book publishers employing direct marketing to their consumer and business subscribers. The council holds educational programs during the year through which a wide variety of issues and hot topics are addressed.

Relationship Marketing Council
This council is for members who use direct response marketing media and technologies in integrated campaigns to build relationships with their customers. Through regular breakfast meetings and the Relationship Marketing Conference, the council provides education and insight into this fast-growing, multi-disciplinary area.

CDMA Special Interest Councils

Glossary of Terms

A

Active buyer
A customer who has an existing purchase commitment.

Allowable margin (AM)
The margin remaining after the cost of goods, shipping and handling, and bad debt considerations have been subtracted from revenue.

Attrition rates
The percentage of customers who are not likely to renew or complete their commitment.

B

Back-end
The measurement of a buyer's performance after the order has been placed.

Bangtail
A promotional or payment envelope with a second flap that is perforated and designed to be used as an additional order form or change of address form.

Bill enclosure
Any promotional piece or notice enclosed with a bill, invoice, or statement that is used to offer additional purchases.

Bounce back
An additional offer enclosed within a product shipment made to your customer.

Bulk mail
A category of third-class mail that refers to a quantity of identical pieces, but addressed to different names. A term used in reference to postal standards.

Business list
Any list of individuals or titles that is based on a business-associated interest, inquiry, membership, subscription, or purchase.

Business reply card (BRC)
A pre-addressed response card with postage prepaid.

Business reply envelope (BRE)
A pre-addressed return envelope usually with postage prepaid.

Business-to-business
Marketing efforts directed from one business to another.

C

Canadian Direct Marketing Association (CDMA)
The national association representing direct marketers in Canada. Its purpose is to present a unified voice in matters of technology, postal affairs, education, training, and recruitment.

Campaign
Refers to a multi-media program.

Catalogue
A book or booklet offering more than one product for order by the mail or phone. A catalogue can also drive the purchaser into a retail outlet.

Catalogue buyer
One who buys merchandise from a catalogue.

Catalogue request
One who requests a catalogue be sent to him or her. The catalogue may be free or there may be a nominal charge for shipping and handling.

CDMA Do Not Mail/Do Not Call
A service provided by CDMA, which allows individuals or companies to remove their names and addresses from all Canadian lists. This list is made available to all CDMA members and non-members to be used prior to any project. This eliminates consumers who do not wish to receive any solicitations by mail or phone.

Cheshire label
Specially prepared paper, which can come in rolls, fanfold or accordion folded, used by computer bureaus to reproduce names and addresses that will be mechanically affixed to a mailing piece.

Cleaning
The process of correcting, editing, and/or removing a name and address from a list because it is no longer entirely correct.

Coding
A device used to identify the list, offer, or some other form of testing, which is linked back to a name and address. Or a structure of letters and numbers used to classify address characteristics on a list.

Compiled lists
Names and addresses derived from databases, directories, newspapers, public records, trade show registrations, which identifies groups of people or companies with something in common.

Computer service bureau
An internal or external facility providing general or specific data-processing services.

Consumer list
A list of names at a home address.

Contributor list
Names and addresses of individuals who have given to a specific fundraising effort.

Controlled circulation
Distribution of a publication or newspaper to individuals or companies on the basis of their titles or occupations. Typically distributed free of charge. Recipients are asked from time to time to verify the information that qualifies them to continue receiving the publication or newspaper.

Conversion rates
The ratio of inquiries converted to buyers. This ratio is used to track two-step programs, such as trial offers or lead generation.

Co-op mailing
A mailing of more than one offer included in the same envelope. Each participating mailer shares the overall mailing costs.

Cost per inquiry (CPI)
A simple formula derived by dividing the total cost by the number of *inquiries* received.

Cost per order (CPO)
Similar to cost per inquiry, except the formula is based on actual *orders* rather than inquiries.

Cost per response (CPR)
Reflects the actual cost of obtaining one response or lead.

Cost per thousand (CPM)
Refers to the cost of reaching one thousand prospects. Common to printing, list rental, and media circulation.

Coupon
The part of an advertisement or mailer that is intended to be filled in by the respondent and returned to the advertiser.

Customer profile
A description of your customer. Usually the result of analysis based on existing purchase behaviour as well as demographic, geographic, and outside data.

D

Database
A compilation of customers, inquiries, or leads. There are three types of databases: 1) private; 2) public; 3) co-op.

Demographics
Socio-economic characteristics pertaining to a geographic unit. Can include country, city, postal code, group of households, education, ethnicity, and income level.

Direct marketing
An information-driven marketing process managed by database technology, that enables marketers to develop, test, implement, measure, and appropriately modify customised marketing programs and strategies.

Direct response advertising
Response-driven advertising.

Donor list
A list of individuals or companies that have given money to one or more charitable or fundraising organisations.

DRTV
Direct response television identified by a 1-800 (888) number for response.

Dupe
Two or more name and address records that are found to be equal under the list user's basis of comparison (match code, mathematical formula, etc.).

Duplication elimination
A specific kind of controlled duplication, which, no matter how many times a name and address appears on a list, and/or on how many different lists, it will only be accepted once. Also referred to as dupe-elimination.

E

Exchange
A mutual agreement by mailers to trade lists rather than renting for a fixed price.

Expiration date
A date an offer expires.

Expire(s)
A former customer who is no longer considered an active buyer.

F

Fixed cost
Includes the cost of all promotion or advertising as

well as any allocated overhead costs.

Fixed field
A way of laying out or formatting a computer file that puts every piece of data in a specific position relative to every other piece of data.

Free fall insert (FFI) or free standing insert (FSI)
A pre-printed piece loosely inserted or nested in a newspaper or magazine.

Frequency
The number of times an individual has ordered within a specific period of time. May also refer to your media plan as to the specific number of insertions within a given period.

Friend-get-a-friend (member-get-a-member)
A marketing term used when you request one existing customer to refer the name of a potential customer.

Front-end response/back-end performance
The profit or loss associated with a first-time order or response. Back end performance is the ongoing profitability of a customer. Factors to consider are: collection costs, conversion costs, renewal rates, lifetime value, returns, and cost of payment plans.

Front-end
The up-front activities in your campaign that lead to an order or contribution.

Fulfillment (fulfilling)
The activities performed once an order is received. The term is also used to refer to the physical handling and shipping of an order.

G

Guarantee
A pledge of customer satisfaction.

H

Handling charge
Refers to a charge for processing an order.

Hotline list
The most recent names added to your mailing list. These names are usually not any older than three to six months.

House list
Your own customer file.

House list duplicate
A match to an outside rented list based on your own house list.

I

Indicia
A mark representing a postal permit.

Inquiry
Not a firm order. It is used to reference customers who have asked for a brochure or more information without making any order commitment.

J

Johnson box
Wording that appears at the top of a letter highlighting the key benefits and offer of a program.

K

Key code
Numbers or letters that appear on a label, order form, or TV/radio tag, which indicate the source of the name or segmentation.

L

Labels one-up
Vertical strips of single labels containing customer names and addresses.

Laser addressing
The personalising of individual pieces by laser equipment.

Laser letters
Letters that are printed and personalised on high-speed computerised imaging equipment.

Layout
An artist's rendition that demonstrates the creative idea and its relative position in the promotional piece.

Lettershop
An external or internal service that handles the insertion of mailing components and prepares them for delivery to the post office.

Level of confidence (probability theory)
The size and accuracy of your test governed by the statistical probability theory based on a confidence level of 95 or 99 percent accuracy.

Lift letter/memo. Also referred to as a publisher's lift memo
A separate piece added to your mailing package to

convince your prospects to purchase.

List
Names and addresses of individuals or companies that have something in common.

List maintenance
A system for keeping names and addresses or other relevant customer data up to date.

List owner
The company that owns the mailing list you want to rent.

List segment
Smaller sub-groups within a list, defined by recency, frequency, monetary, geographic, demographic, and/or other characteristics.

List selection
The selection of particular characteristics within a list, usually chosen based on your target market and method of payment, source of name, sex, etc.

List test
A portion of a list selected to determine the effectiveness of the entire list or universe.

M

Merge/purge (dupe elimination)
Combining two or more lists for the purpose of eliminating duplicate names. Reports are issued indicating, by list, the number of unique names, inter-file duplicates, assigned multi-buyers, and other pertinent information.

N

Name value
An allowance for the future value of a name based on potential sales as part of the house list or from contribution to list rental income.

Negative option
A purchase plan in which your customers agree to buy and pay for products or services at regular intervals, unless they notify you to stop shipping.

Net name agreement
Usually used when making arrangements for list rental. This is an adjusted list price to reflect a percentage of names shipped, or, for a percentage of names mailed, whichever is greater.

Nth name selection
A fractional unit that is repeated in sampling a list.

O

Offer
Your terms (price, premium, trial offer) which promote a specific product or service.

Order card
Also referred to as a reply card, it is the piece that initiates the order. It is printed on heavy stock and does not need a return envelope.

Order form
Designed to contain your customer's ordering information and is returned in a reply envelope.

Outside list
The use of rented names from any company other than your own.

Overlay
The process by which external data is added to a file for the purpose of either enhancement of the existing information or to allow for more specialised selection.

P

Package insert
Promotional enclosures in outgoing product shipments.

Package
An all inclusive term used to define the assembled enclosures of a mailing effort.

Paid circulation
The distribution of publications to individuals or companies that have paid subscriptions or purchased the magazine or newspaper on the newsstand.

Premium
An additional item offered to your customers as an inducement to product purchase or trial.

Pre-print insert
A supplied advertising insert that is printed in advance and supplied to the newspaper or magazine.

Pressure sensitive labels
A label with a dual purpose. It is used as the initial addressing portion of a mailing, then removed from its addressing position by the consumer and re-affixed to an order form for return.

Probability theory
The size and accuracy of your test governed by this statistical theory.

Glossary of Terms

Glossary of Terms

Profit per response (PPR)
Subtracting the cost per response (CPR) from the allowable margin (AM).

Psychographics
Any characteristics or qualities used to denote the life style(s) or attitude(s) of your customers or prospective customers.

R

R^2
A proportion of variance that is explained by the model variables.

Renewal rates
Indicates the number of people who have renewed their commitment. Often used in reference to subscription products.

Retention
Refers specifically to customers you want to keep.

Return on promotion (ROP)
By dividing the profit per response (PPR) by the total amount of all the money at risk (cost of goods, shipping and handling, postage, advertising costs, etc.), equals the return on promotion (ROP).

Revenue
Gross average order value, plus shipping and handling plus any deferred payments, minus returns, equals net revenue per order.

Roll-out
The remaining portion of a list (house or rented), after having successfully tested a portion of it.

Run of press or run of paper (ROP)
Advertising that is run on-page as part of a newspaper or magazine.

S

Seeding
Deliberately placing dummy names on your mailing list to track its usage.

Self-mailer
A direct mail piece, self-contained, that does not require an outer envelope for mailing.

Slippage
A discrepancy between test and volume mailings.

Source code
Unique alphabetical or numeric identification for distinguishing one list or media source from another.

Standard industry classification (SIC)
Classification of the business category, such as manufacturing, communications, education, etc.

Statement stuffer
A small, printed piece carried in a customer's invoice or monthly statement.

Step-testing
A plan that allows you to test in small increments prior to a roll-out of a larger number.

T

Teaser
Information on the outer envelope designed to entice the customer into opening the envelope to find out more about the offer.

Tenure
The length of time of the customer relationship.

Title
A prefix or suffix of a name that more accurately identifyies an individual, e.g., Mr., Mrs., Dr., or, chairman, president, sales manager.

U

Universe
The total number of available names that fit into a pre-determined selection.

Update
Adding recent transactions and current information to a list that reflects a more current status of each record.

V

Variable cost
Includes cost of merchandise, cost of returns, reply postage, order processing, credit card fee, credit check costs, customer service, fulfillment, returns, bad debt, collection effort, and premiums.